HARLEY LOVES JOKER

BY PAUL DINI

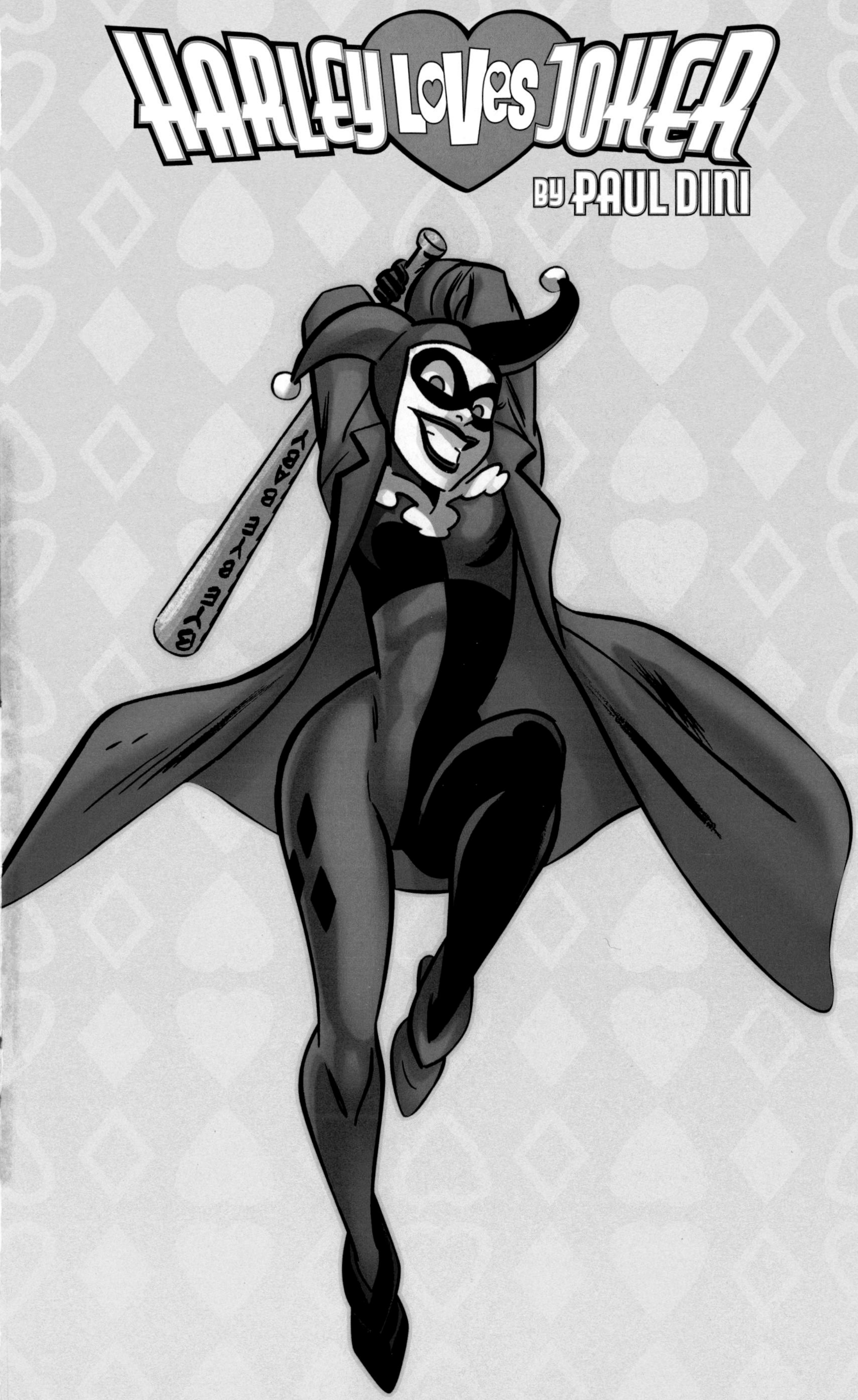

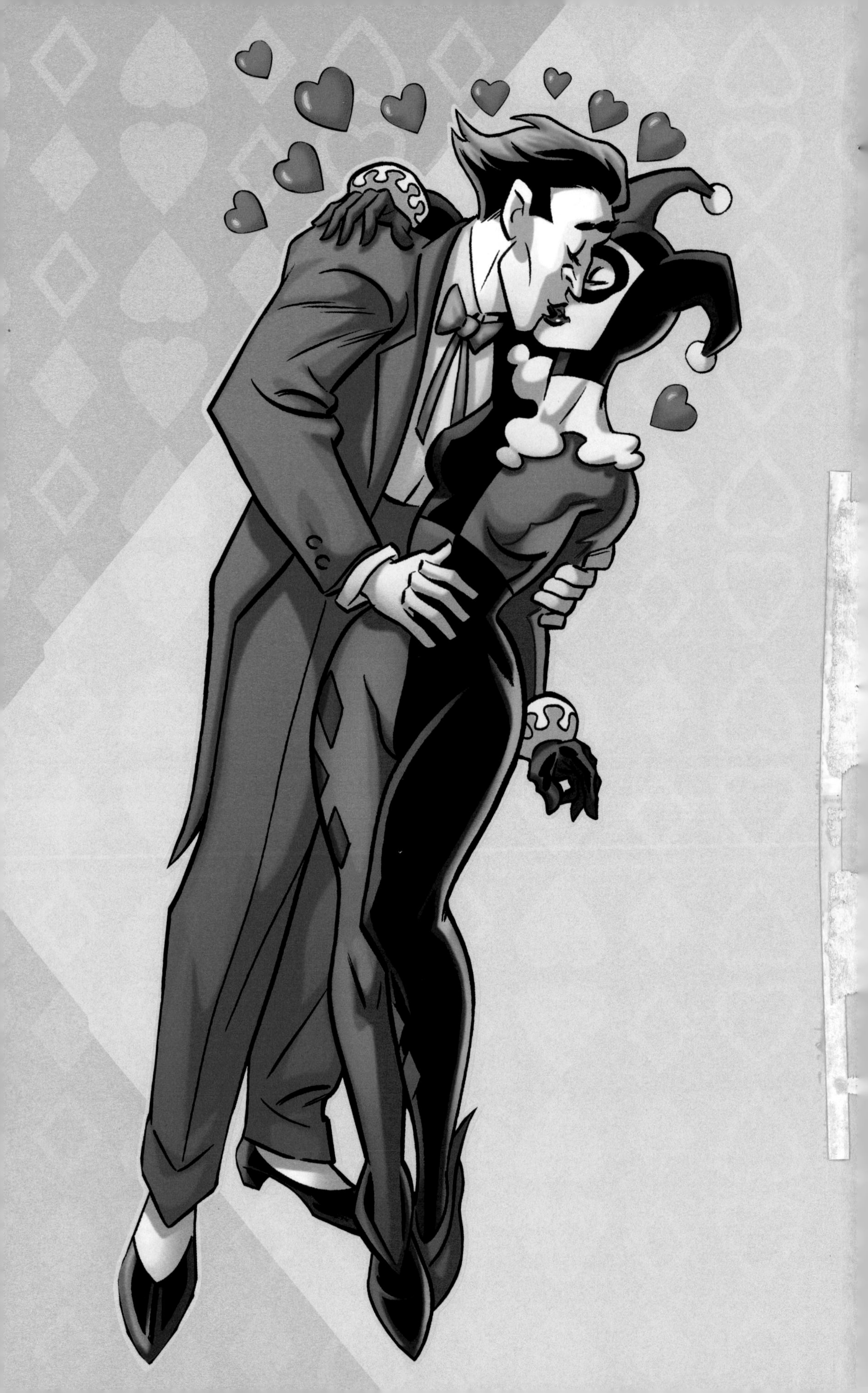

HARLEY LOVES JOKER BY PAUL DINI

PAUL DINI
JIMMY PALMIOTTI
writers

BRET BLEVINS
penciller

J. BONE
BRET BLEVINS
inkers

ALEX SINCLAIR
colorist

DAVE SHARPE
COREY BREEN
letterers

AMANDA CONNER & ALEX SINCLAIR
collection cover artists

HARLEY QUINN created by PAUL DINI & BRUCE TIMM

CHRIS CONROY Editor – Original Series ◊ **DAVE WIELGOSZ** Assistant Editor – Original Series
JEB WOODARD Group Editor – Collected Editions ◊ **ROBIN WILDMAN** Editor – Collected Edition
STEVE COOK Design Director – Books ◊ **SHANNON STEWART** Publication Design

BOB HARRAS Senior VP – Editor-in-Chief, DC Comics ◊ **PAT McCALLUM** Executive Editor, DC Comics

DAN DiDIO Publisher ◊ **JIM LEE** Publisher & Chief Creative Officer
AMIT DESAI Executive VP – Business & Marketing Strategy, Direct to Consumer & Global Franchise Management
BOBBIE CHASE VP & Executive Editor, Young Reader & Talent Development
MARK CHIARELLO Senior VP – Art, Design & Collected Editions ◊ **JOHN CUNNINGHAM** Senior VP – Sales & Trade Marketing
BRIAR DARDEN VP – Business Affairs ◊ **ANNE DePIES** Senior VP – Business Strategy, Finance & Administration
DON FALLETTI VP – Manufacturing Operations ◊ **LAWRENCE GANEM** VP – Editorial Administration & Talent Relations
ALISON GILL Senior VP – Manufacturing & Operations ◊ **JASON GREENBERG** VP – Business Strategy & Finance
HANK KANALZ Senior VP – Editorial Strategy & Administration ◊ **JAY KOGAN** Senior VP – Legal Affairs
NICK J. NAPOLITANO VP – Manufacturing Administration ◊ **LISETTE OSTERLOH** VP – Digital Marketing & Events
EDDIE SCANNELL VP – Consumer Marketing ◊ **COURTNEY SIMMONS** Senior VP – Publicity & Communications
JIM (SKI) SOKOLOWSKI VP – Comic Book Specialty Sales & Trade Marketing
NANCY SPEARS VP – Mass, Book, Digital Sales & Trade Marketing ◊ **MICHELE R. WELLS** VP – Content Strategy

HARLEY LOVES JOKER BY PAUL DINI

Published by DC Comics. Compilation and all new material Copyright © 2018 DC Comics. All Rights Reserved.
Originally published in single magazine form in HARLEY QUINN 17-25,
HARLEY QUINN: HARLEY LOVES JOKER 1-2. Copyright © 2017, 2018 DC Comics. All Rights Reserved.
All characters, their distinctive likenesses and related elements featured in this publication are trademarks of DC Comics.
The stories, characters and incidents featured in this publication are entirely fictional.
DC Comics does not read or accept unsolicited submissions of ideas, stories or artwork.

DC Comics, 2900 West Alameda Ave., Burbank, CA 91505
Printed by LSC Communications, Kendallville, IN, USA. 11/9/18. First Printing.
ISBN: 978-1-4012-8349-0

Library of Congress Cataloging-in-Publication Data is available.

HARLEY LOVES JOKER
PART ONE

PAUL DINI & JIMMY PALMIOTTI writers BRET BLEVINS pencils
J. BONE inks ALEX SINCLAIR colors DAVE SHARPE letters
HARLEY QUINN created by PAUL DINI and BRUCE TIMM

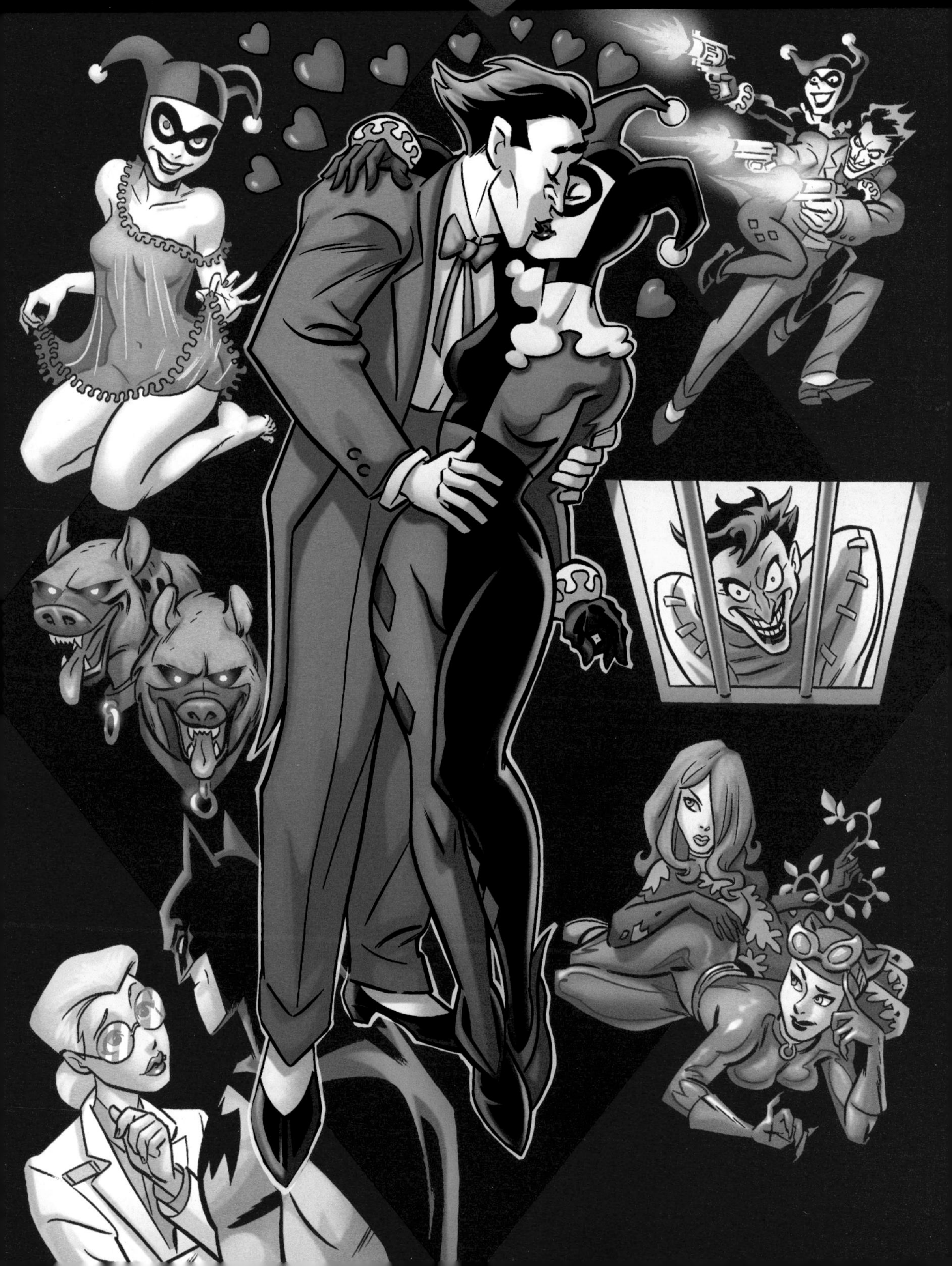

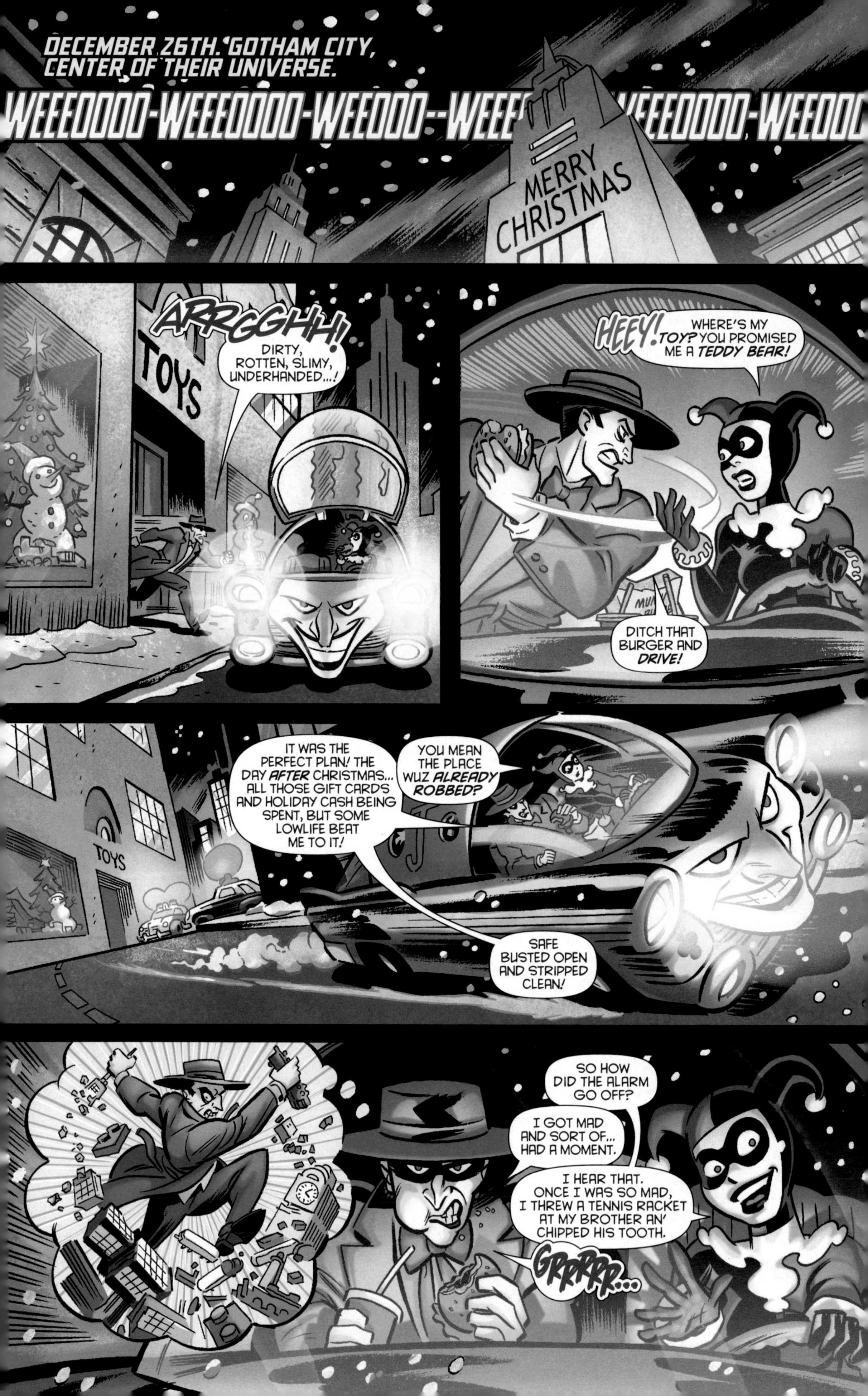
DECEMBER 26TH. GOTHAM CITY, CENTER OF THEIR UNIVERSE.
WEEEOOOO-WEEEOOOO-WEEOOO--WEEE
WEEEOOOO-WEEOO
MERRY CHRISTMAS
TOYS
ARRRGGHH!
DIRTY, ROTTEN, SLIMY, UNDERHANDED...!
HEEY!
WHERE'S MY TOY? YOU PROMISED ME A TEDDY BEAR!
DITCH THAT BURGER AND DRIVE!
IT WAS THE PERFECT PLAN! THE DAY AFTER CHRISTMAS... ALL THOSE GIFT CARDS AND HOLIDAY CASH BEING SPENT, BUT SOME LOWLIFE BEAT ME TO IT!
YOU MEAN THE PLACE WUZ ALREADY ROBBED?
SAFE BUSTED OPEN AND STRIPPED CLEAN!
TOYS
SO HOW DID THE ALARM GO OFF?
I GOT MAD AND SORT OF... HAD A MOMENT.
I HEAR THAT. ONCE I WAS SO MAD, I THREW A TENNIS RACKET AT MY BROTHER AN' CHIPPED HIS TOOTH.
GRRRRR...

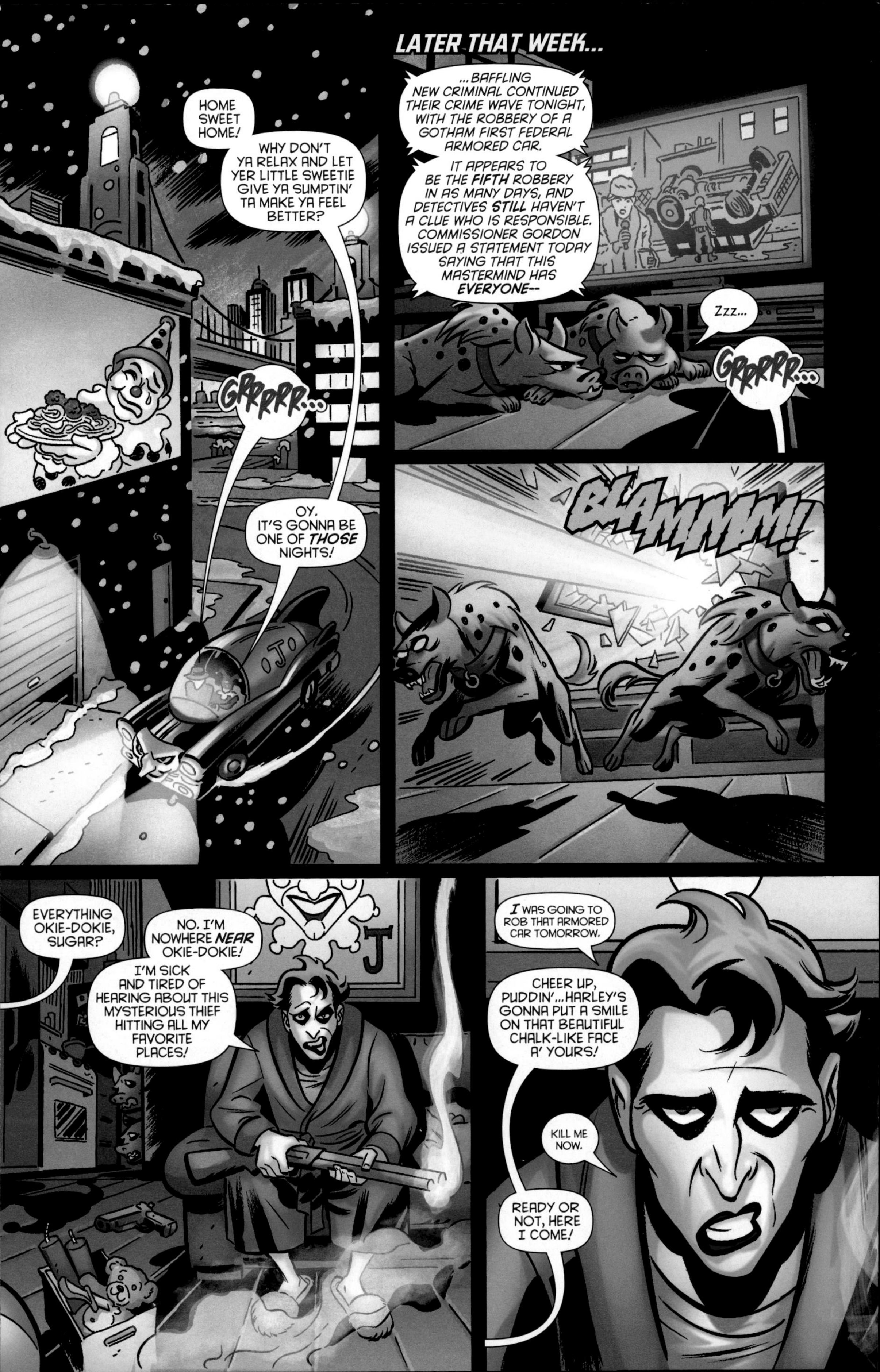

LATER THAT WEEK...
HOME SWEET HOME!
WHY DON'T YA RELAX AND LET YER LITTLE SWEETIE GIVE YA SUMPTIN' TA MAKE YA FEEL BETTER?
GRRRRR...
OY. IT'S GONNA BE ONE OF THOSE NIGHTS!
...BAFFLING NEW CRIMINAL CONTINUED THEIR CRIME WAVE TONIGHT, WITH THE ROBBERY OF A GOTHAM FIRST FEDERAL ARMORED CAR.
IT APPEARS TO BE THE FIFTH ROBBERY IN AS MANY DAYS, AND DETECTIVES STILL HAVEN'T A CLUE WHO IS RESPONSIBLE. COMMISSIONER GORDON ISSUED A STATEMENT TODAY SAYING THAT THIS MASTERMIND HAS EVERYONE--
Zzz...
GRRRRR...
BLAMMMM!
EVERYTHING OKIE-DOKIE, SUGAR?
NO. I'M NOWHERE NEAR OKIE-DOKIE!
I'M SICK AND TIRED OF HEARING ABOUT THIS MYSTERIOUS THIEF HITTING ALL MY FAVORITE PLACES!
I WAS GOING TO ROB THAT ARMORED CAR TOMORROW.
CHEER UP, PUDDIN'...HARLEY'S GONNA PUT A SMILE ON THAT BEAUTIFUL CHALK-LIKE FACE A' YOURS!
KILL ME NOW.
READY OR NOT, HERE I COME!

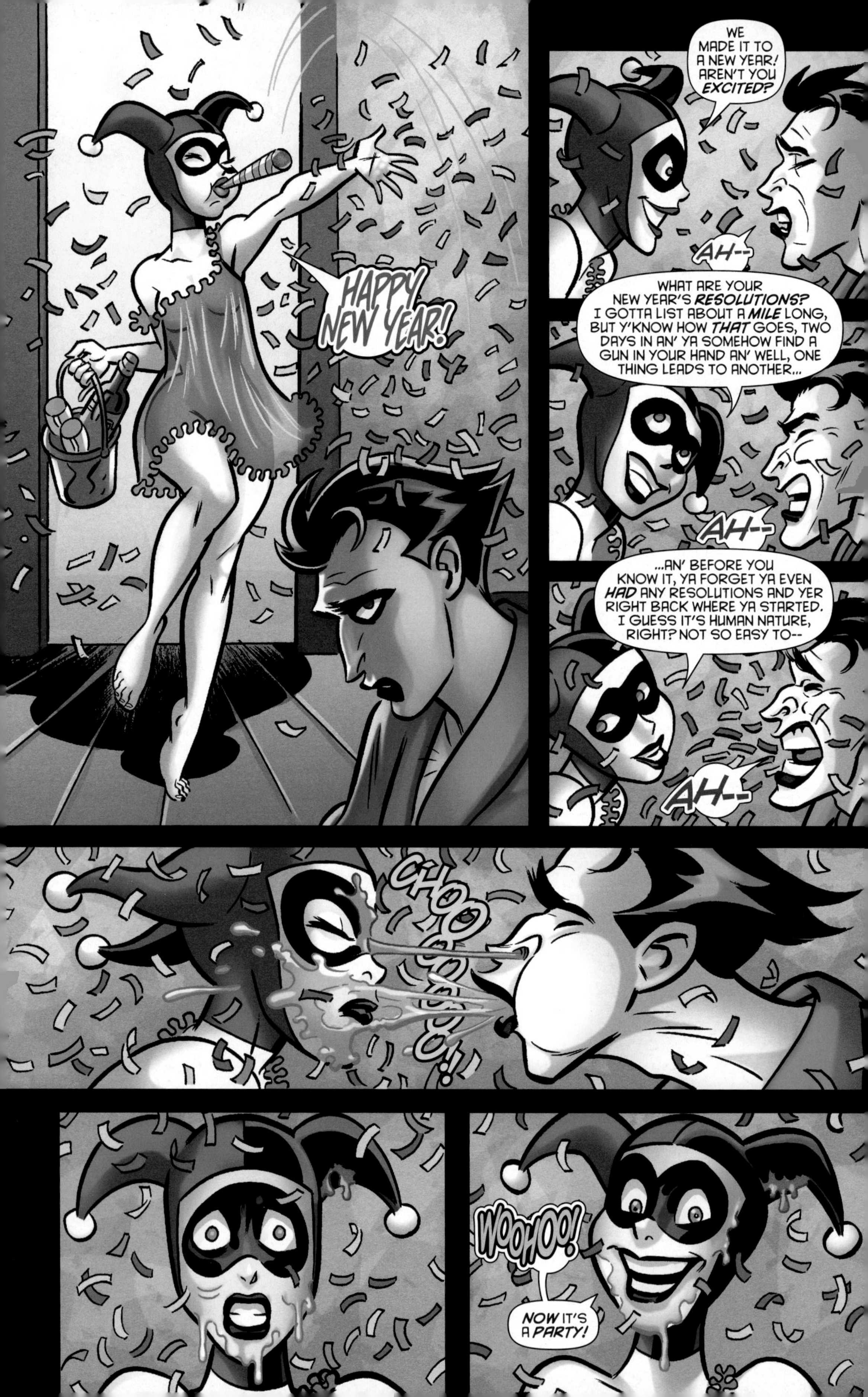

HAPPY NEW YEAR!
WE MADE IT TO A NEW YEAR! AREN'T YOU EXCITED?
AH--
WHAT ARE YOUR NEW YEAR'S RESOLUTIONS? I GOTTA LIST ABOUT A MILE LONG, BUT Y'KNOW HOW THAT GOES, TWO DAYS IN AN' YA SOMEHOW FIND A GUN IN YOUR HAND AN' WELL, ONE THING LEADS TO ANOTHER...
AH--
...AN' BEFORE YOU KNOW IT, YA FORGET YA EVEN HAD ANY RESOLUTIONS AND YER RIGHT BACK WHERE YA STARTED. I GUESS IT'S HUMAN NATURE, RIGHT? NOT SO EASY TO--
AH--
CHOOOOOOOO!!
WOOHOO!
NOW IT'S A PARTY!

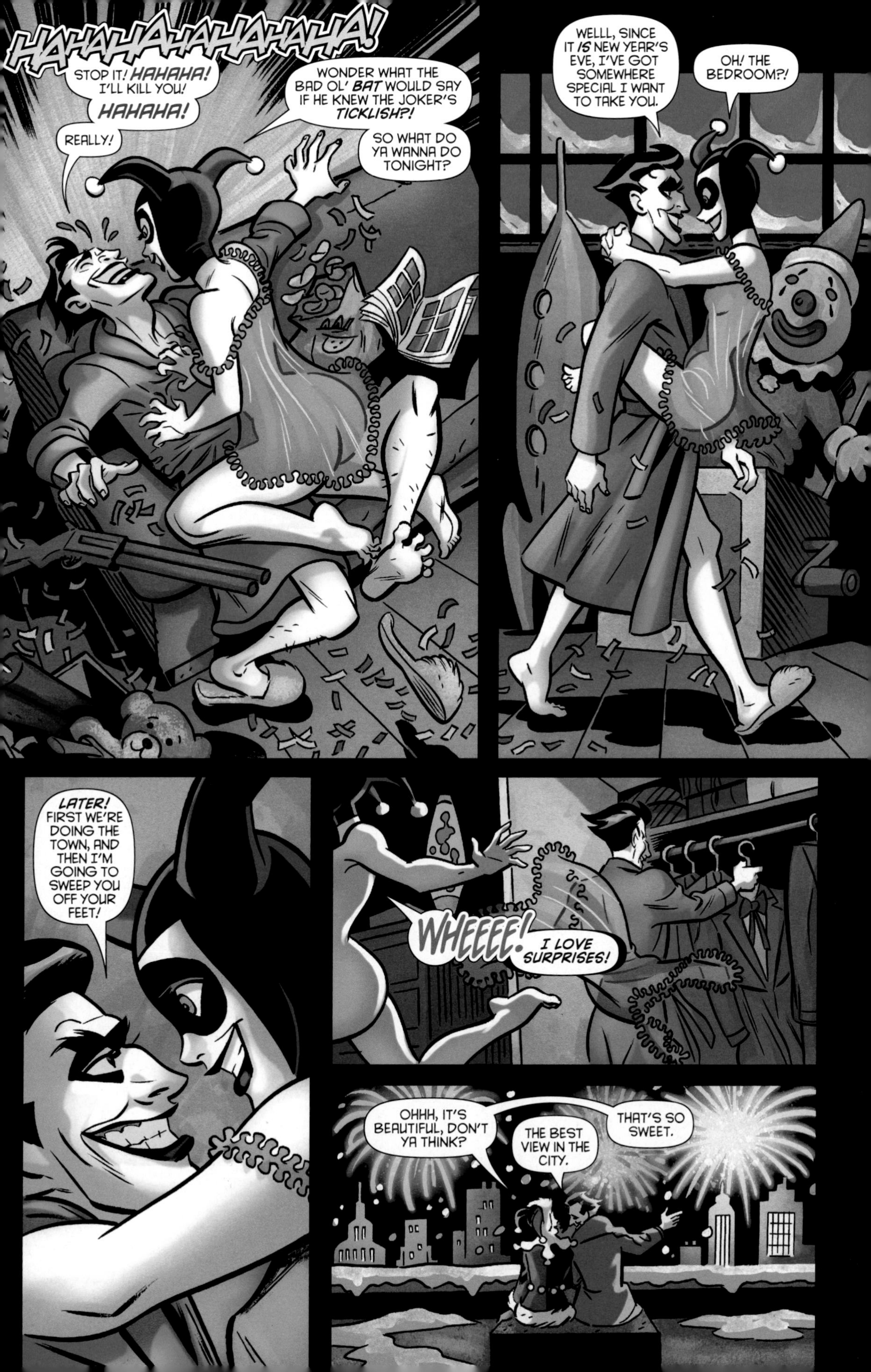
HAHAHAHAHAHAHAHA!
STOP IT! HAHAHA! I'LL KILL YOU! HAHAHA!
REALLY!
WONDER WHAT THE BAD OL' BAT WOULD SAY IF HE KNEW THE JOKER'S TICKLISH?!
SO WHAT DO YA WANNA DO TONIGHT?
WELLL, SINCE IT IS NEW YEAR'S EVE, I'VE GOT SOMEWHERE SPECIAL I WANT TO TAKE YOU.
OH! THE BEDROOM?!
LATER! FIRST WE'RE DOING THE TOWN, AND THEN I'M GOING TO SWEEP YOU OFF YOUR FEET!
WHEEEE!
I LOVE SURPRISES!
OHHH, IT'S BEAUTIFUL, DON'T YA THINK?
THE BEST VIEW IN THE CITY.
THAT'S SO SWEET.

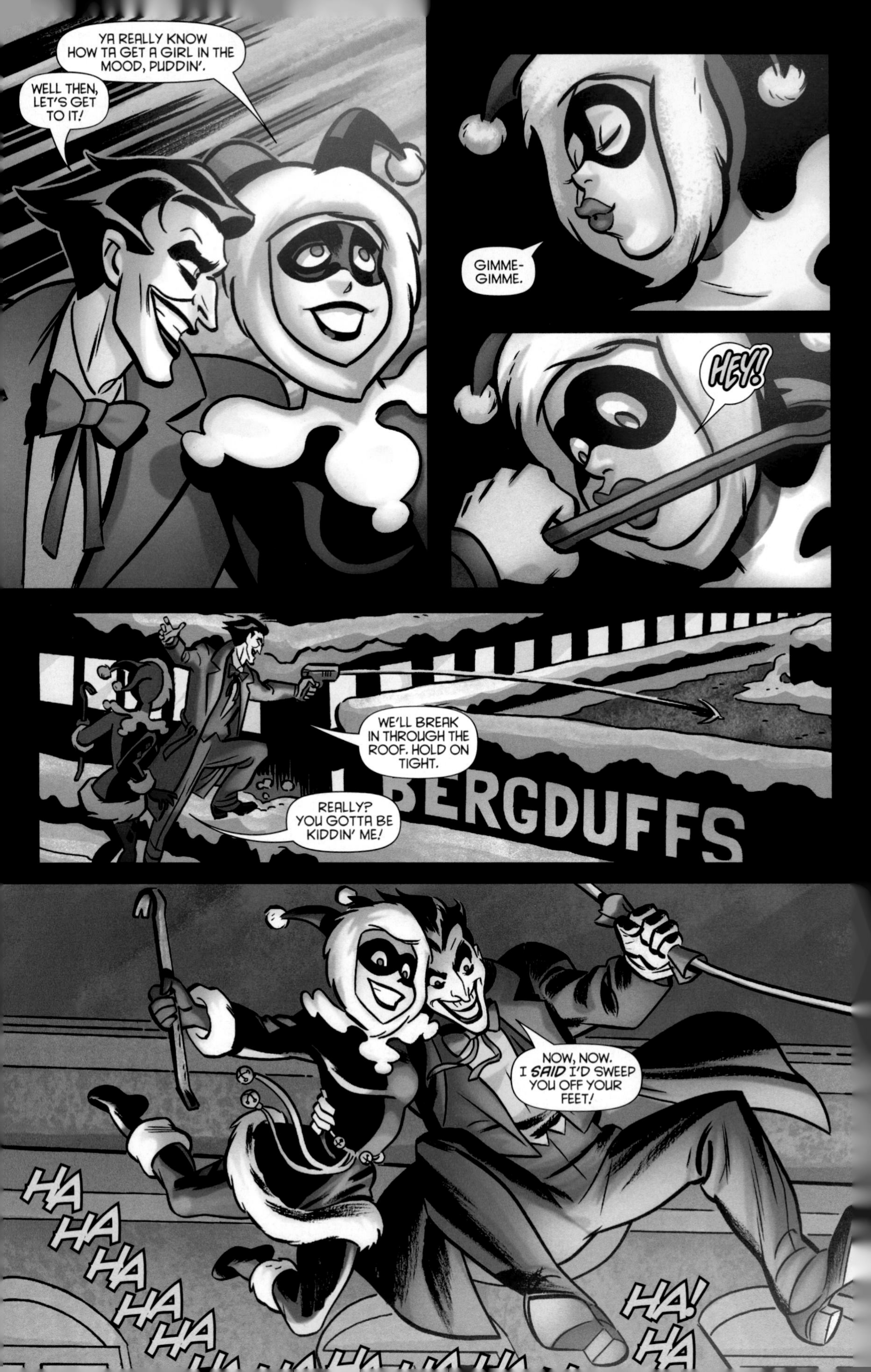
YA REALLY KNOW HOW TA GET A GIRL IN THE MOOD, PUDDIN'.
WELL THEN, LET'S GET TO IT!
GIMME-GIMME.
HEY!!
WE'LL BREAK IN THROUGH THE ROOF. HOLD ON TIGHT.
REALLY? YOU GOTTA BE KIDDIN' ME!
BERGDUFFS
NOW, NOW. I *SAID* I'D SWEEP YOU OFF YOUR FEET!
HA HA HA HA HA HA
HA! HA

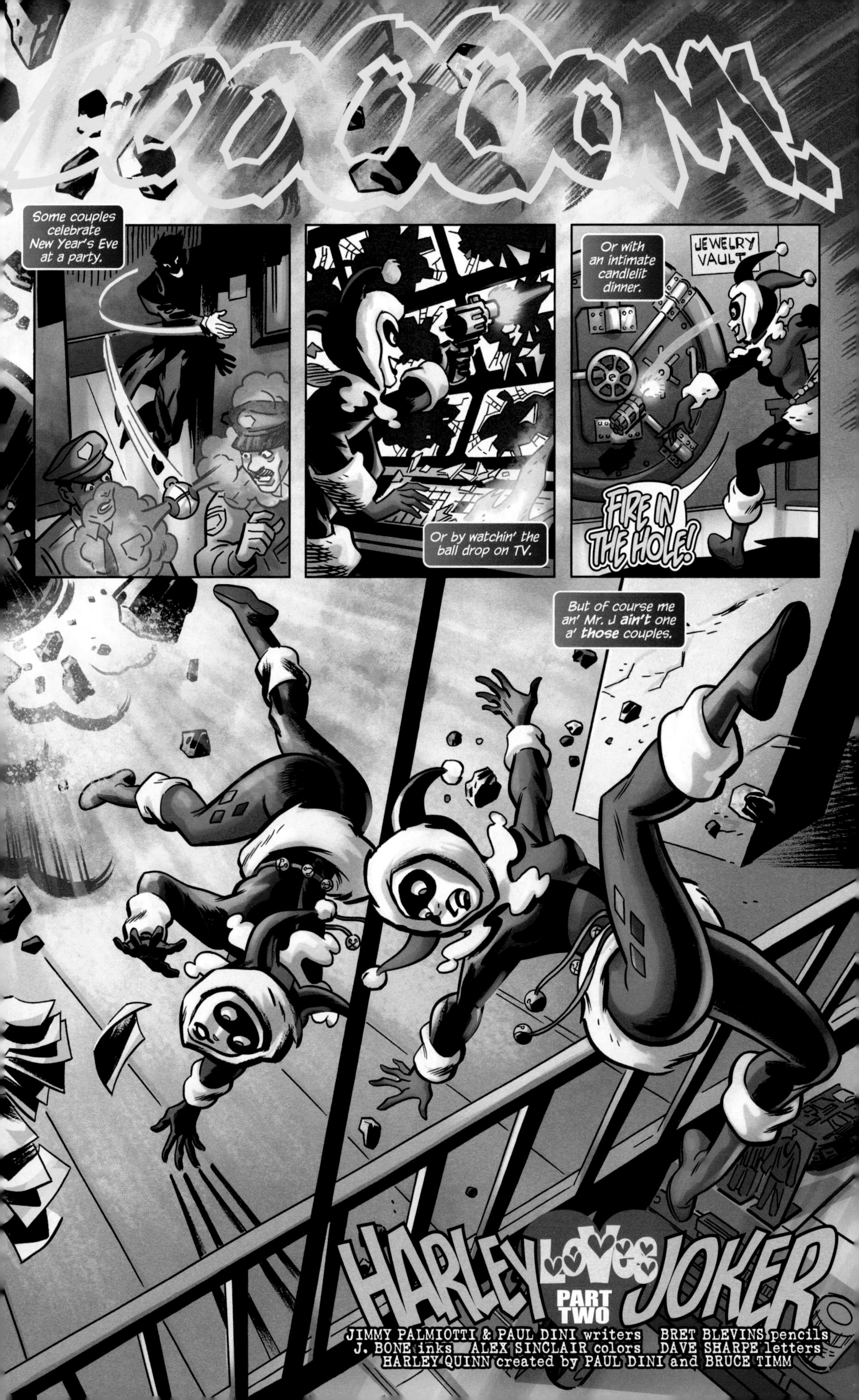
Some couples celebrate New Year's Eve at a party.
Or by watchin' the ball drop on TV.
Or with an intimate candlelit dinner.
JEWELRY VAULT
FIRE IN THE HOLE!
But of course me an' Mr. J ain't one a' those couples.
HARLEY LOVES JOKER
PART TWO
JIMMY PALMIOTTI & PAUL DINI writers BRET BLEVINS pencils
J. BONE inks ALEX SINCLAIR colors DAVE SHARPE letters
HARLEY QUINN created by PAUL DINI and BRUCE TIMM

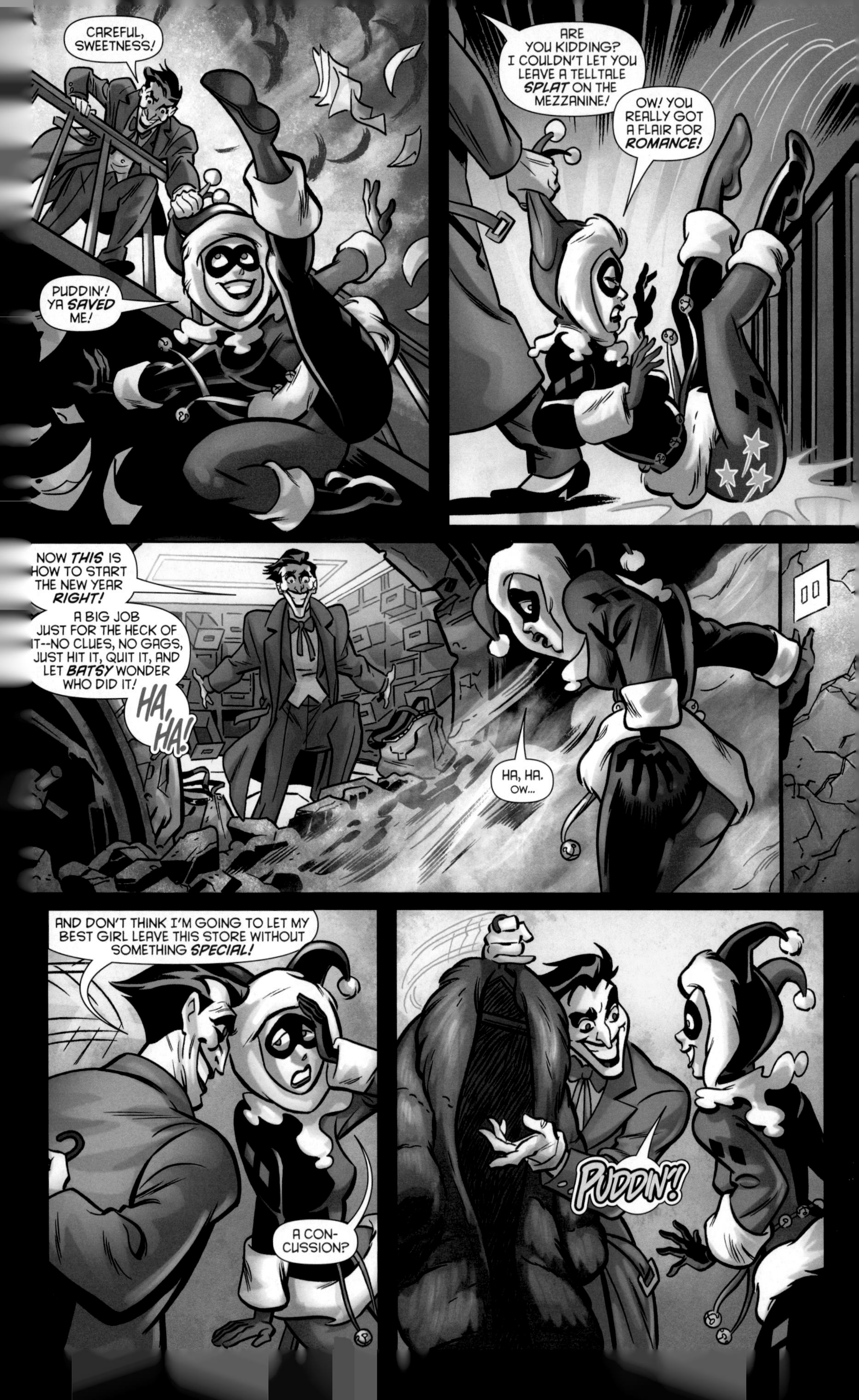
CAREFUL, SWEETNESS!
PUDDIN'! YA SAVED ME!
ARE YOU KIDDING? I COULDN'T LET YOU LEAVE A TELLTALE SPLAT ON THE MEZZANINE!
OW! YOU REALLY GOT A FLAIR FOR ROMANCE!
NOW THIS IS HOW TO START THE NEW YEAR RIGHT!
A BIG JOB JUST FOR THE HECK OF IT--NO CLUES, NO GAGS, JUST HIT IT, QUIT IT, AND LET BATSY WONDER WHO DID IT!
HA, HA!
HA, HA. OW...
AND DON'T THINK I'M GOING TO LET MY BEST GIRL LEAVE THIS STORE WITHOUT SOMETHING SPECIAL!
A CON-CUSSION?
PUDDIN'!

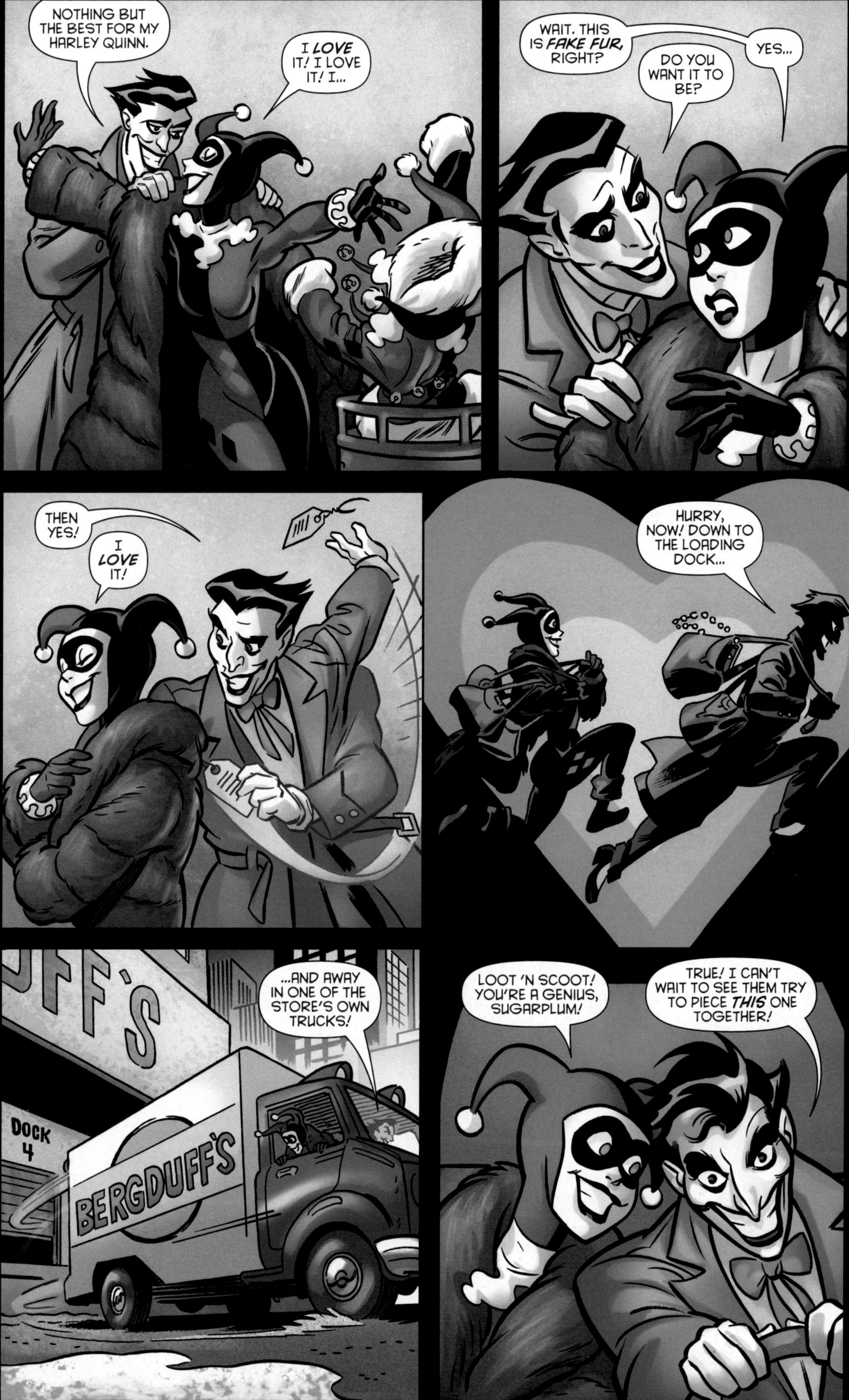
NOTHING BUT THE BEST FOR MY HARLEY QUINN.
I LOVE IT! I LOVE IT! I...
WAIT. THIS IS FAKE FUR, RIGHT?
DO YOU WANT IT TO BE?
YES...
THEN YES!
I LOVE IT!
HURRY, NOW! DOWN TO THE LOADING DOCK...
...AND AWAY IN ONE OF THE STORE'S OWN TRUCKS!
DOCK 4
BERGDUFF'S
LOOT 'N SCOOT! YOU'RE A GENIUS, SUGARPLUM!
TRUE! I CAN'T WAIT TO SEE THEM TRY TO PIECE THIS ONE TOGETHER!

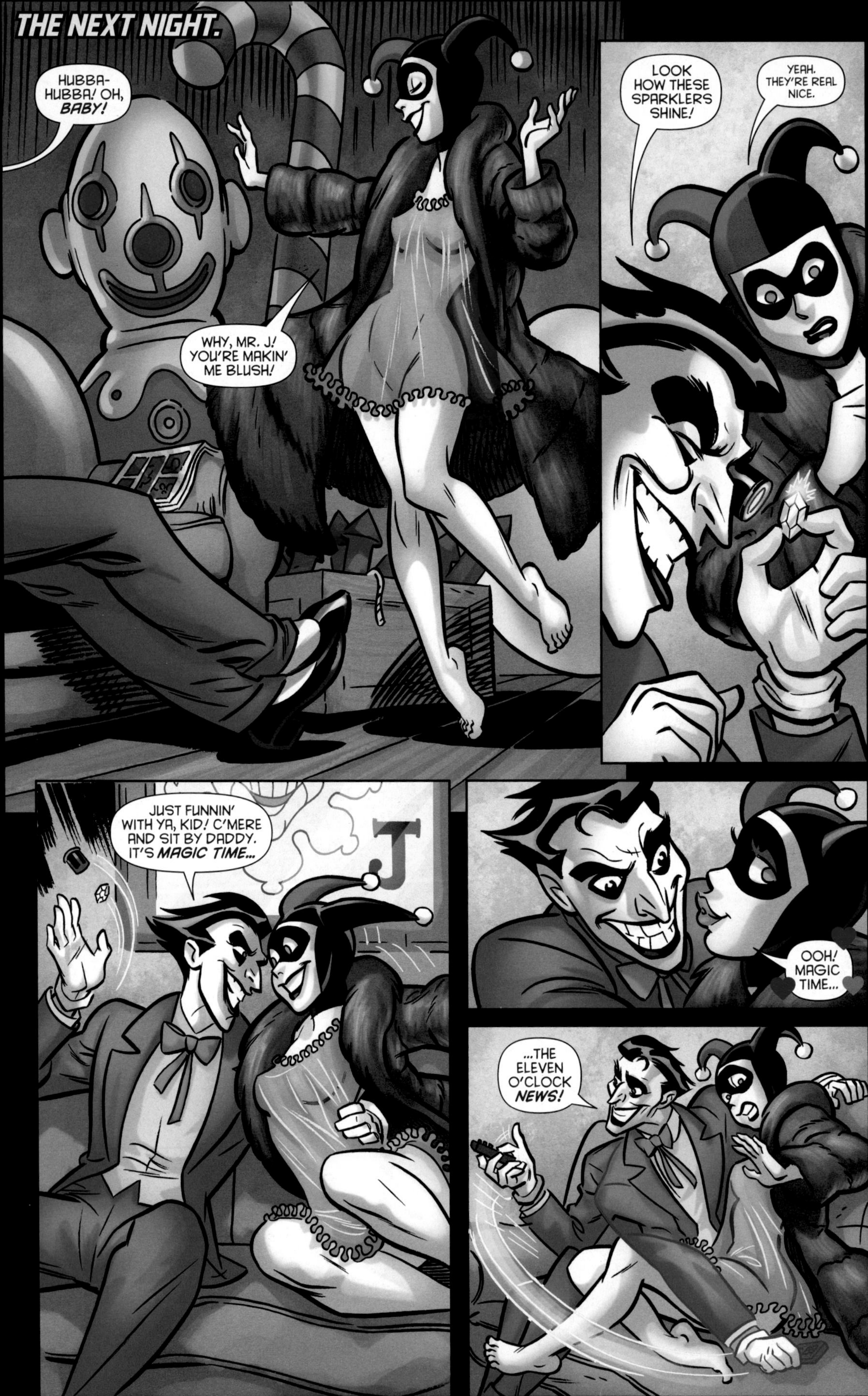
THE NEXT NIGHT.
HUBBA-HUBBA! OH, BABY!
WHY, MR. J! YOU'RE MAKIN' ME BLUSH!
LOOK HOW THESE SPARKLERS SHINE!
YEAH. THEY'RE REAL NICE.
JUST FUNNIN' WITH YA, KID! C'MERE AND SIT BY DADDY. IT'S MAGIC TIME...
OOH! MAGIC TIME...
...THE ELEVEN O'CLOCK NEWS!

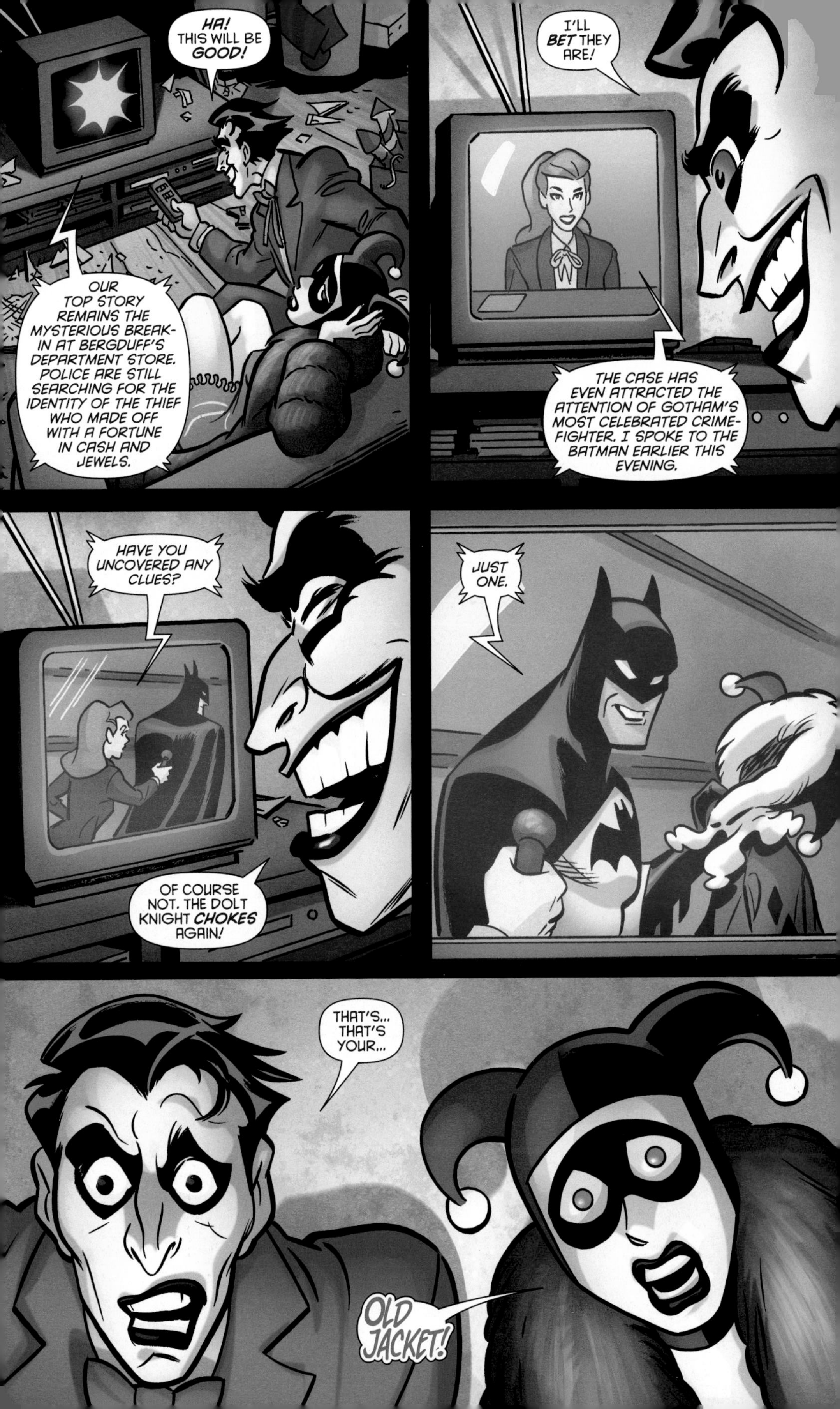
HA! THIS WILL BE GOOD!
OUR TOP STORY REMAINS THE MYSTERIOUS BREAK-IN AT BERGDUFF'S DEPARTMENT STORE. POLICE ARE STILL SEARCHING FOR THE IDENTITY OF THE THIEF WHO MADE OFF WITH A FORTUNE IN CASH AND JEWELS.
I'LL BET THEY ARE!
THE CASE HAS EVEN ATTRACTED THE ATTENTION OF GOTHAM'S MOST CELEBRATED CRIME-FIGHTER. I SPOKE TO THE BATMAN EARLIER THIS EVENING.
HAVE YOU UNCOVERED ANY CLUES?
OF COURSE NOT. THE DOLT KNIGHT CHOKES AGAIN!
JUST ONE.
THAT'S... THAT'S YOUR...
OLD JACKET!

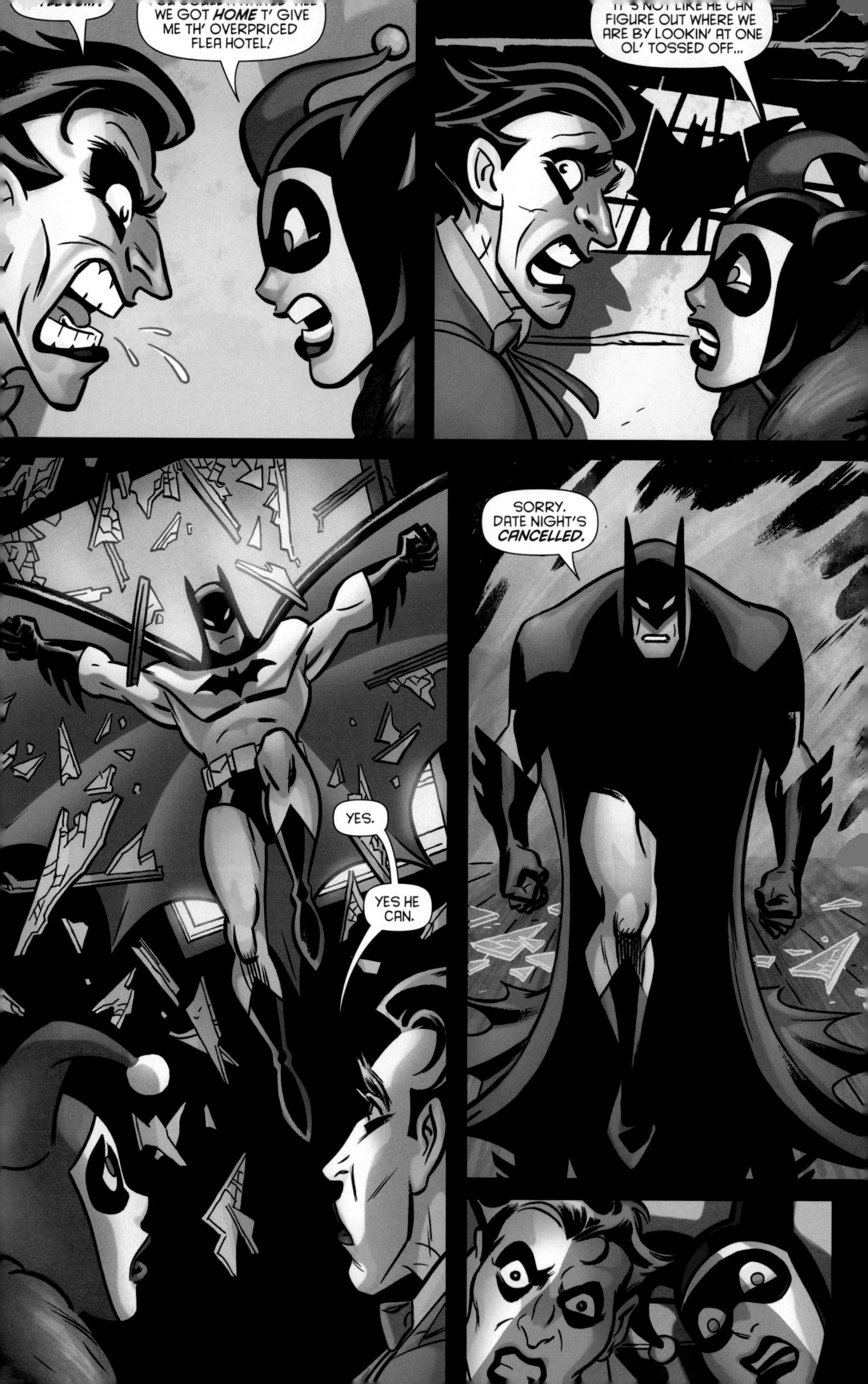

WE GOT *HOME* T' GIVE
ME TH' OVERPRICED
FLEA HOTEL!
FIGURE OUT WHERE WE
ARE BY LOOKIN' AT ONE
OL' TOSSED OFF...
YES.
YES HE CAN.
SORRY. DATE NIGHT'S *CANCELLED.*

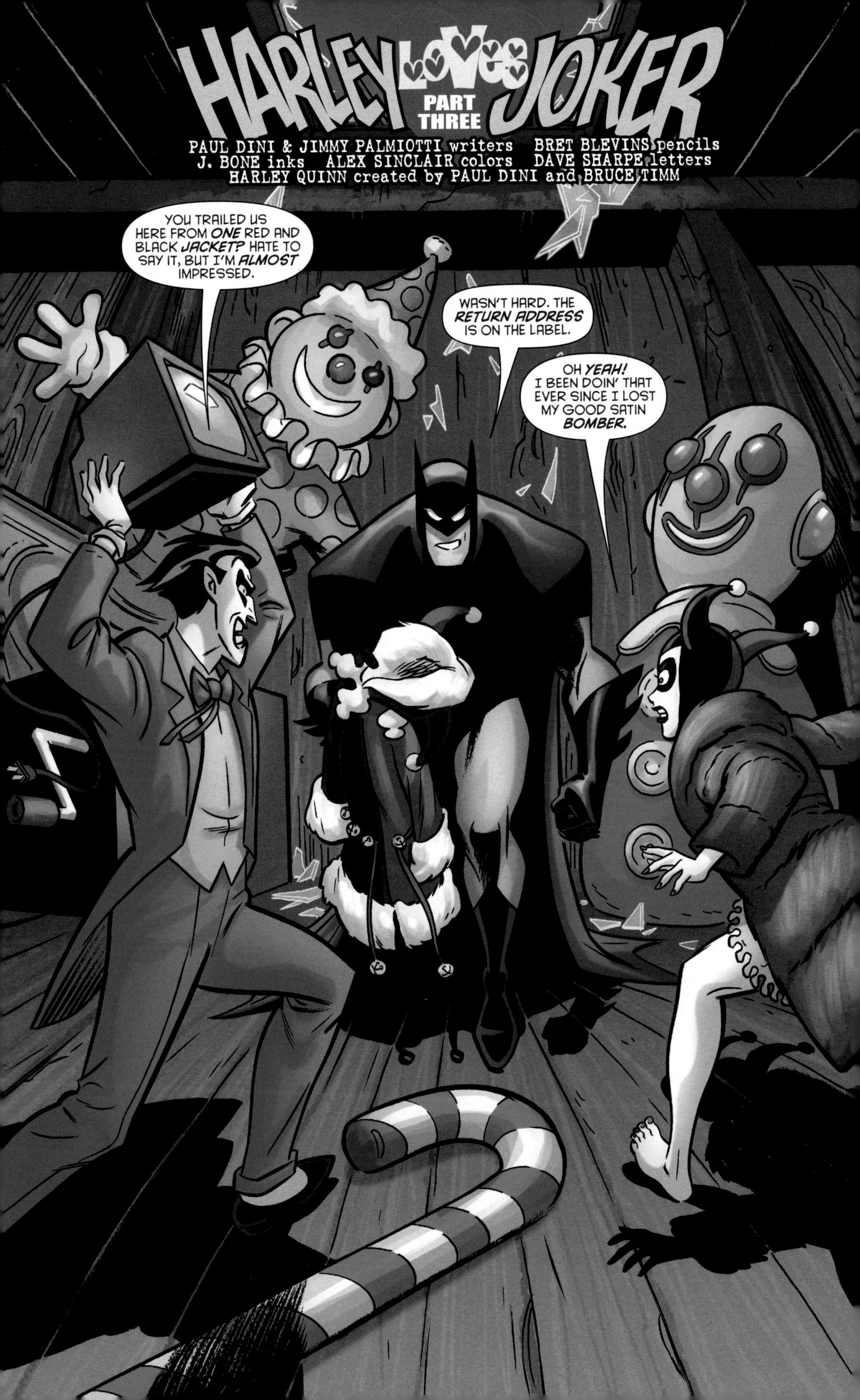
HARLEY LOVES JOKER
PART THREE
PAUL DINI & JIMMY PALMIOTTI writers BRET BLEVINS pencils
J. BONE inks ALEX SINCLAIR colors DAVE SHARPE letters
HARLEY QUINN created by PAUL DINI and BRUCE TIMM
YOU TRAILED US HERE FROM ONE RED AND BLACK JACKET? HATE TO SAY IT, BUT I'M ALMOST IMPRESSED.
WASN'T HARD. THE RETURN ADDRESS IS ON THE LABEL.
OH YEAH! I BEEN DOIN' THAT EVER SINCE I LOST MY GOOD SATIN BOMBER.

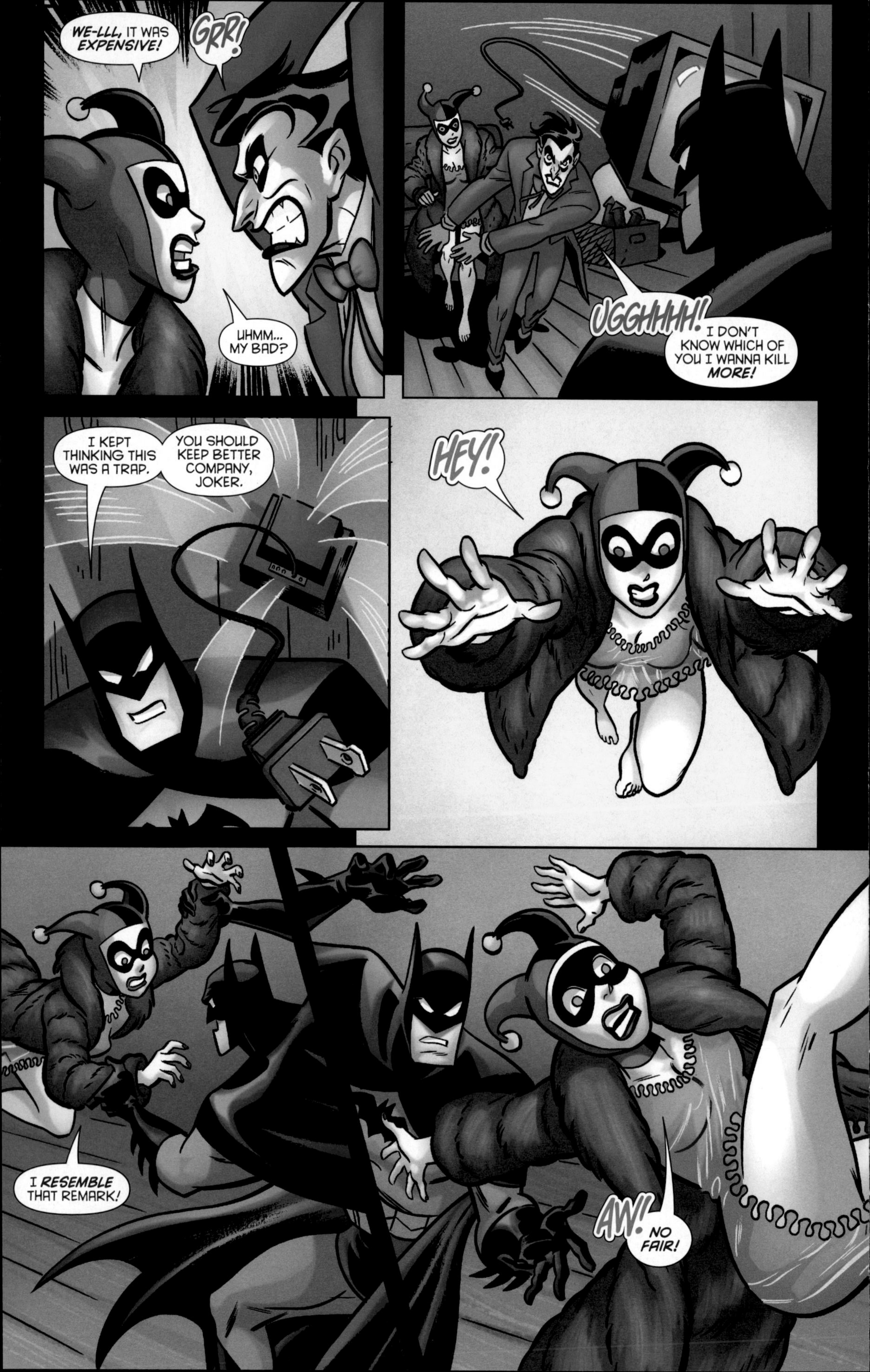

WE-LLL, IT WAS EXPENSIVE!
GRR!
UHMM... MY BAD?
UGGHHHH!
I DON'T KNOW WHICH OF YOU I WANNA KILL MORE!
I KEPT THINKING THIS WAS A TRAP.
YOU SHOULD KEEP BETTER COMPANY, JOKER.
HEY!
I RESEMBLE THAT REMARK!
AW!
NO FAIR!

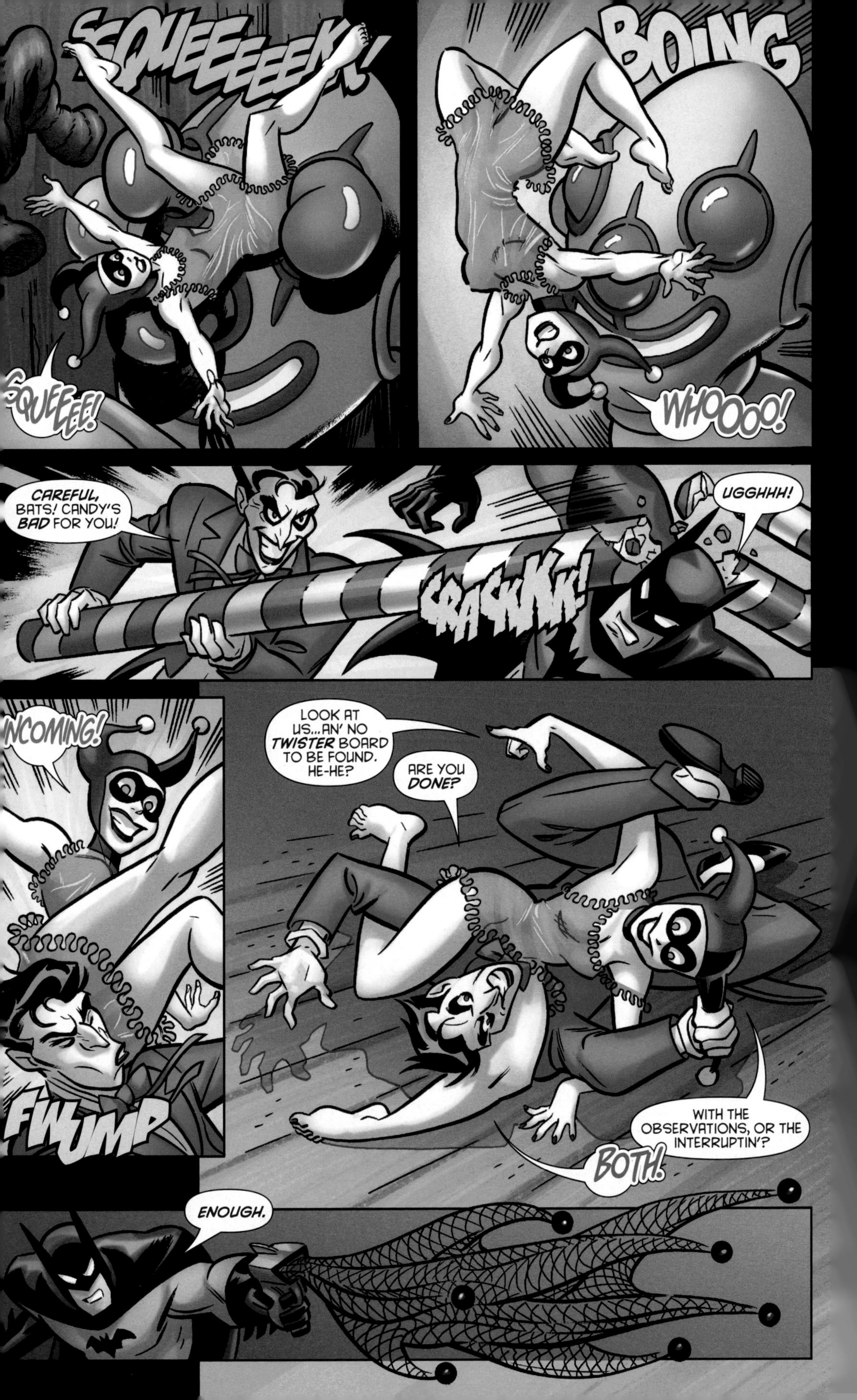
SQUEEEEEEEK!
SQUEEEE!
BOING
WHOOOOO!
CAREFUL, BATS! CANDY'S BAD FOR YOU!
UGGHHH!
CRACKKK!
INCOMING!
FWUMP
LOOK AT US...AN' NO TWISTER BOARD TO BE FOUND. HE-HE?
ARE YOU DONE?
WITH THE OBSERVATIONS, OR THE INTERRUPTIN'?
BOTH.
ENOUGH.

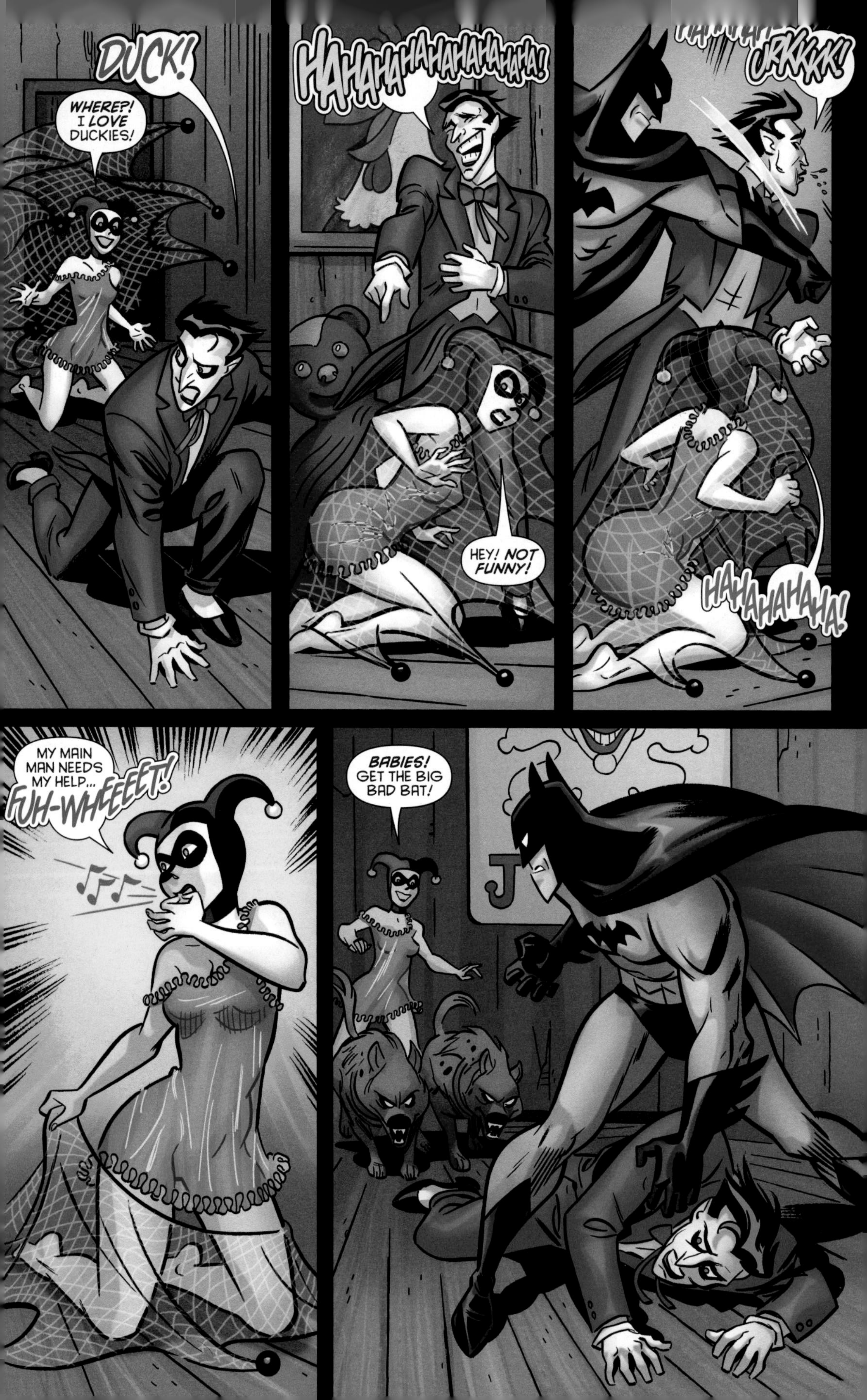

DUCK!
WHERE?! I LOVE DUCKIES!
HAHAHAHAHAHAHAHAHAHA!
HEY! NOT FUNNY!
URKKKK!
HAHAHAHAHA!
MY MAIN MAN NEEDS MY HELP...
FUH-WHEEEEET!
BABIES! GET THE BIG BAD BAT!

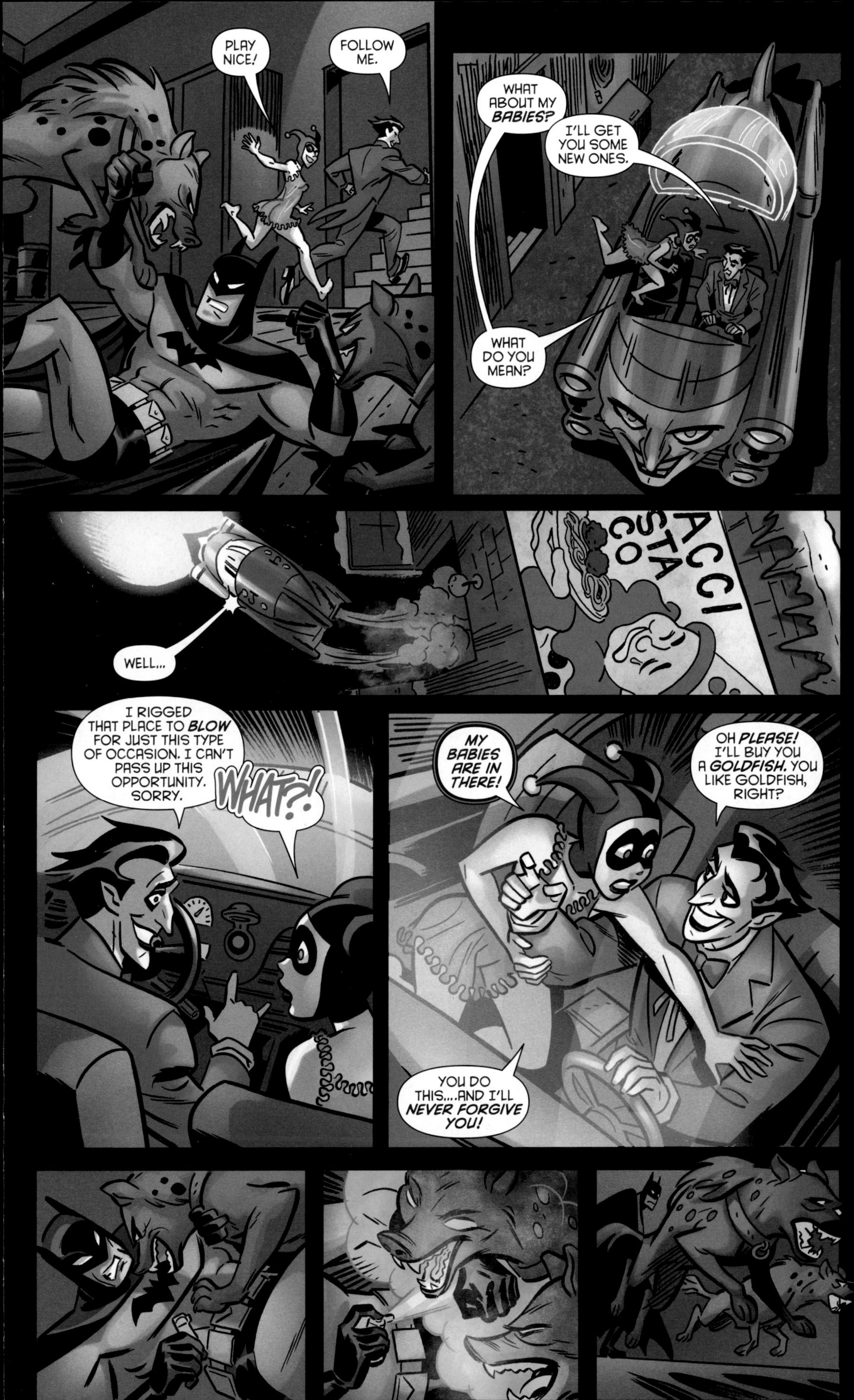
PLAY NICE!
FOLLOW ME.
WHAT ABOUT MY BABIES?
I'LL GET YOU SOME NEW ONES.
WHAT DO YOU MEAN?
WELL...
ACCI
STA
CO
I RIGGED THAT PLACE TO BLOW FOR JUST THIS TYPE OF OCCASION. I CAN'T PASS UP THIS OPPORTUNITY. SORRY.
WHAT?!
MY BABIES ARE IN THERE!
OH PLEASE! I'LL BUY YOU A GOLDFISH. YOU LIKE GOLDFISH, RIGHT?
YOU DO THIS....AND I'LL NEVER FORGIVE YOU!

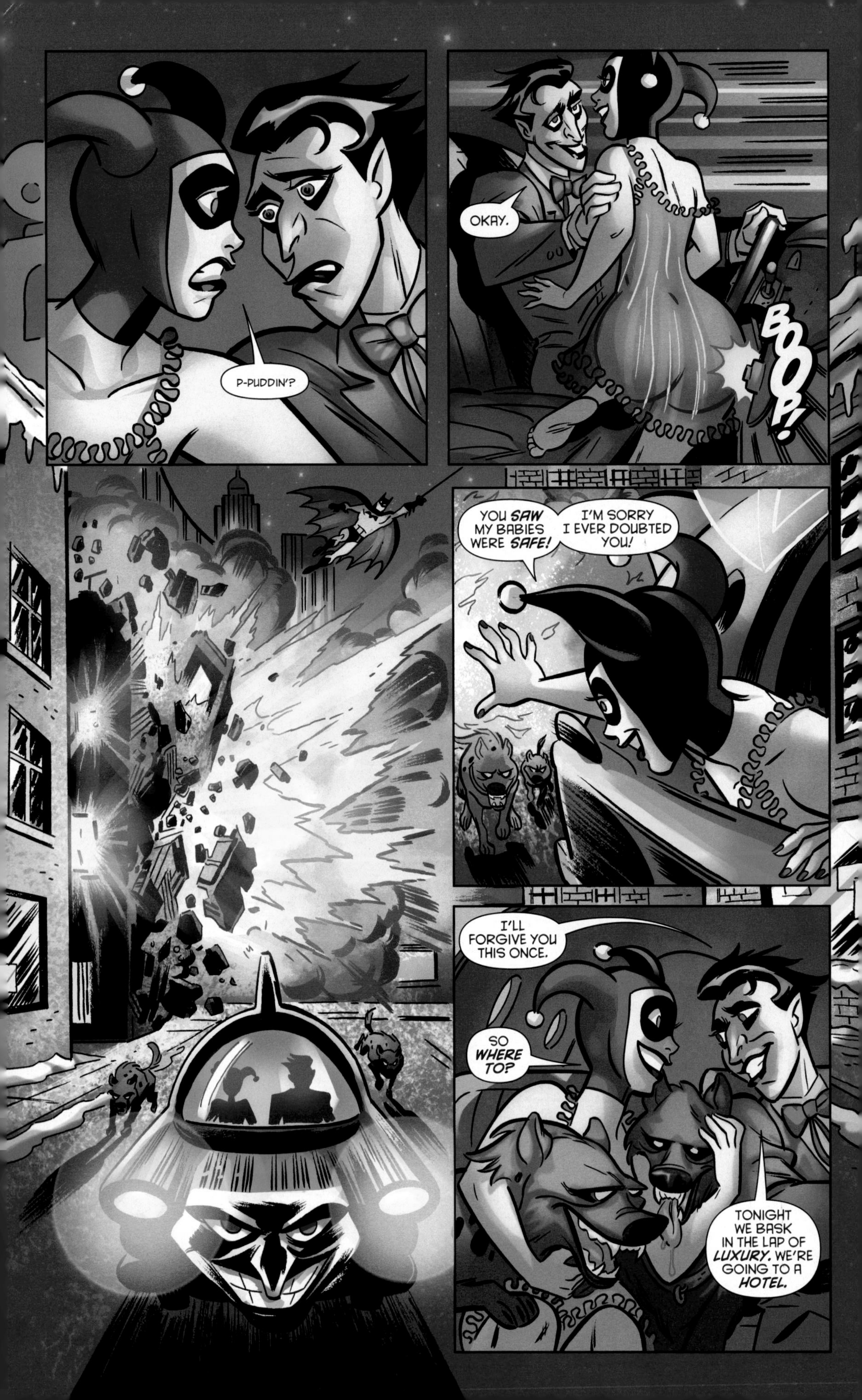
P-PUDDIN'?
OKAY.
BOOP!
YOU SAW MY BABIES WERE SAFE!
I'M SORRY I EVER DOUBTED YOU!
I'LL FORGIVE YOU THIS ONCE.
SO WHERE TO?
TONIGHT WE BASK IN THE LAP OF LUXURY. WE'RE GOING TO A HOTEL.

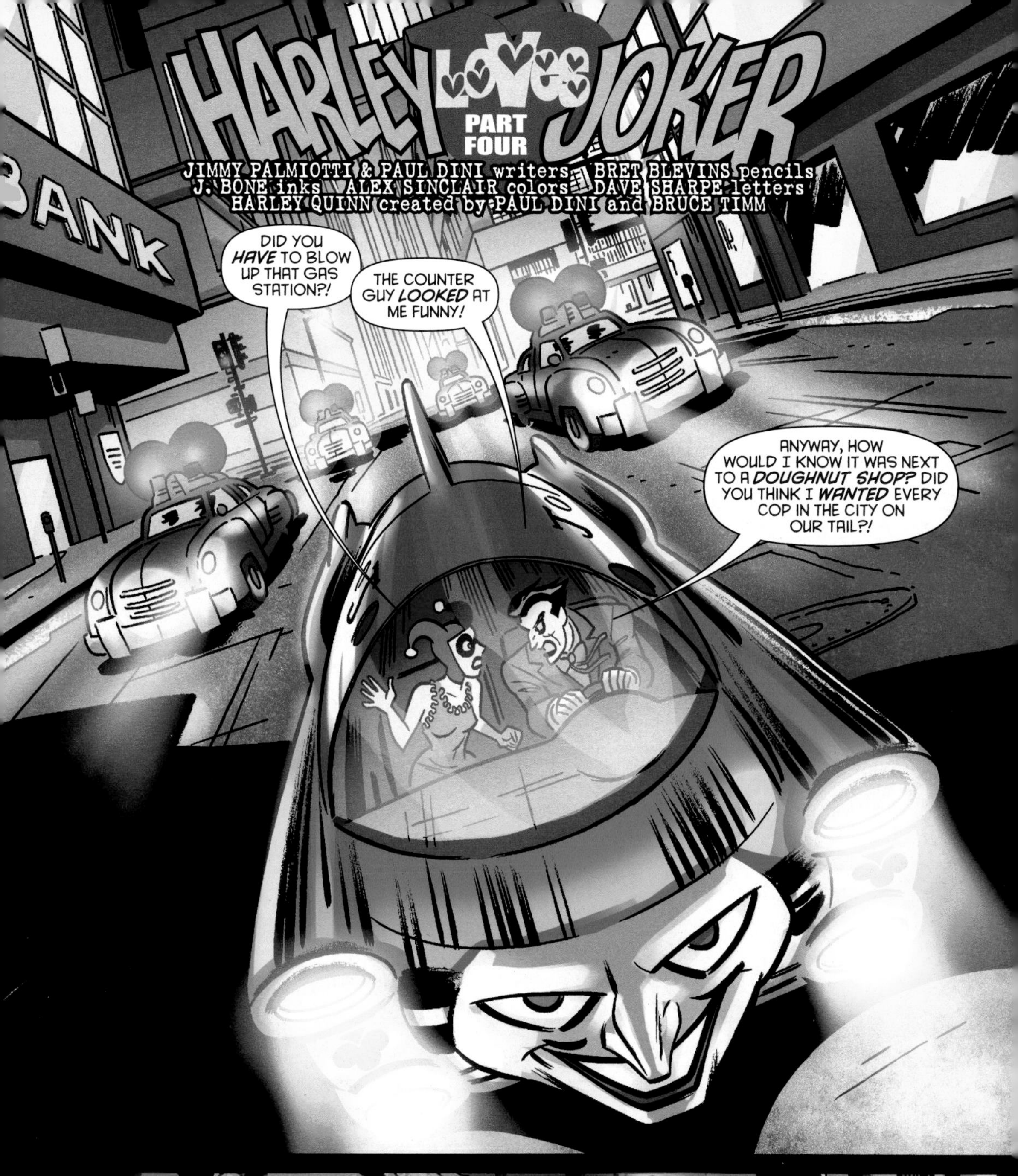
HARLEY LOVES JOKER
PART FOUR
JIMMY PALMIOTTI & PAUL DINI writers BRET BLEVINS pencils
J. BONE inks ALEX SINCLAIR colors DAVE SHARPE letters
HARLEY QUINN created by PAUL DINI and BRUCE TIMM
BANK
DID YOU *HAVE* TO BLOW UP THAT GAS STATION?!
THE COUNTER GUY *LOOKED* AT ME FUNNY!
ANYWAY, HOW WOULD I KNOW IT WAS NEXT TO A *DOUGHNUT SHOP?* DID YOU THINK I *WANTED* EVERY COP IN THE CITY ON OUR TAIL?!

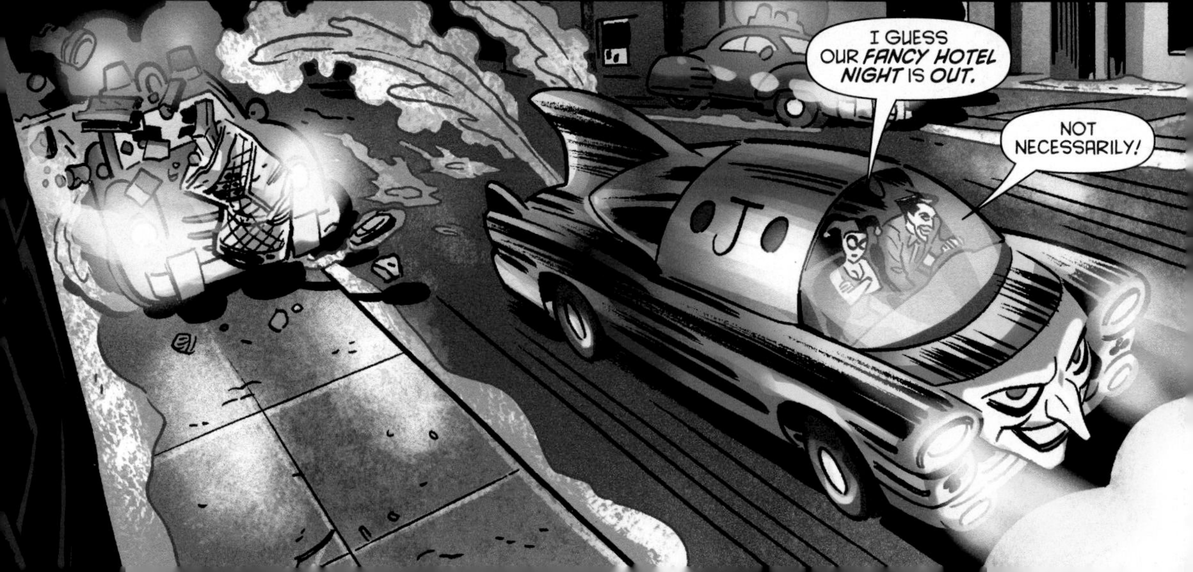
I GUESS OUR *FANCY HOTEL NIGHT* IS *OUT.*
NOT NECESSARILY!

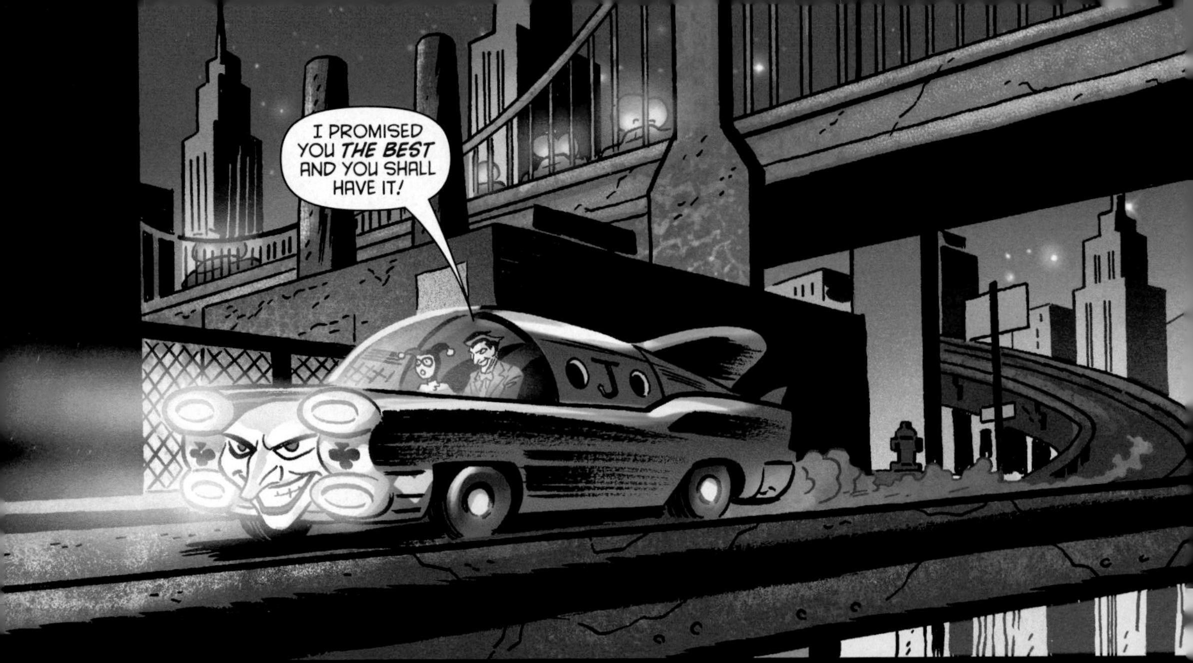
I PROMISED YOU THE BEST AND YOU SHALL HAVE IT!
J

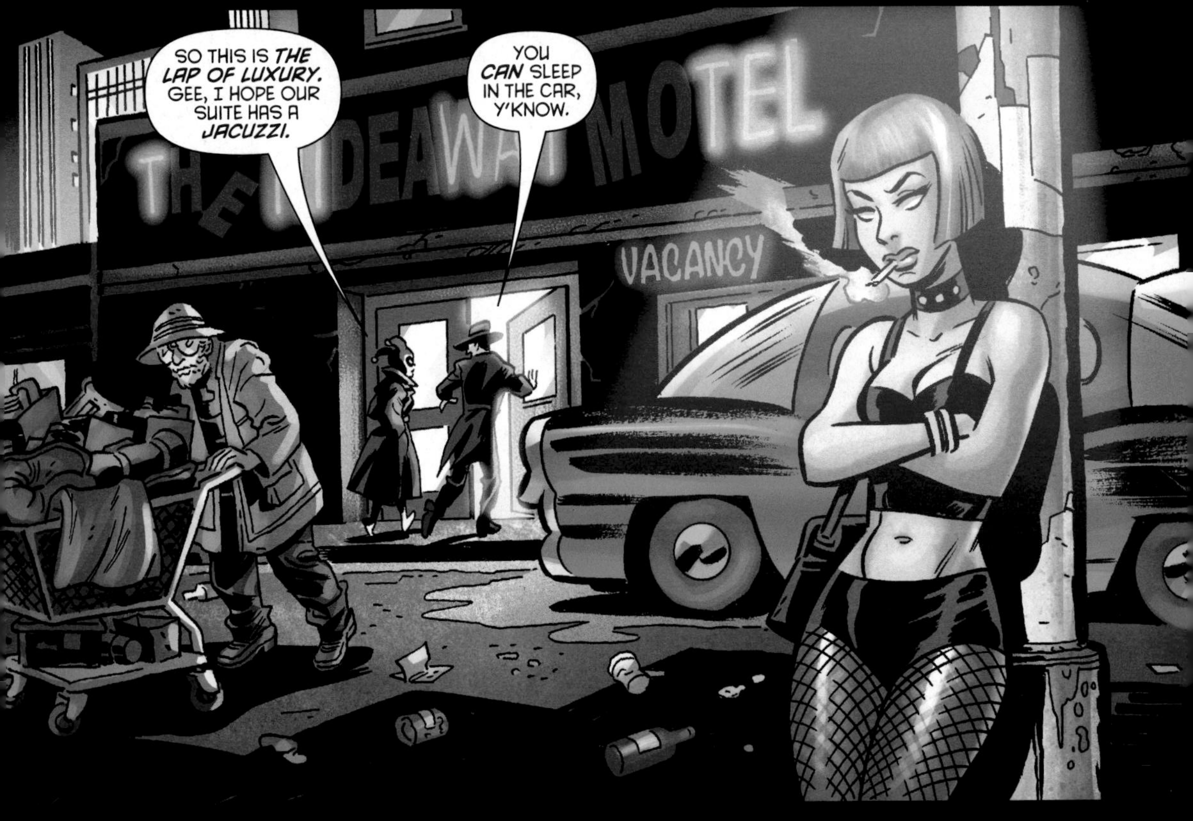
SO THIS IS THE LAP OF LUXURY. GEE, I HOPE OUR SUITE HAS A JACUZZI.
YOU CAN SLEEP IN THE CAR, Y'KNOW.
THE HIDEAWAY MOTEL
VACANCY

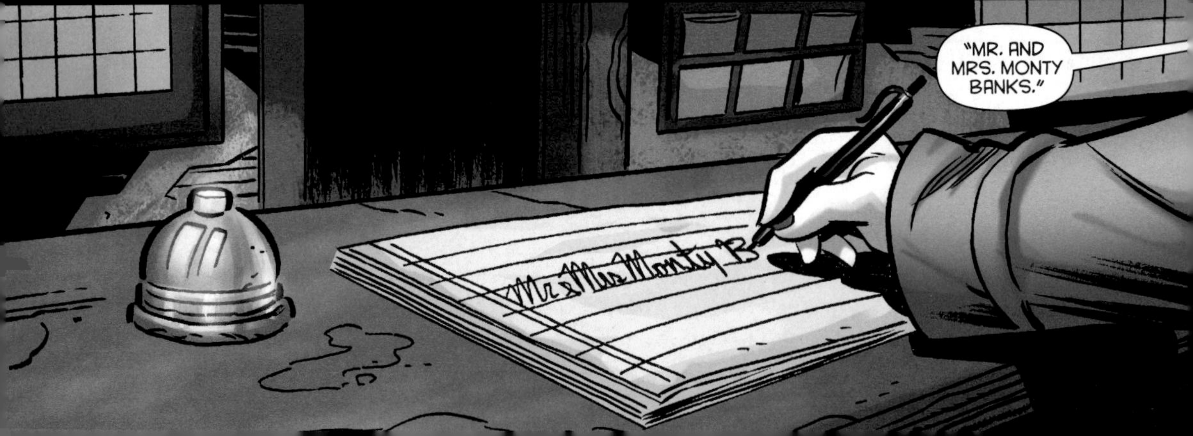
"MR. AND MRS. MONTY BANKS."

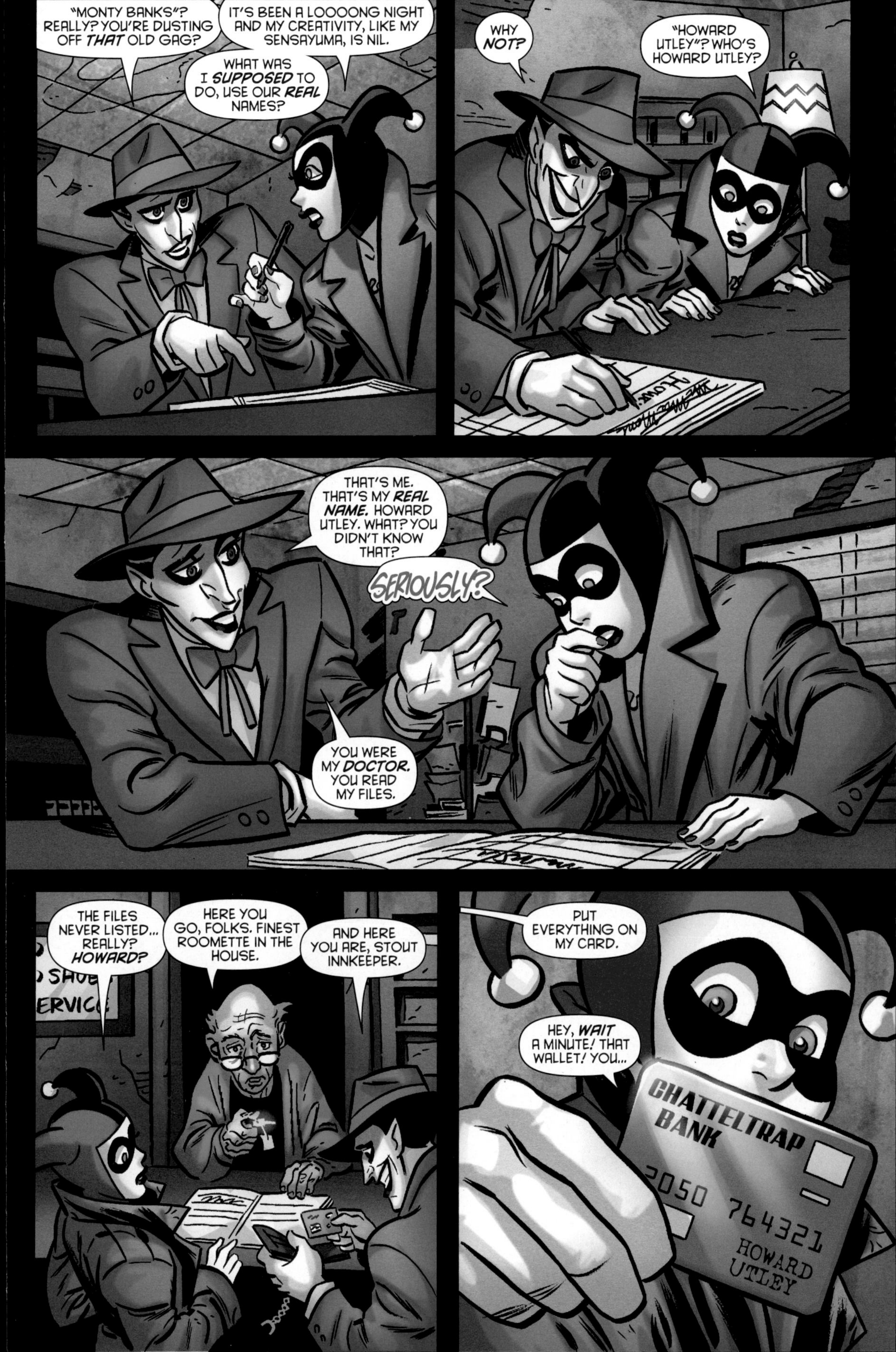
"MONTY BANKS"? REALLY? YOU'RE DUSTING OFF *THAT* OLD GAG?
IT'S BEEN A LOOOONG NIGHT AND MY CREATIVITY, LIKE MY SENSAYUMA, IS NIL.
WHAT WAS I *SUPPOSED* TO DO, USE OUR *REAL* NAMES?
WHY *NOT?*
"HOWARD UTLEY"? WHO'S HOWARD UTLEY?
THAT'S ME. THAT'S MY *REAL NAME.* HOWARD UTLEY. WHAT? YOU DIDN'T KNOW THAT?
SERIOUSLY?
YOU WERE MY *DOCTOR.* YOU READ MY FILES.
THE FILES NEVER LISTED... REALLY? *HOWARD?*
HERE YOU GO, FOLKS. FINEST ROOMETTE IN THE HOUSE.
AND HERE YOU ARE, STOUT INNKEEPER.
PUT EVERYTHING ON MY CARD.
HEY, *WAIT* A MINUTE! THAT WALLET! YOU...
CHATTELTRAP BANK
2050 764321
HOWARD UTLEY

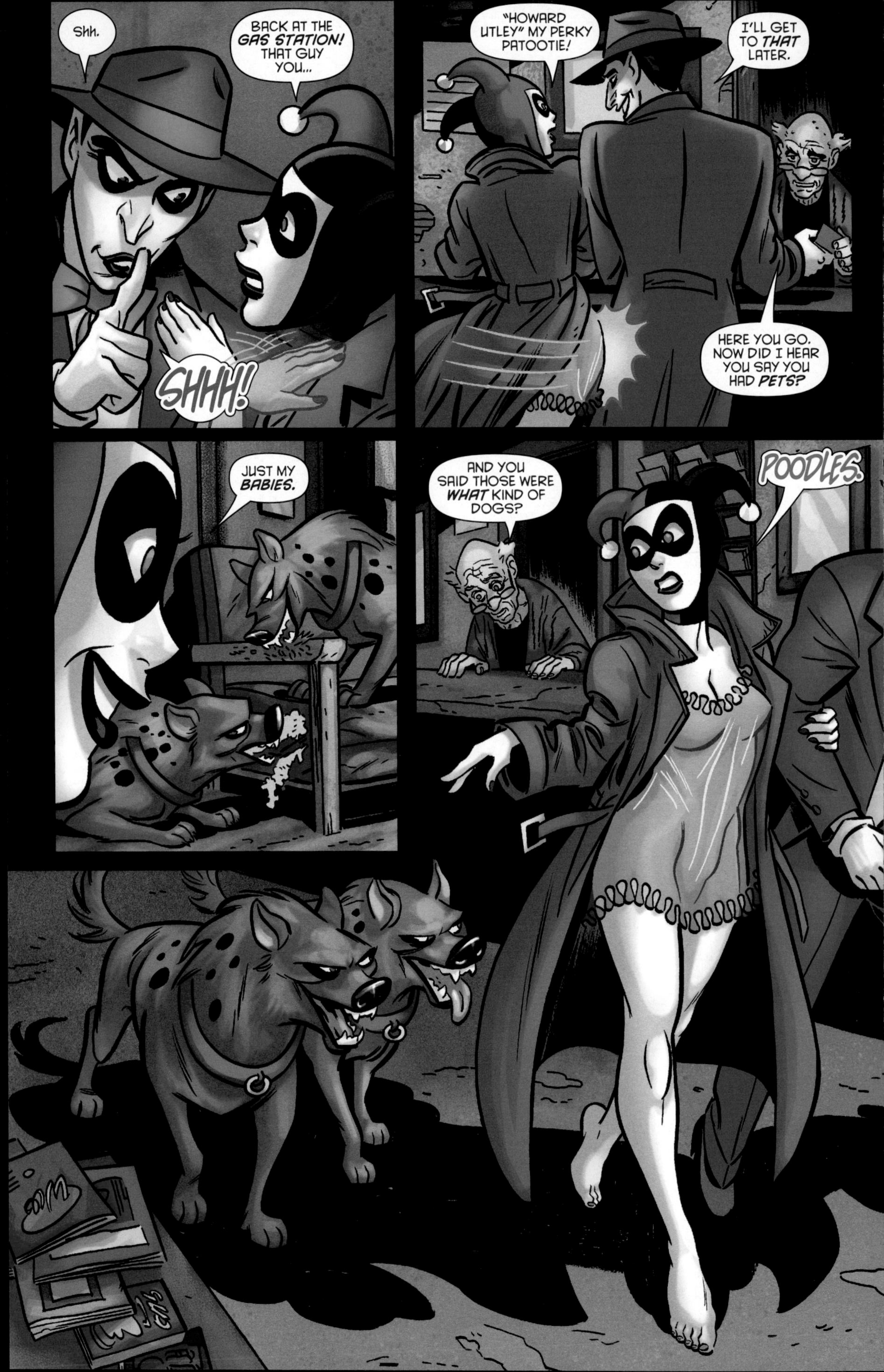
Shh.
BACK AT THE GAS STATION! THAT GUY YOU...
SHHH!
"HOWARD UTLEY" MY PERKY PATOOTIE!
I'LL GET TO THAT LATER.
HERE YOU GO. NOW DID I HEAR YOU SAY YOU HAD PETS?
JUST MY BABIES.
AND YOU SAID THOSE WERE WHAT KIND OF DOGS?
POODLES.

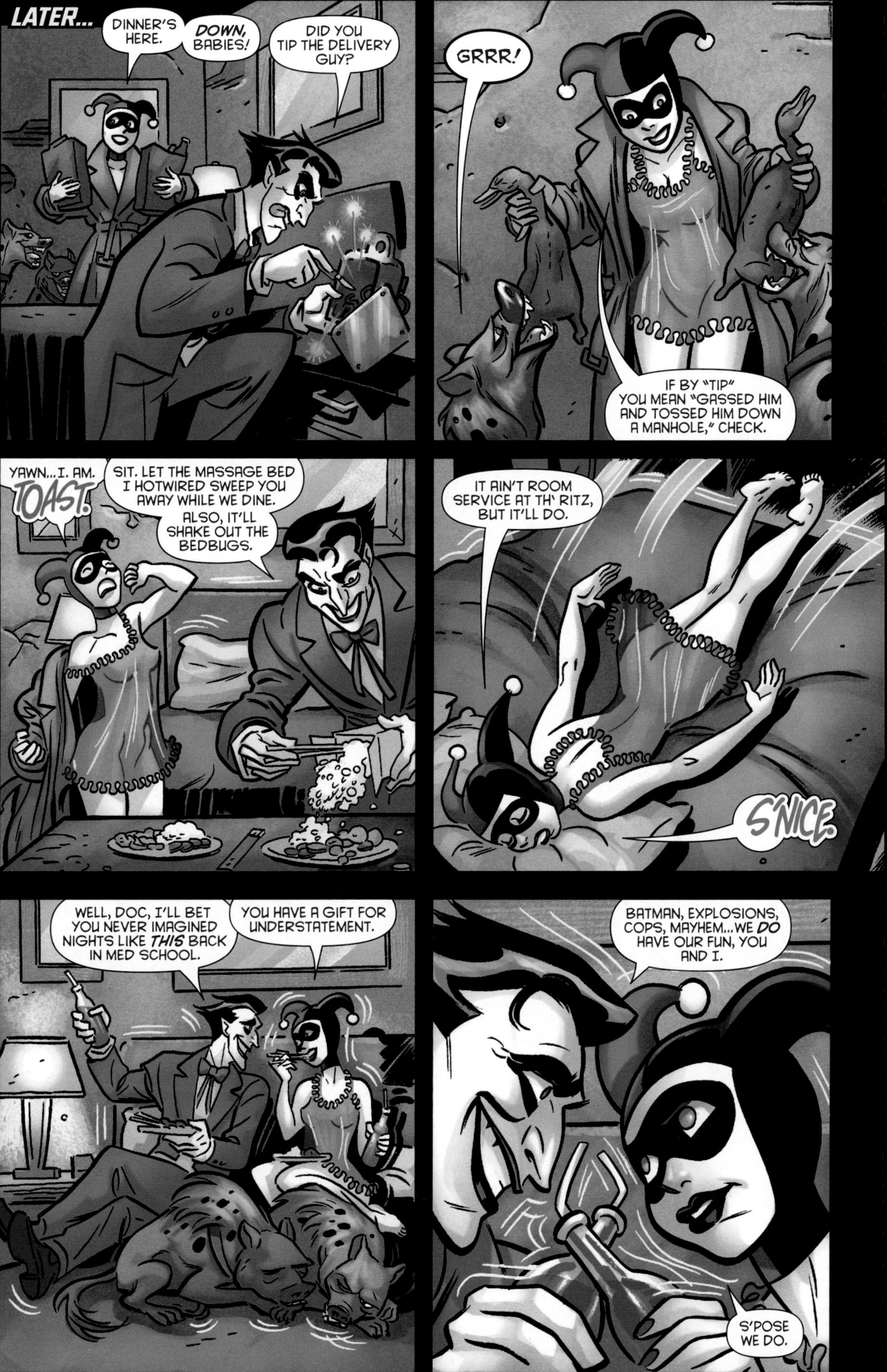
LATER...
DINNER'S HERE.
DOWN, BABIES!
DID YOU TIP THE DELIVERY GUY?
GRRR!
IF BY "TIP" YOU MEAN "GASSED HIM AND TOSSED HIM DOWN A MANHOLE," CHECK.
YAWN...I. AM. TOAST.
SIT. LET THE MASSAGE BED I HOTWIRED SWEEP YOU AWAY WHILE WE DINE.
ALSO, IT'LL SHAKE OUT THE BEDBUGS.
IT AIN'T ROOM SERVICE AT TH' RITZ, BUT IT'LL DO.
S'NICE.
WELL, DOC, I'LL BET YOU NEVER IMAGINED NIGHTS LIKE THIS BACK IN MED SCHOOL.
YOU HAVE A GIFT FOR UNDERSTATEMENT.
BATMAN, EXPLOSIONS, COPS, MAYHEM...WE DO HAVE OUR FUN, YOU AND I.
S'POSE WE DO.

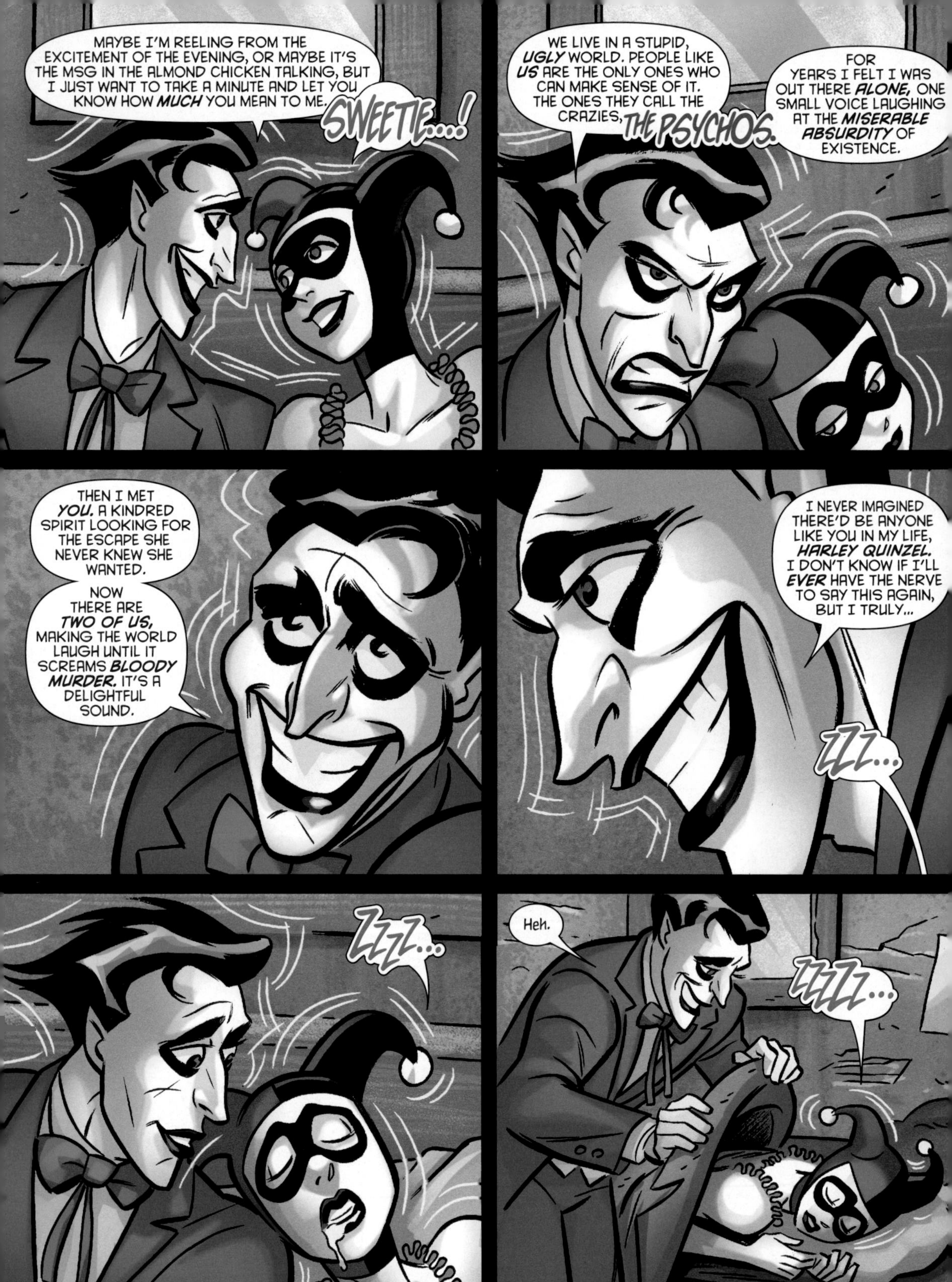
MAYBE I'M REELING FROM THE EXCITEMENT OF THE EVENING, OR MAYBE IT'S THE MSG IN THE ALMOND CHICKEN TALKING, BUT I JUST WANT TO TAKE A MINUTE AND LET YOU KNOW HOW MUCH YOU MEAN TO ME.
SWEETIE...!
WE LIVE IN A STUPID, UGLY WORLD. PEOPLE LIKE US ARE THE ONLY ONES WHO CAN MAKE SENSE OF IT. THE ONES THEY CALL THE CRAZIES, THE PSYCHOS.
FOR YEARS I FELT I WAS OUT THERE ALONE, ONE SMALL VOICE LAUGHING AT THE MISERABLE ABSURDITY OF EXISTENCE.
THEN I MET YOU. A KINDRED SPIRIT LOOKING FOR THE ESCAPE SHE NEVER KNEW SHE WANTED.
NOW THERE ARE TWO OF US, MAKING THE WORLD LAUGH UNTIL IT SCREAMS BLOODY MURDER. IT'S A DELIGHTFUL SOUND.
I NEVER IMAGINED THERE'D BE ANYONE LIKE YOU IN MY LIFE, HARLEY QUINZEL. I DON'T KNOW IF I'LL EVER HAVE THE NERVE TO SAY THIS AGAIN, BUT I TRULY...
ZZZ...
ZZZZ...
Heh.
ZZZZZ...

Shhh...Harley is sleeping.

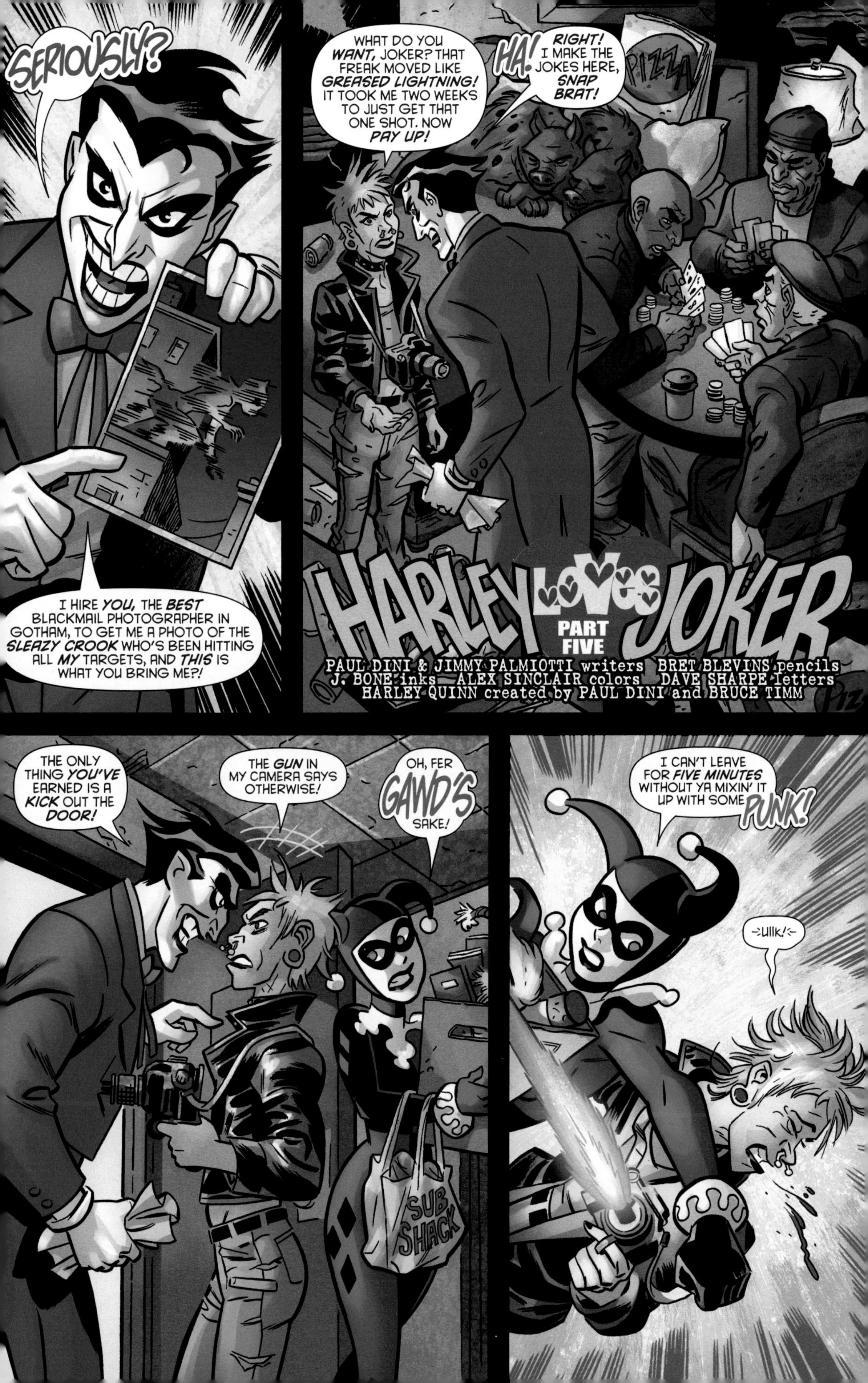
SERIOUSLY?
I HIRE YOU, THE BEST BLACKMAIL PHOTOGRAPHER IN GOTHAM, TO GET ME A PHOTO OF THE SLEAZY CROOK WHO'S BEEN HITTING ALL MY TARGETS, AND THIS IS WHAT YOU BRING ME?!
WHAT DO YOU WANT, JOKER? THAT FREAK MOVED LIKE GREASED LIGHTNING! IT TOOK ME TWO WEEKS TO JUST GET THAT ONE SHOT. NOW PAY UP!
HA! RIGHT! I MAKE THE JOKES HERE, SNAP BRAT!
PIZZA
HARLEY LOVES JOKER
PART FIVE
PAUL DINI & JIMMY PALMIOTTI writers BRET BLEVINS pencils
J. BONE inks ALEX SINCLAIR colors DAVE SHARPE letters
HARLEY QUINN created by PAUL DINI and BRUCE TIMM
THE ONLY THING YOU'VE EARNED IS A KICK OUT THE DOOR!
THE GUN IN MY CAMERA SAYS OTHERWISE!
OH, FER GAWD'S SAKE!
SUB SHACK
I CAN'T LEAVE FOR FIVE MINUTES WITHOUT YA MIXIN' IT UP WITH SOME PUNK!
-UlIK!-

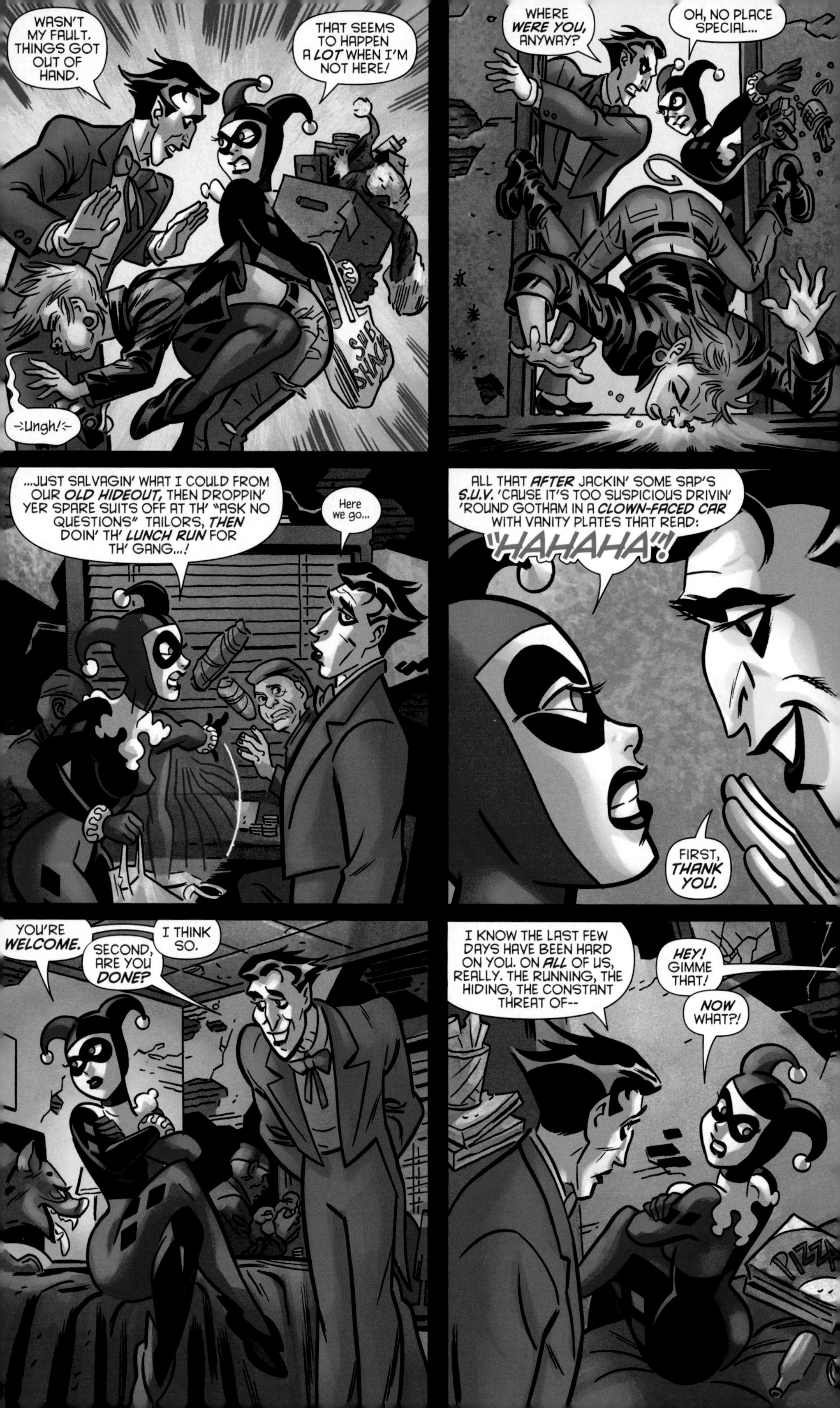

WASN'T MY FAULT. THINGS GOT OUT OF HAND.
THAT SEEMS TO HAPPEN A *LOT* WHEN I'M NOT HERE!
SUB SHACK
Ungh!
WHERE *WERE YOU,* ANYWAY?
OH, NO PLACE SPECIAL...
...JUST SALVAGIN' WHAT I COULD FROM OUR *OLD HIDEOUT,* THEN DROPPIN' YER SPARE SUITS OFF AT TH' "ASK NO QUESTIONS" TAILORS, *THEN* DOIN' TH' *LUNCH RUN* FOR TH' GANG...!
Here we go...
ALL THAT *AFTER* JACKIN' SOME SAP'S *S.U.V.* 'CAUSE IT'S TOO SUSPICIOUS DRIVIN' 'ROUND GOTHAM IN A *CLOWN-FACED CAR* WITH VANITY PLATES THAT READ: "HAHAHA"!
FIRST, *THANK YOU.*
YOU'RE *WELCOME.*
SECOND, ARE YOU *DONE?*
I THINK SO.
I KNOW THE LAST FEW DAYS HAVE BEEN HARD ON YOU. ON *ALL* OF US, REALLY. THE RUNNING, THE HIDING, THE CONSTANT THREAT OF--
HEY! GIMME THAT!
NOW WHAT?!

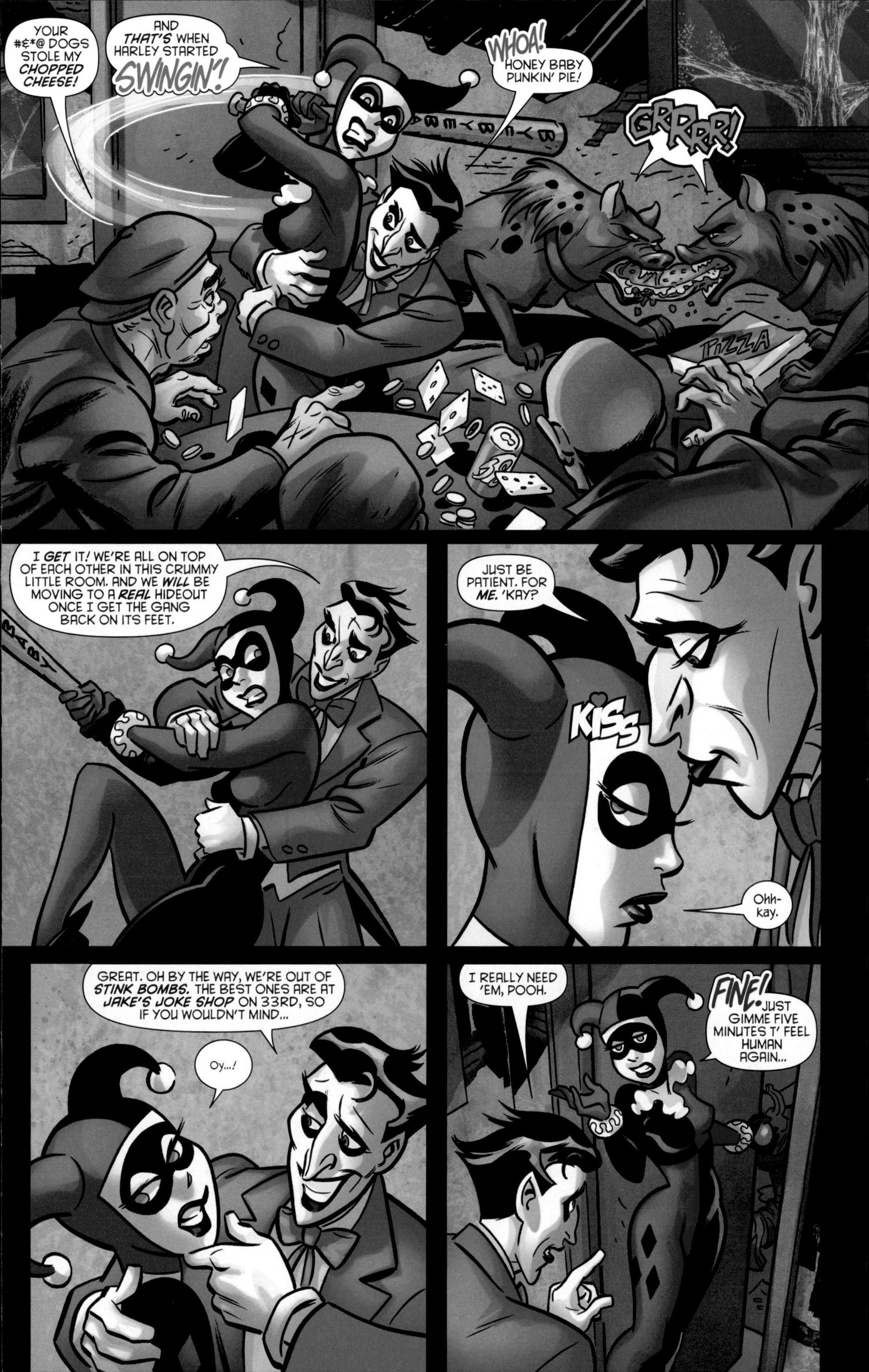
YOUR #&*@ DOGS STOLE MY CHOPPED CHEESE!
AND THAT'S WHEN HARLEY STARTED SWINGIN'!
WHOA! HONEY BABY PUNKIN' PIE!
GRRRR!
PIZZA
I GET IT! WE'RE ALL ON TOP OF EACH OTHER IN THIS CRUMMY LITTLE ROOM. AND WE WILL BE MOVING TO A REAL HIDEOUT ONCE I GET THE GANG BACK ON ITS FEET.
JUST BE PATIENT. FOR ME. 'KAY?
KISS
Ohh-kay.
GREAT. OH BY THE WAY, WE'RE OUT OF STINK BOMBS. THE BEST ONES ARE AT JAKE'S JOKE SHOP ON 33RD, SO IF YOU WOULDN'T MIND...
Oy...!
I REALLY NEED 'EM, POOH.
FINE! JUST GIMME FIVE MINUTES T' FEEL HUMAN AGAIN...

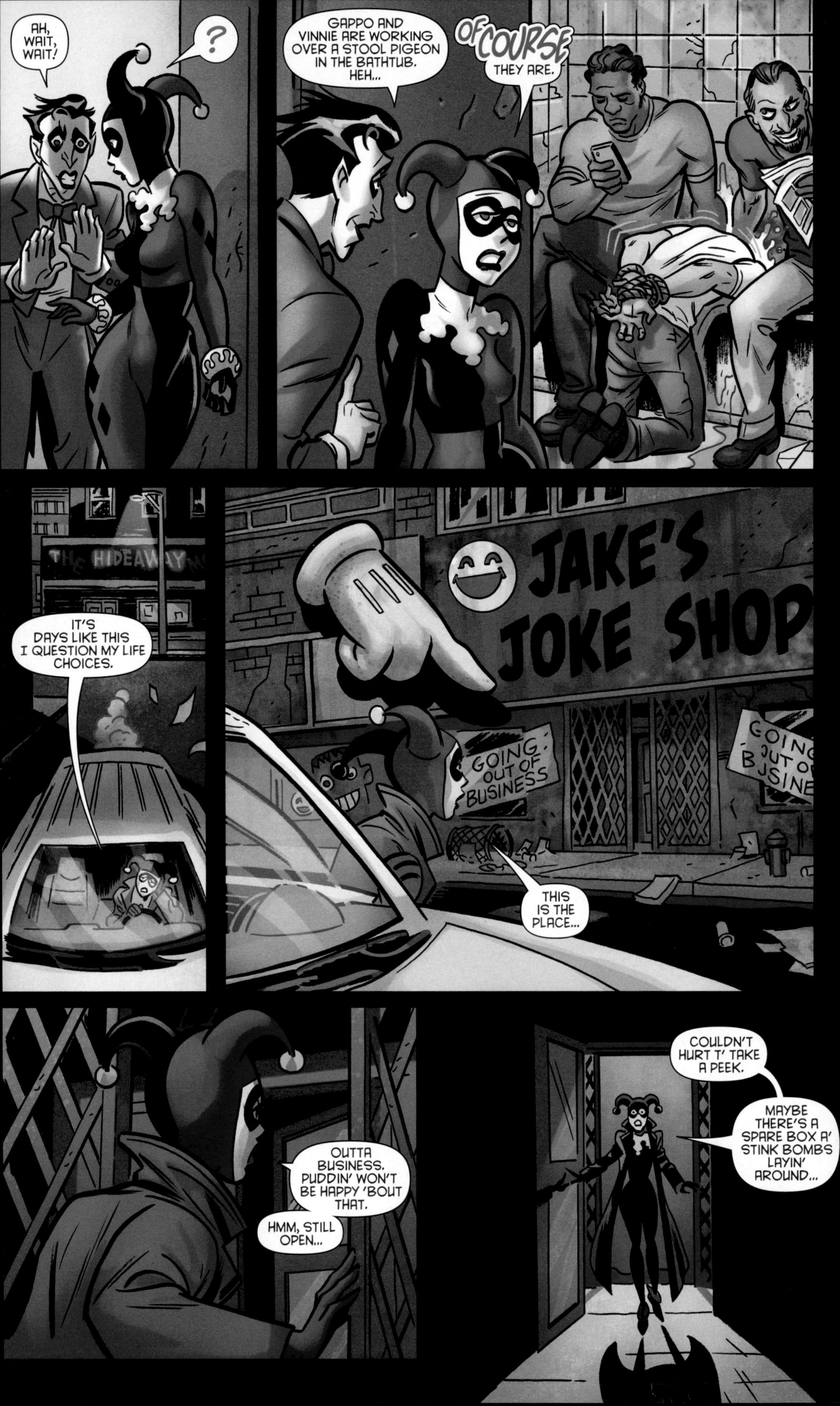

AH, WAIT, WAIT!
?
GAPPO AND VINNIE ARE WORKING OVER A STOOL PIGEON IN THE BATHTUB. HEH...
OF COURSE THEY ARE.
THE HIDEAWAY
IT'S DAYS LIKE THIS I QUESTION MY LIFE CHOICES.
JAKE'S JOKE SHOP
GOING OUT OF BUSINESS
THIS IS THE PLACE...
OUTTA BUSINESS. PUDDIN' WON'T BE HAPPY 'BOUT THAT.
HMM, STILL OPEN...
COULDN'T HURT T' TAKE A PEEK.
MAYBE THERE'S A SPARE BOX A' STINK BOMBS LAYIN' AROUND...

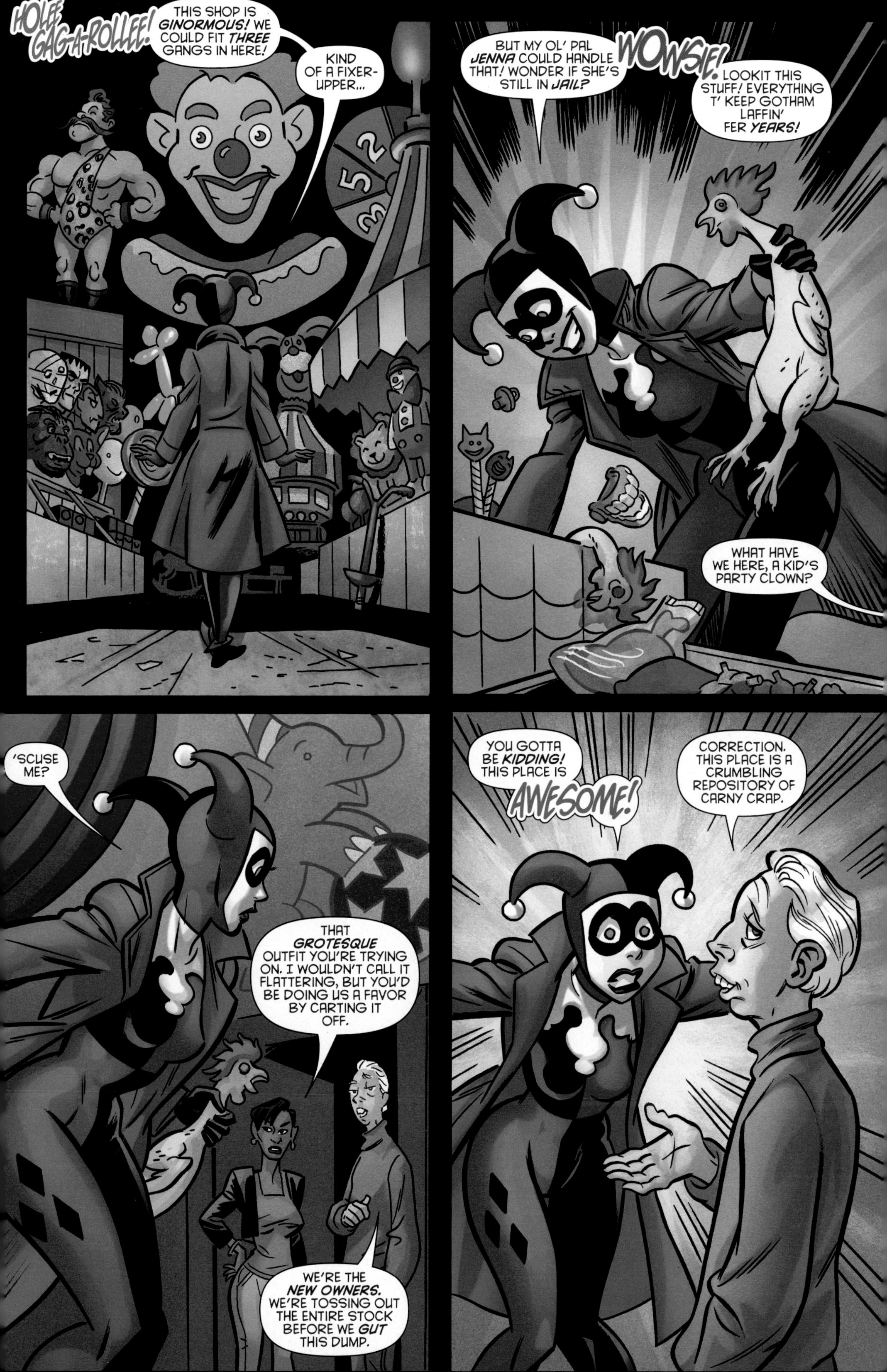
HOLEE GAG-A-ROLLEE!
THIS SHOP IS GINORMOUS! WE COULD FIT THREE GANGS IN HERE!
KIND OF A FIXER-UPPER...
BUT MY OL' PAL JENNA COULD HANDLE THAT! WONDER IF SHE'S STILL IN JAIL?
WOWSIE!
LOOKIT THIS STUFF! EVERYTHING T' KEEP GOTHAM LAFFIN' FER YEARS!
WHAT HAVE WE HERE, A KID'S PARTY CLOWN?
'SCUSE ME?
THAT GROTESQUE OUTFIT YOU'RE TRYING ON. I WOULDN'T CALL IT FLATTERING, BUT YOU'D BE DOING US A FAVOR BY CARTING IT OFF.
WE'RE THE NEW OWNERS. WE'RE TOSSING OUT THE ENTIRE STOCK BEFORE WE GUT THIS DUMP.
YOU GOTTA BE KIDDING! THIS PLACE IS AWESOME!
CORRECTION. THIS PLACE IS A CRUMBLING REPOSITORY OF CARNY CRAP.

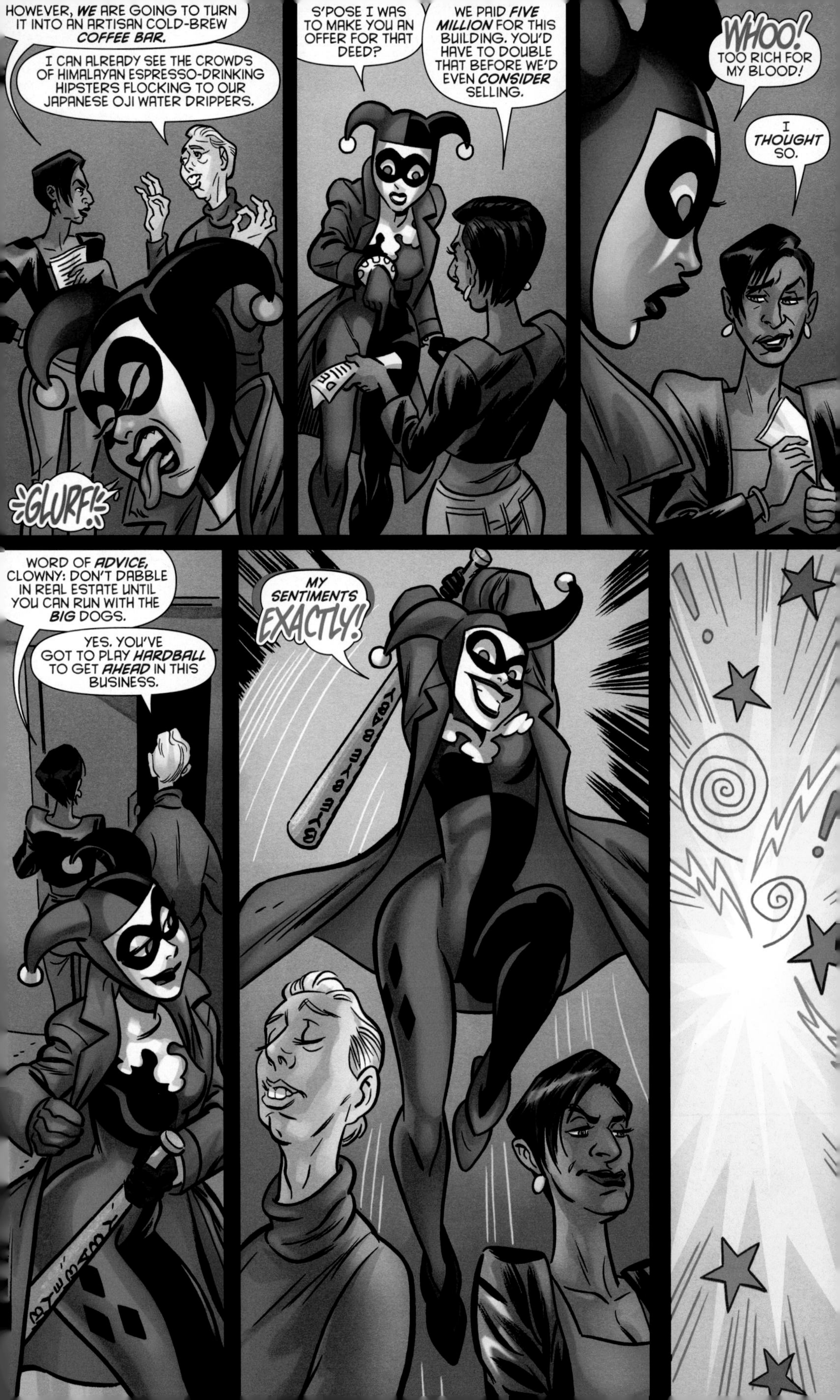
HOWEVER, WE ARE GOING TO TURN IT INTO AN ARTISAN COLD-BREW COFFEE BAR.
I CAN ALREADY SEE THE CROWDS OF HIMALAYAN ESPRESSO-DRINKING HIPSTERS FLOCKING TO OUR JAPANESE OJI WATER DRIPPERS.
GLURF!
S'POSE I WAS TO MAKE YOU AN OFFER FOR THAT DEED?
WE PAID FIVE MILLION FOR THIS BUILDING. YOU'D HAVE TO DOUBLE THAT BEFORE WE'D EVEN CONSIDER SELLING.
WHOO! TOO RICH FOR MY BLOOD!
I THOUGHT SO.
WORD OF ADVICE, CLOWNY: DON'T DABBLE IN REAL ESTATE UNTIL YOU CAN RUN WITH THE BIG DOGS.
YES. YOU'VE GOT TO PLAY HARDBALL TO GET AHEAD IN THIS BUSINESS.
MY SENTIMENTS EXACTLY!

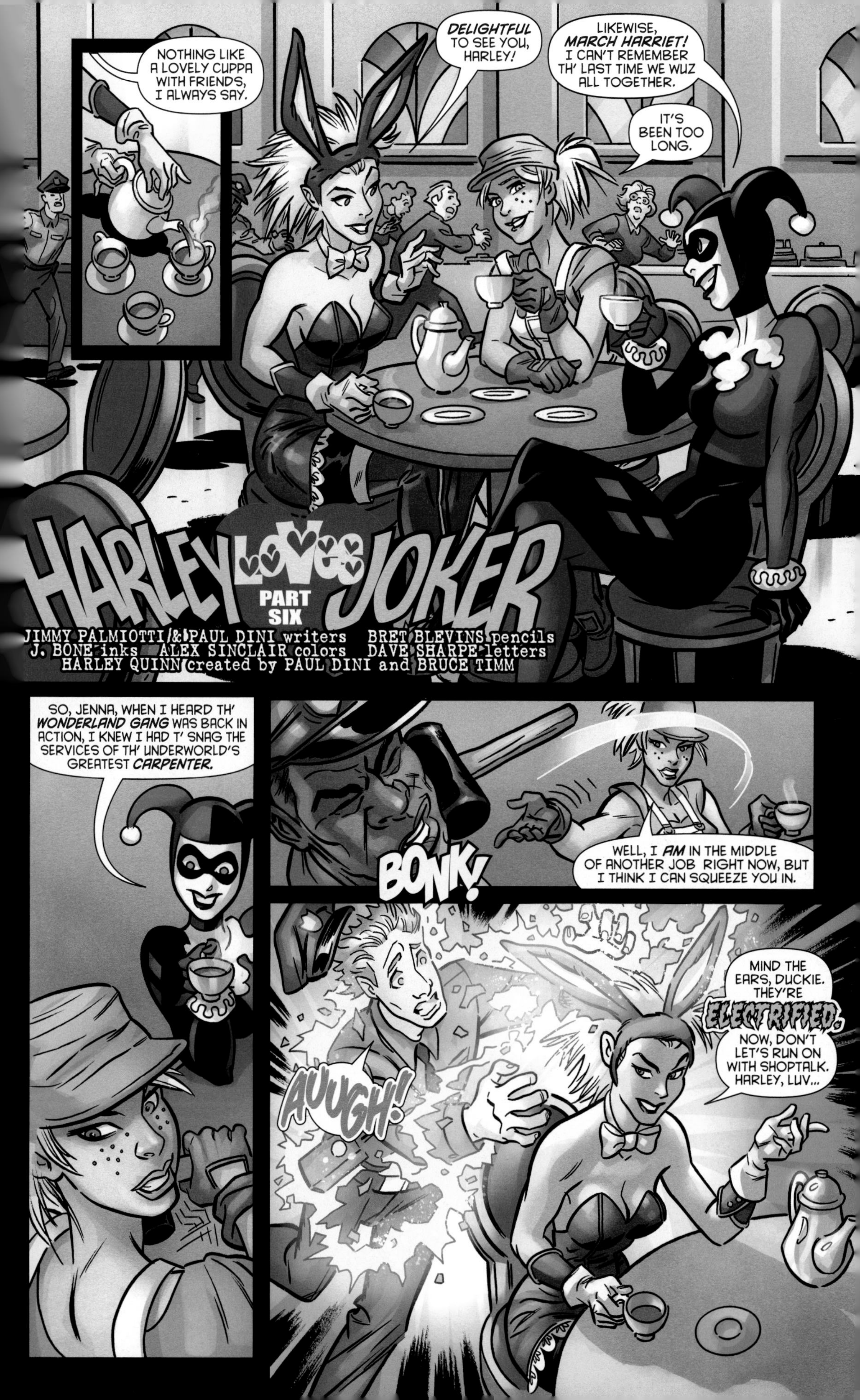
NOTHING LIKE A LOVELY CUPPA WITH FRIENDS, I ALWAYS SAY.
DELIGHTFUL TO SEE YOU, HARLEY!
LIKEWISE, MARCH HARRIET! I CAN'T REMEMBER TH' LAST TIME WE WUZ ALL TOGETHER.
IT'S BEEN TOO LONG.
HARLEY LOVES JOKER
PART SIX
JIMMY PALMIOTTI & PAUL DINI writers BRET BLEVINS pencils
J. BONE inks ALEX SINCLAIR colors DAVE SHARPE letters
HARLEY QUINN created by PAUL DINI and BRUCE TIMM
SO, JENNA, WHEN I HEARD TH' WONDERLAND GANG WAS BACK IN ACTION, I KNEW I HAD T' SNAG THE SERVICES OF TH' UNDERWORLD'S GREATEST CARPENTER.
WELL, I AM IN THE MIDDLE OF ANOTHER JOB RIGHT NOW, BUT I THINK I CAN SQUEEZE YOU IN.
BONK!
MIND THE EARS, DUCKIE. THEY'RE ELECTRIFIED.
NOW, DON'T LET'S RUN ON WITH SHOPTALK. HARLEY, LUV...
AUUGH!

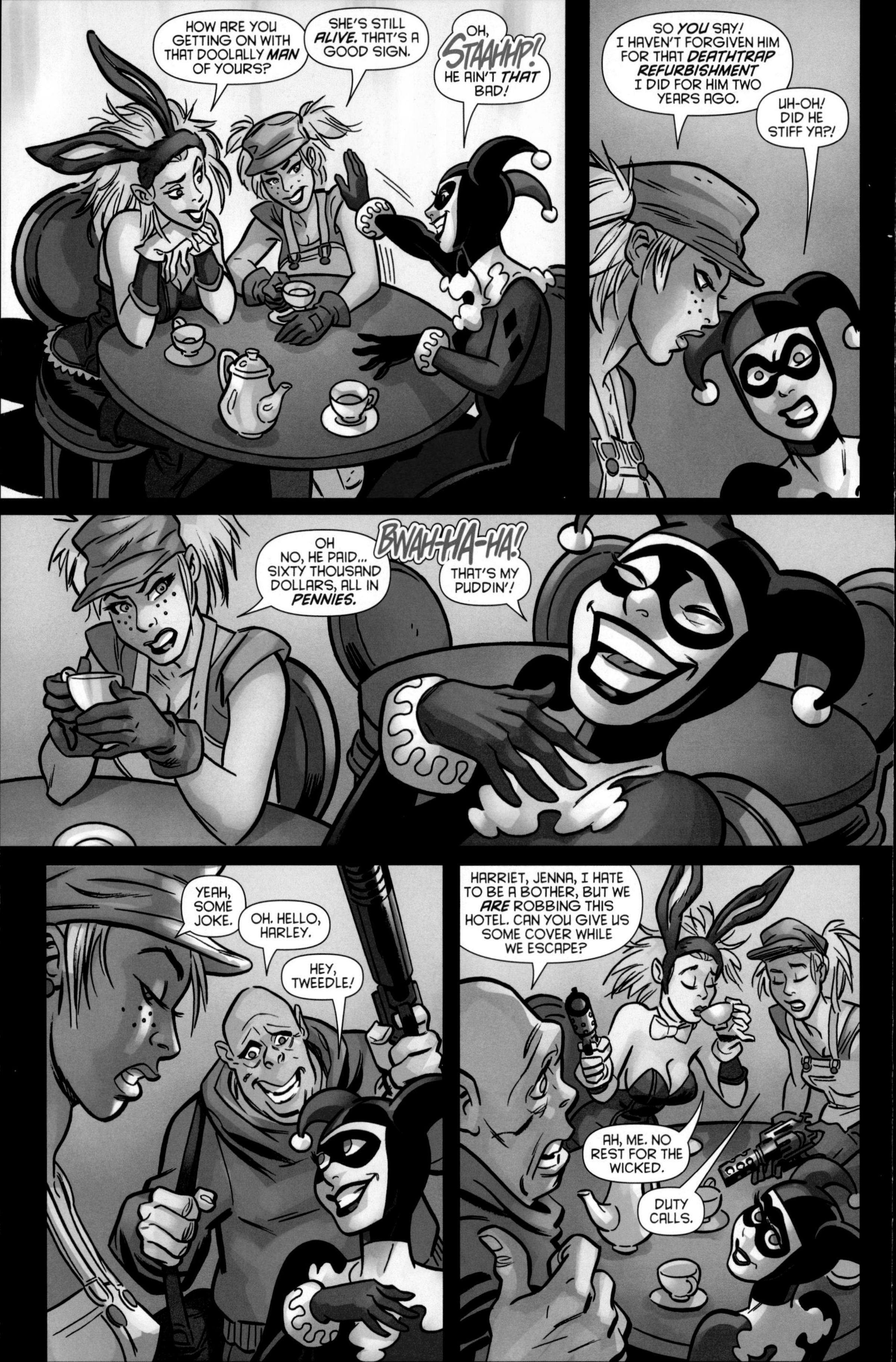

HOW ARE YOU GETTING ON WITH THAT DOOLALLY MAN OF YOURS?
SHE'S STILL ALIVE. THAT'S A GOOD SIGN.
OH, STAAHHP! HE AIN'T THAT BAD!
SO YOU SAY! I HAVEN'T FORGIVEN HIM FOR THAT DEATHTRAP REFURBISHMENT I DID FOR HIM TWO YEARS AGO.
UH-OH! DID HE STIFF YA?!
OH NO, HE PAID... SIXTY THOUSAND DOLLARS, ALL IN PENNIES.
BWAH-HA-HA!
THAT'S MY PUDDIN'!
YEAH, SOME JOKE.
OH. HELLO, HARLEY.
HEY, TWEEDLE!
HARRIET, JENNA, I HATE TO BE A BOTHER, BUT WE ARE ROBBING THIS HOTEL. CAN YOU GIVE US SOME COVER WHILE WE ESCAPE?
AH, ME. NO REST FOR THE WICKED.
DUTY CALLS.

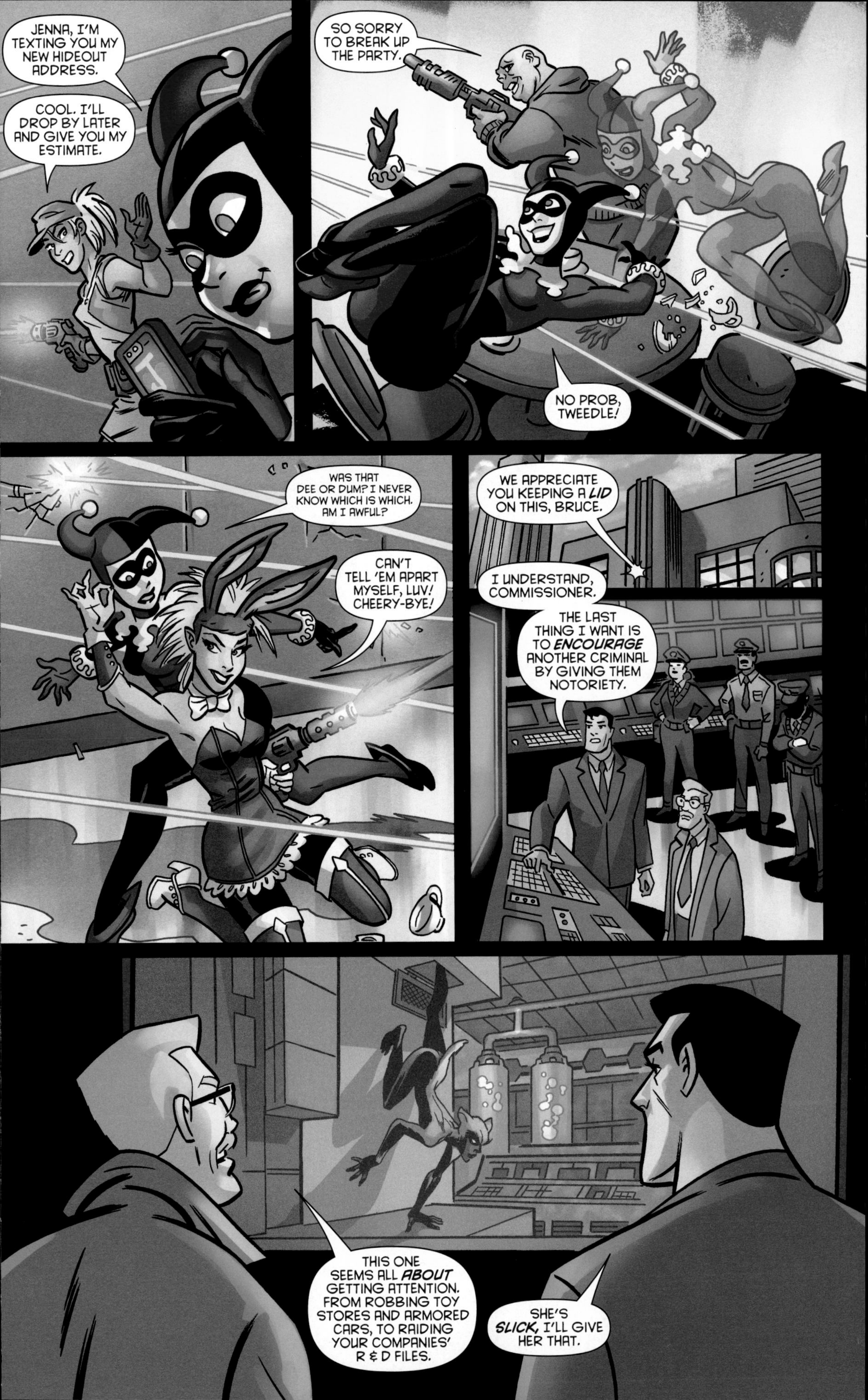
JENNA, I'M TEXTING YOU MY NEW HIDEOUT ADDRESS.
COOL. I'LL DROP BY LATER AND GIVE YOU MY ESTIMATE.
SO SORRY TO BREAK UP THE PARTY.
NO PROB, TWEEDLE!
WAS THAT DEE OR DUM? I NEVER KNOW WHICH IS WHICH. AM I AWFUL?
CAN'T TELL 'EM APART MYSELF, LUV! CHEERY-BYE!
WE APPRECIATE YOU KEEPING A LID ON THIS, BRUCE.
I UNDERSTAND, COMMISSIONER.
THE LAST THING I WANT IS TO ENCOURAGE ANOTHER CRIMINAL BY GIVING THEM NOTORIETY.
THIS ONE SEEMS ALL ABOUT GETTING ATTENTION. FROM ROBBING TOY STORES AND ARMORED CARS, TO RAIDING YOUR COMPANIES' R & D FILES.
SHE'S SLICK, I'LL GIVE HER THAT.

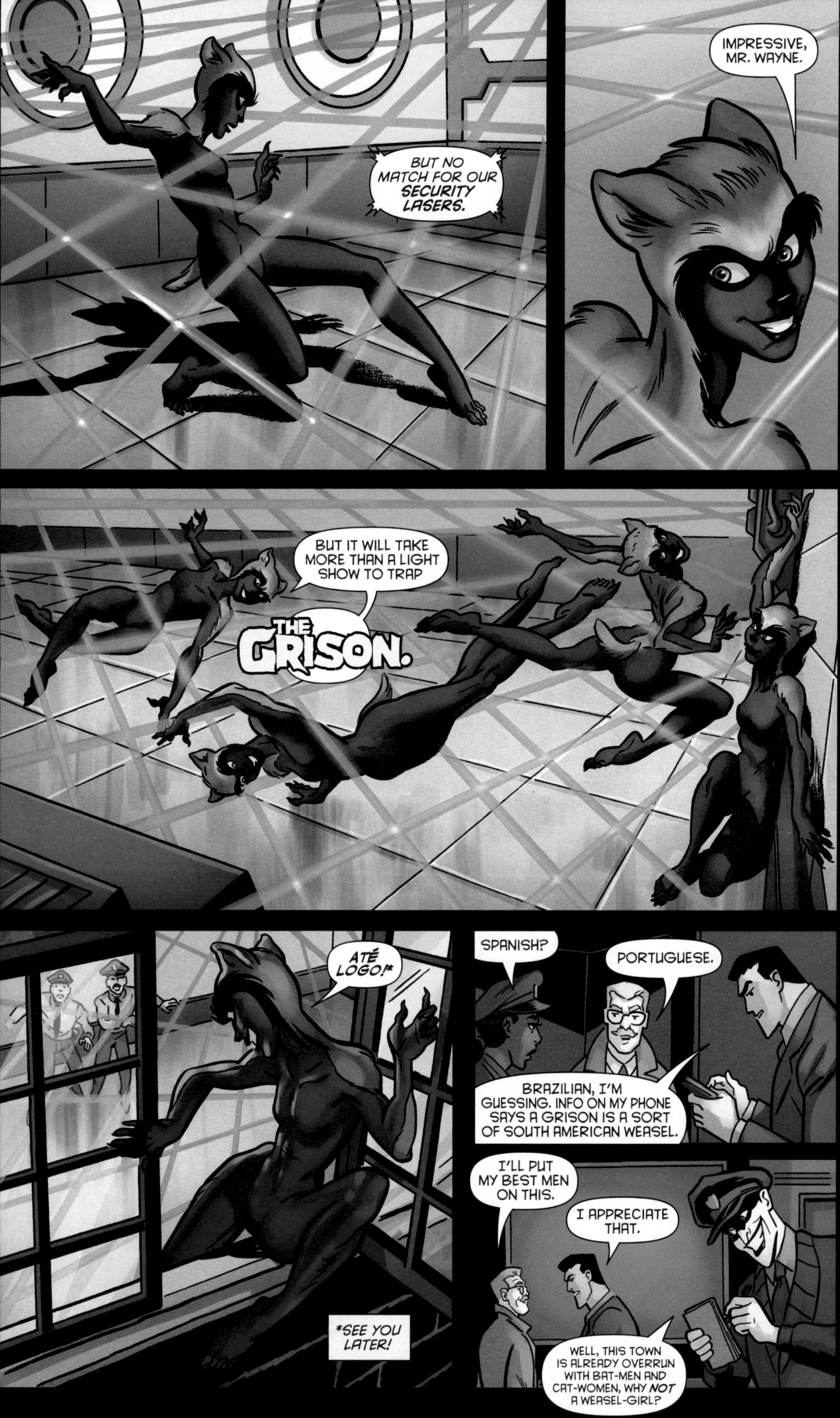
BUT NO MATCH FOR OUR SECURITY LASERS.
IMPRESSIVE, MR. WAYNE.
BUT IT WILL TAKE MORE THAN A LIGHT SHOW TO TRAP
THE GRISON.
ATÉ LOGO!*
*SEE YOU LATER!
SPANISH?
PORTUGUESE.
BRAZILIAN, I'M GUESSING. INFO ON MY PHONE SAYS A GRISON IS A SORT OF SOUTH AMERICAN WEASEL.
I'LL PUT MY BEST MEN ON THIS.
I APPRECIATE THAT.
WELL, THIS TOWN IS ALREADY OVERRUN WITH BAT-MEN AND CAT-WOMEN, WHY NOT A WEASEL-GIRL?

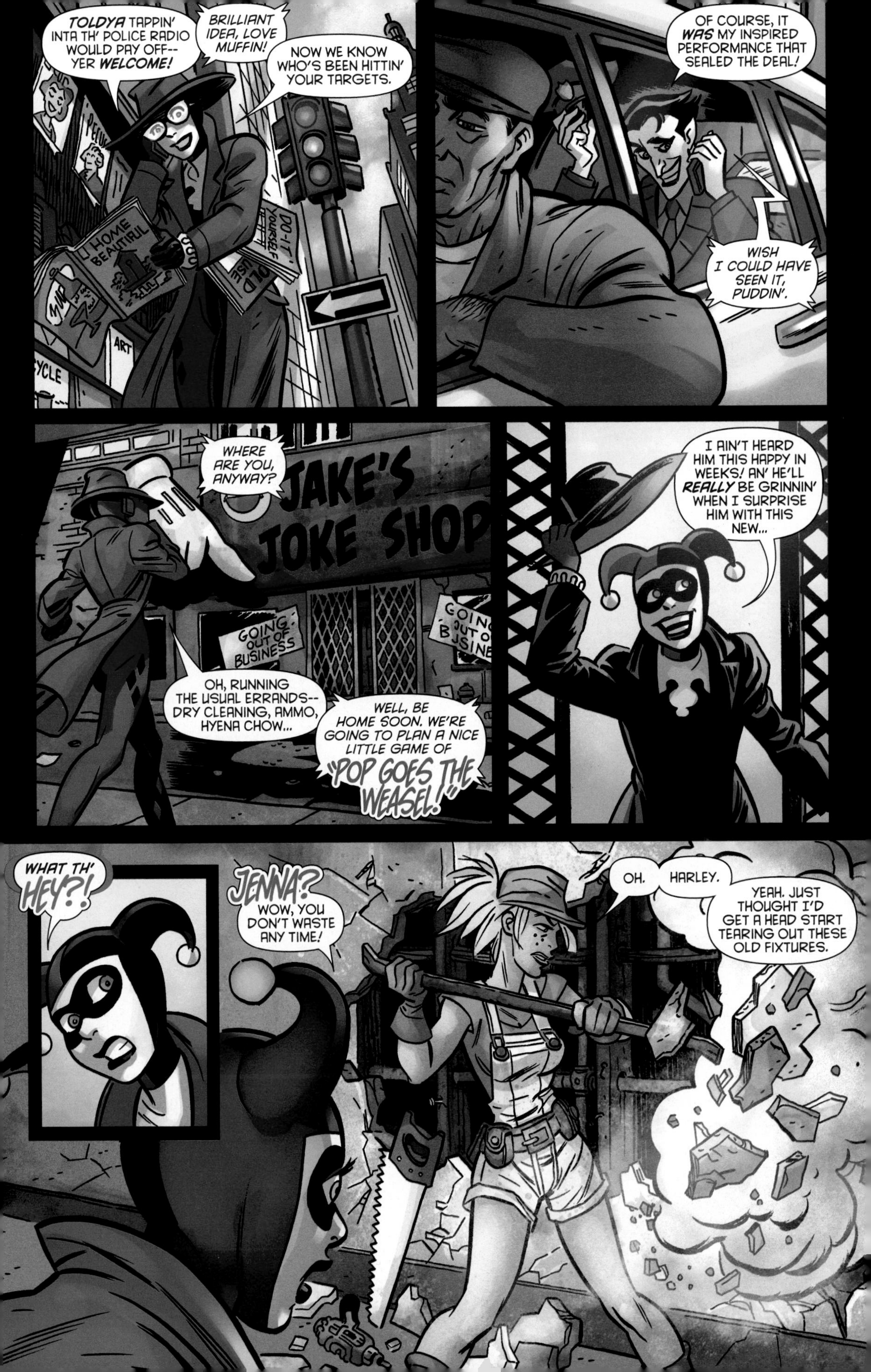
TOLDYA TAPPIN' INTA TH' POLICE RADIO WOULD PAY OFF-- YER WELCOME!
BRILLIANT IDEA, LOVE MUFFIN!
NOW WE KNOW WHO'S BEEN HITTIN' YOUR TARGETS.
HOME BEAUTIFUL
DO-IT YOURSELF
OF COURSE, IT WAS MY INSPIRED PERFORMANCE THAT SEALED THE DEAL!
WISH I COULD HAVE SEEN IT, PUDDIN'.
ART
WHERE ARE YOU, ANYWAY?
JAKE'S JOKE SHOP
GOING OUT OF BUSINESS
OH, RUNNING THE USUAL ERRANDS-- DRY CLEANING, AMMO, HYENA CHOW...
WELL, BE HOME SOON. WE'RE GOING TO PLAN A NICE LITTLE GAME OF "POP GOES THE WEASEL!"
I AIN'T HEARD HIM THIS HAPPY IN WEEKS! AN' HE'LL REALLY BE GRINNIN' WHEN I SURPRISE HIM WITH THIS NEW...
WHAT TH' HEY?!
JENNA? WOW, YOU DON'T WASTE ANY TIME!
OH.
HARLEY.
YEAH. JUST THOUGHT I'D GET A HEAD START TEARING OUT THESE OLD FIXTURES.

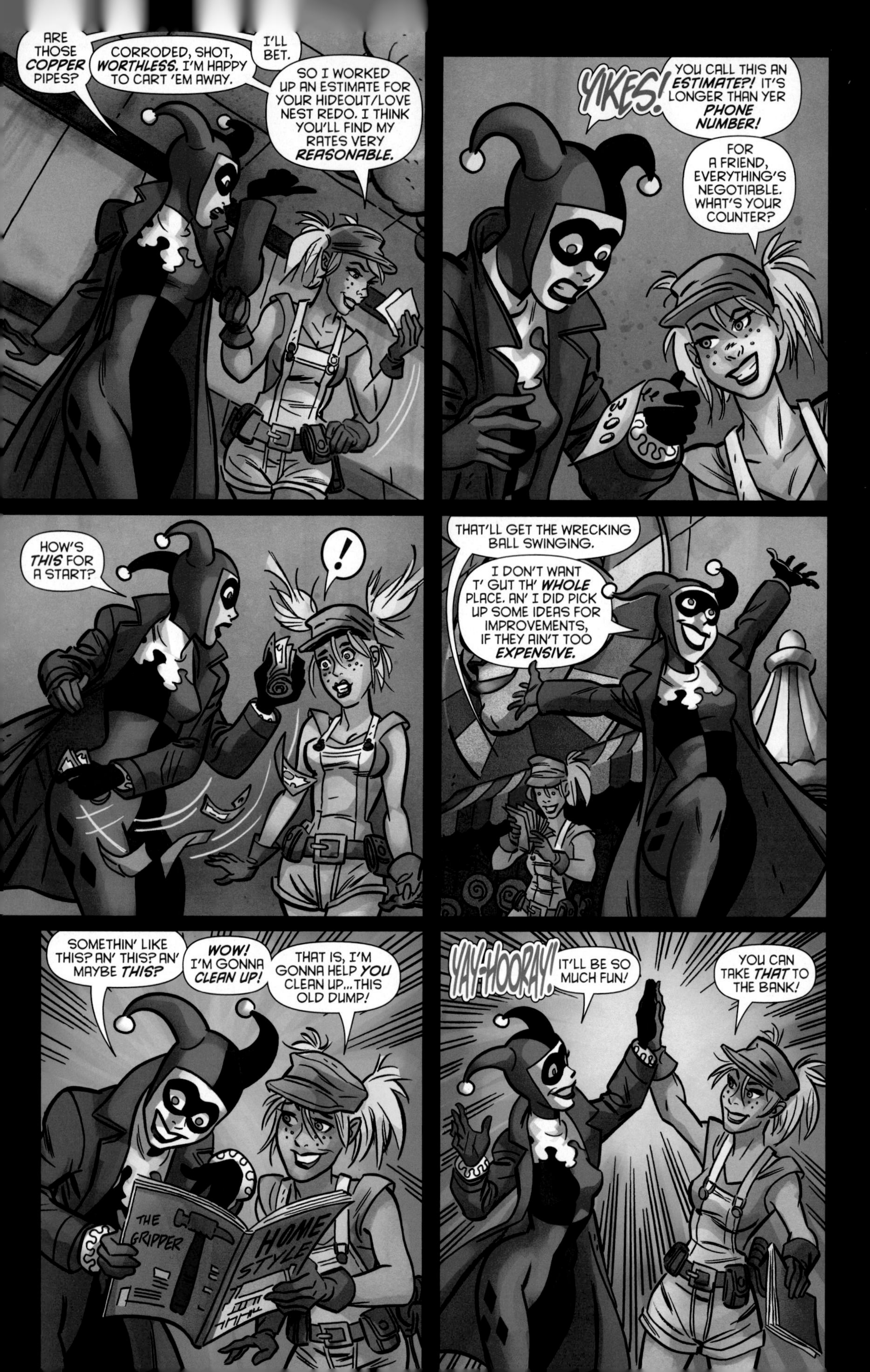
ARE THOSE *COPPER* PIPES?
CORRODED, SHOT, *WORTHLESS.* I'M HAPPY TO CART 'EM AWAY.
I'LL BET.
SO I WORKED UP AN ESTIMATE FOR YOUR HIDEOUT/LOVE NEST REDO. I THINK YOU'LL FIND MY RATES VERY *REASONABLE.*
YIKES!
YOU CALL THIS AN *ESTIMATE?!* IT'S LONGER THAN YER *PHONE NUMBER!*
FOR A FRIEND, EVERYTHING'S NEGOTIABLE. WHAT'S YOUR COUNTER?
HOW'S *THIS* FOR A START?
!
THAT'LL GET THE WRECKING BALL SWINGING.
I DON'T WANT T' GUT TH' *WHOLE* PLACE. AN' I DID PICK UP SOME IDEAS FOR IMPROVEMENTS, IF THEY AIN'T TOO *EXPENSIVE.*
SOMETHIN' LIKE THIS? AN' THIS? AN' MAYBE *THIS?*
WOW! I'M GONNA *CLEAN UP!*
THAT IS, I'M GONNA HELP *YOU* CLEAN UP... THIS OLD DUMP!
THE GRIPPER
HOME STYLE
YAY-HOORAY!
IT'LL BE SO MUCH FUN!
YOU CAN TAKE *THAT* TO THE BANK!

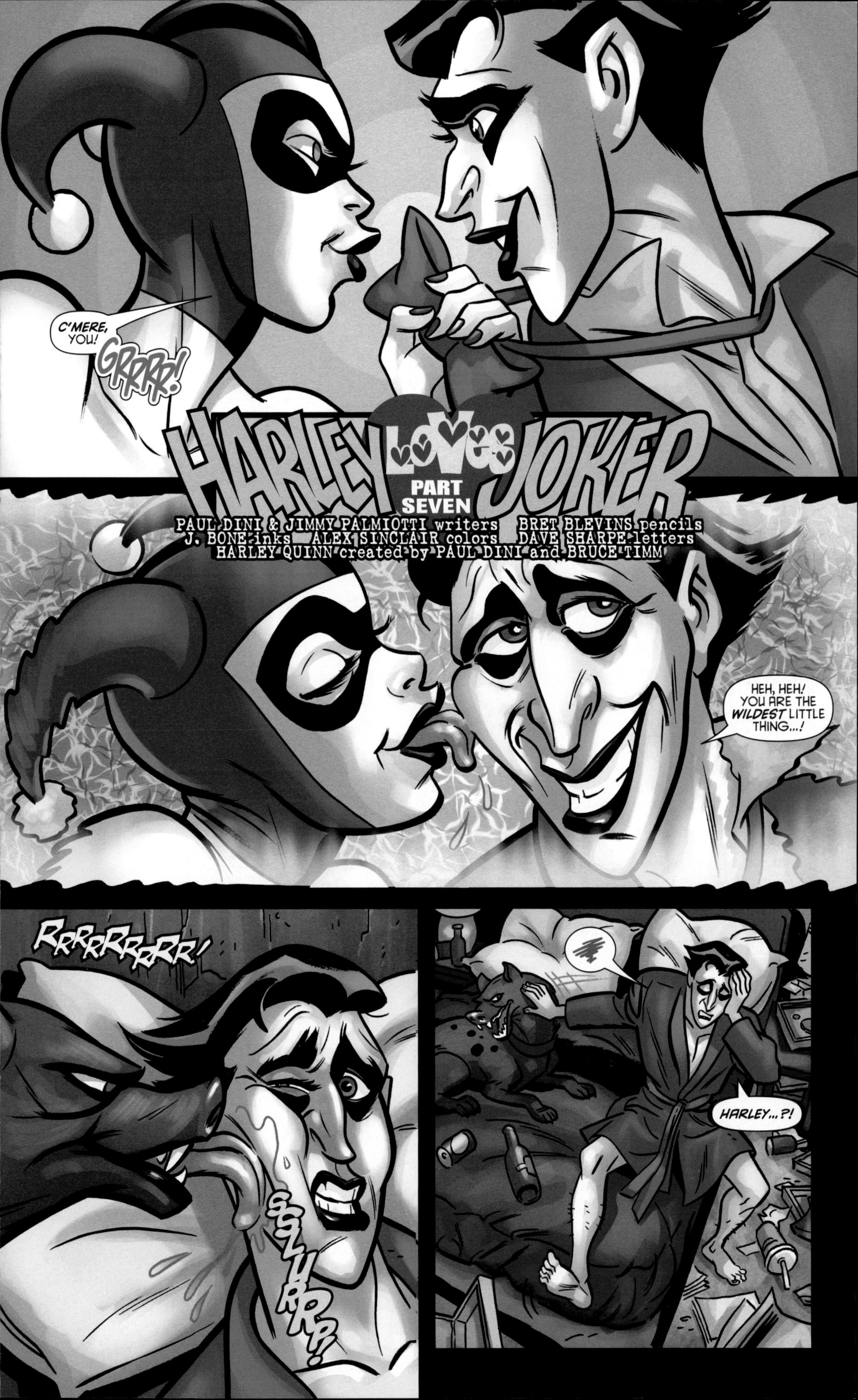
C'MERE, YOU!
GRRRR!
HARLEY LOVES JOKER
PART SEVEN
PAUL DINI & JIMMY PALMIOTTI writers BRET BLEVINS pencils
J. BONE inks ALEX SINCLAIR colors DAVE SHARPE letters
HARLEY QUINN created by PAUL DINI and BRUCE TIMM
HEH, HEH! YOU ARE THE WILDEST LITTLE THING...!
RRRRRRRRR!
SSLURRP!
HARLEY...?!

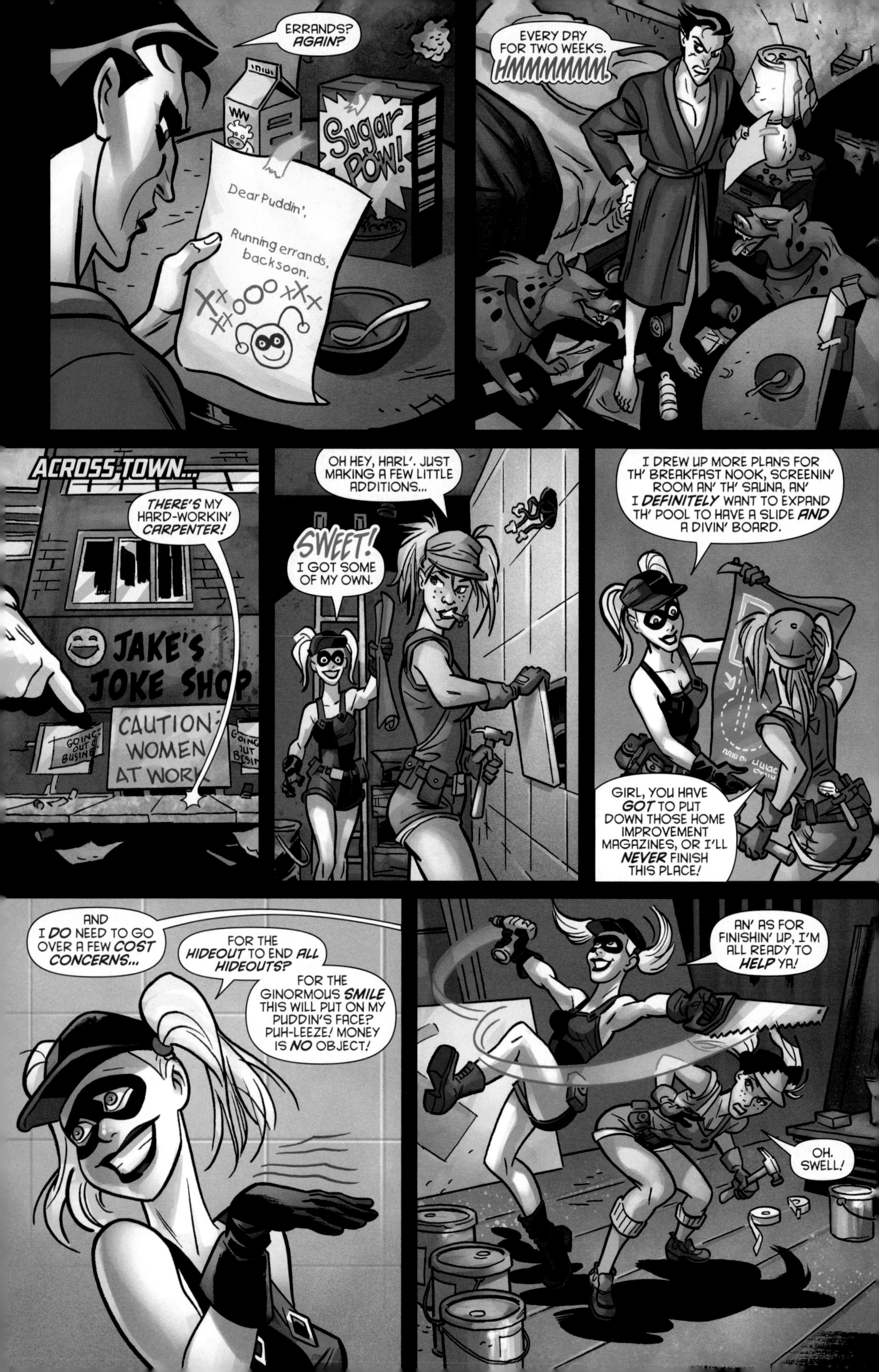
ERRANDS? AGAIN?
Sugar POW!
Dear Puddin',
Running errands, back soon.
XXOOOXXX
EVERY DAY FOR TWO WEEKS.
HMMMMMM.
ACROSS TOWN...
THERE'S MY HARD-WORKIN' CARPENTER!
JAKE'S JOKE SHOP
CAUTION: WOMEN AT WORK
OH HEY, HARL'. JUST MAKING A FEW LITTLE ADDITIONS...
SWEET! I GOT SOME OF MY OWN.
I DREW UP MORE PLANS FOR TH' BREAKFAST NOOK, SCREENIN' ROOM AN' TH' SAUNA, AN' I DEFINITELY WANT TO EXPAND TH' POOL TO HAVE A SLIDE AND A DIVIN' BOARD.
GIRL, YOU HAVE GOT TO PUT DOWN THOSE HOME IMPROVEMENT MAGAZINES, OR I'LL NEVER FINISH THIS PLACE!
AND I DO NEED TO GO OVER A FEW COST CONCERNS...
FOR THE HIDEOUT TO END ALL HIDEOUTS?
FOR THE GINORMOUS SMILE THIS WILL PUT ON MY PUDDIN'S FACE? PUH-LEEZE! MONEY IS NO OBJECT!
AN' AS FOR FINISHIN' UP, I'M ALL READY TO HELP YA!
OH. SWELL!

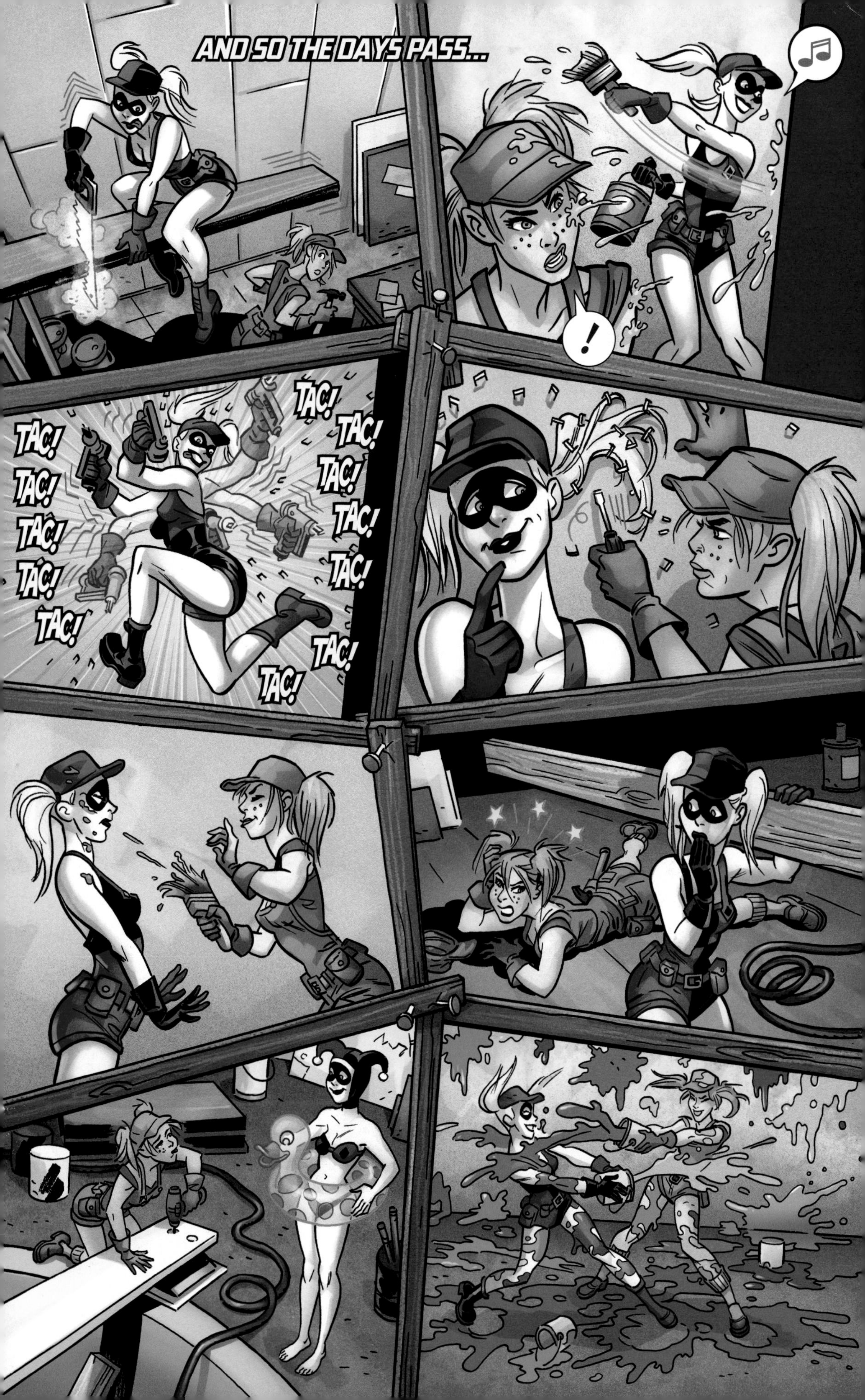
AND SO THE DAYS PASS...
!
TAC!
TAC!
TAC!
TAC!
TAC!
TAC!
TAC!
TAC!
TAC!
TAC!
TAC!
TAC!
TAC!

ARE YOU STILL KEEPING OUR BIG PROJECT A *SECRET* FROM MR. HAPPY?

YEAH, BUT IT AIN'T BEEN EASY. MY PUDDIN' LIKES TO *GIVE* SURPRISES, NOT GET 'EM.

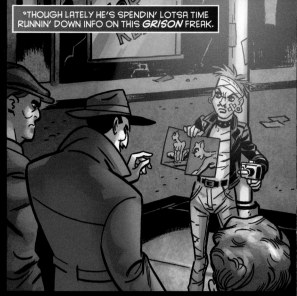

"THOUGH LATELY HE'S SPENDIN' LOTSA TIME RUNNIN' DOWN INFO ON THIS *GRISON* FREAK.

"IF THERE'S ONE THING MR. J LOVES, IT'S WORKIN' UP A *VENDETTA.*"

I DON'T MIND A LITTLE *COMPETITION* BETWEEN OLD *FRIENDS...*

BUT THIS INTERLOPER, THIS... OVER-SIZED *RAT* IS GOING TOO FAR. SHE'S PICKING OFF THE RICHEST SITES IN GOTHAM, LEAVING PRECIOUS LITTLE FOR US *REAL* PLAYERS.

AND YOU HAVE A *SOLUTION,* OF COURSE?

OF *COURSE!* WE SIMPLY BAIT A TRAP WITH A RICH PRIZE, LEAD OUR THIEF TO THE APPROPRIATE LOCATION AND *SNAP!* WASTE ONE WEASEL!

AND NATURALLY THAT LOCATION WOULD BE *HERE,* AT THE *ICEBERG LOUNGE.*

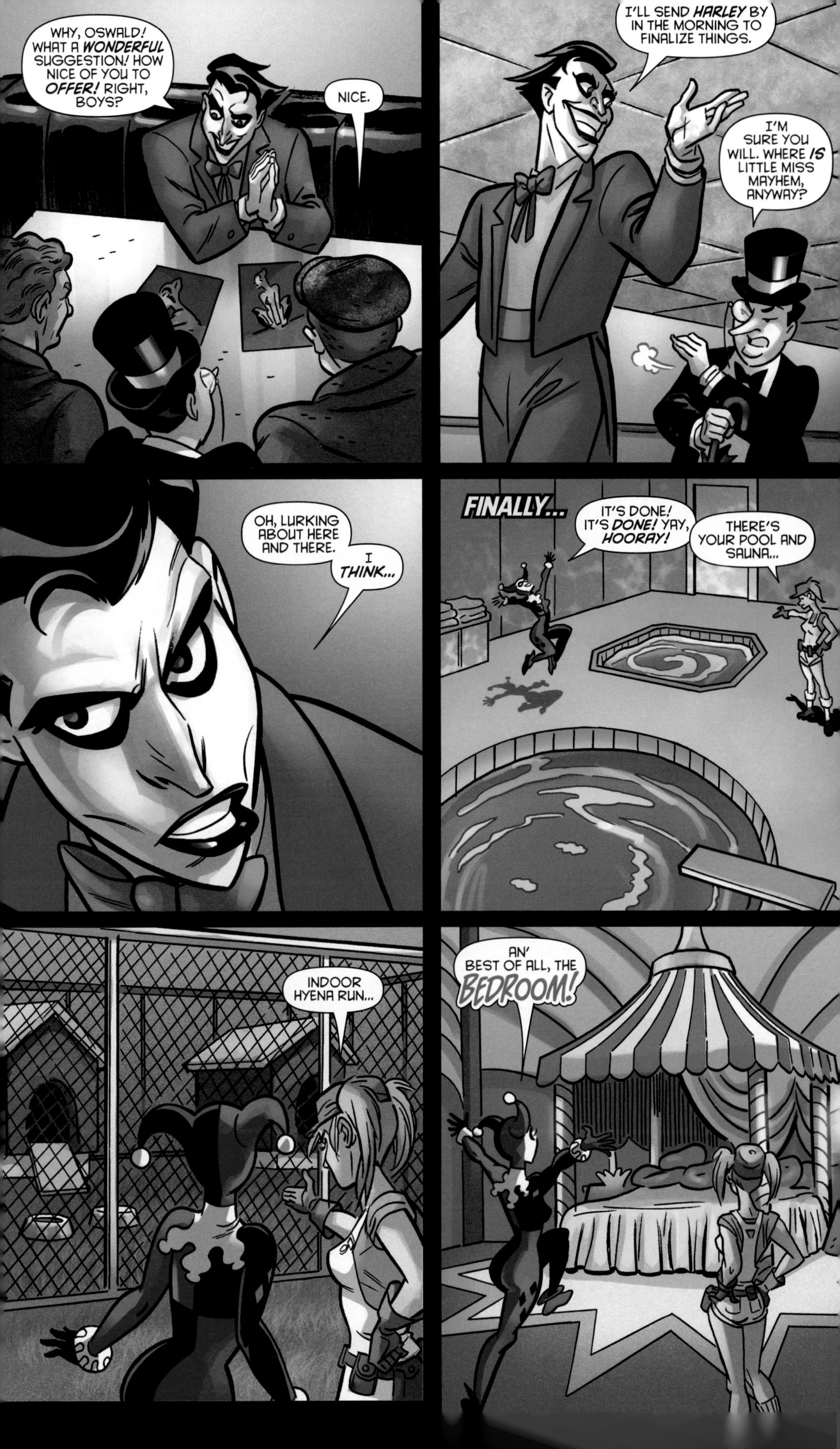
WHY, OSWALD! WHAT A WONDERFUL SUGGESTION! HOW NICE OF YOU TO OFFER! RIGHT, BOYS?
NICE.
I'LL SEND HARLEY BY IN THE MORNING TO FINALIZE THINGS.
I'M SURE YOU WILL. WHERE IS LITTLE MISS MAYHEM, ANYWAY?
OH, LURKING ABOUT HERE AND THERE.
I THINK...
FINALLY...
IT'S DONE! IT'S DONE! YAY, HOORAY!
THERE'S YOUR POOL AND SAUNA...
INDOOR HYENA RUN...
AN' BEST OF ALL, THE BEDROOM!

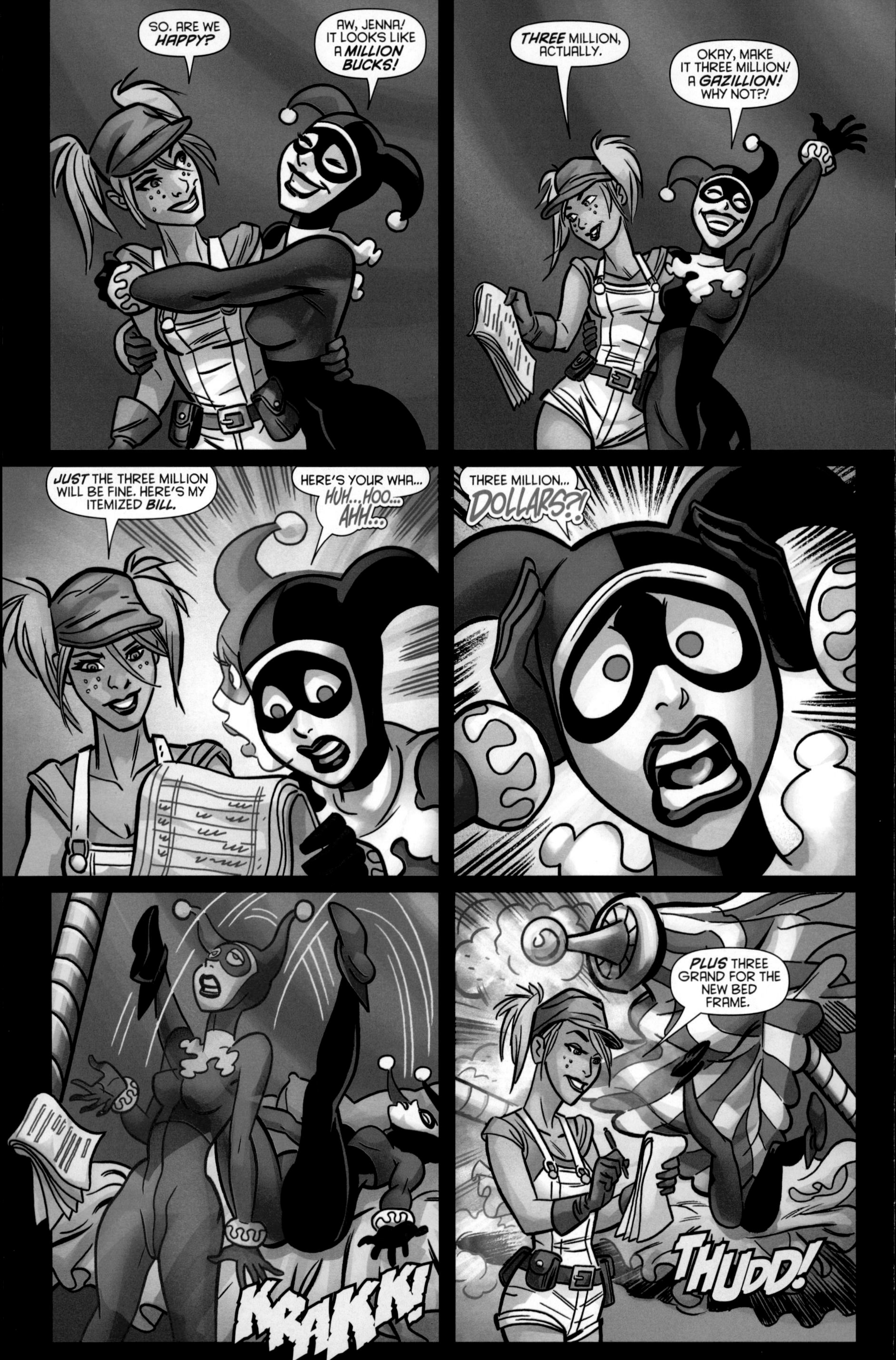

SO. ARE WE HAPPY?
AW, JENNA! IT LOOKS LIKE A MILLION BUCKS!
THREE MILLION, ACTUALLY.
OKAY, MAKE IT THREE MILLION! A GAZILLION! WHY NOT?!
JUST THE THREE MILLION WILL BE FINE. HERE'S MY ITEMIZED BILL.
HERE'S YOUR WHA... HUH...HOO... AHH...
THREE MILLION... DOLLARS?!
KRAKK!
PLUS THREE GRAND FOR THE NEW BED FRAME.
THUDD!

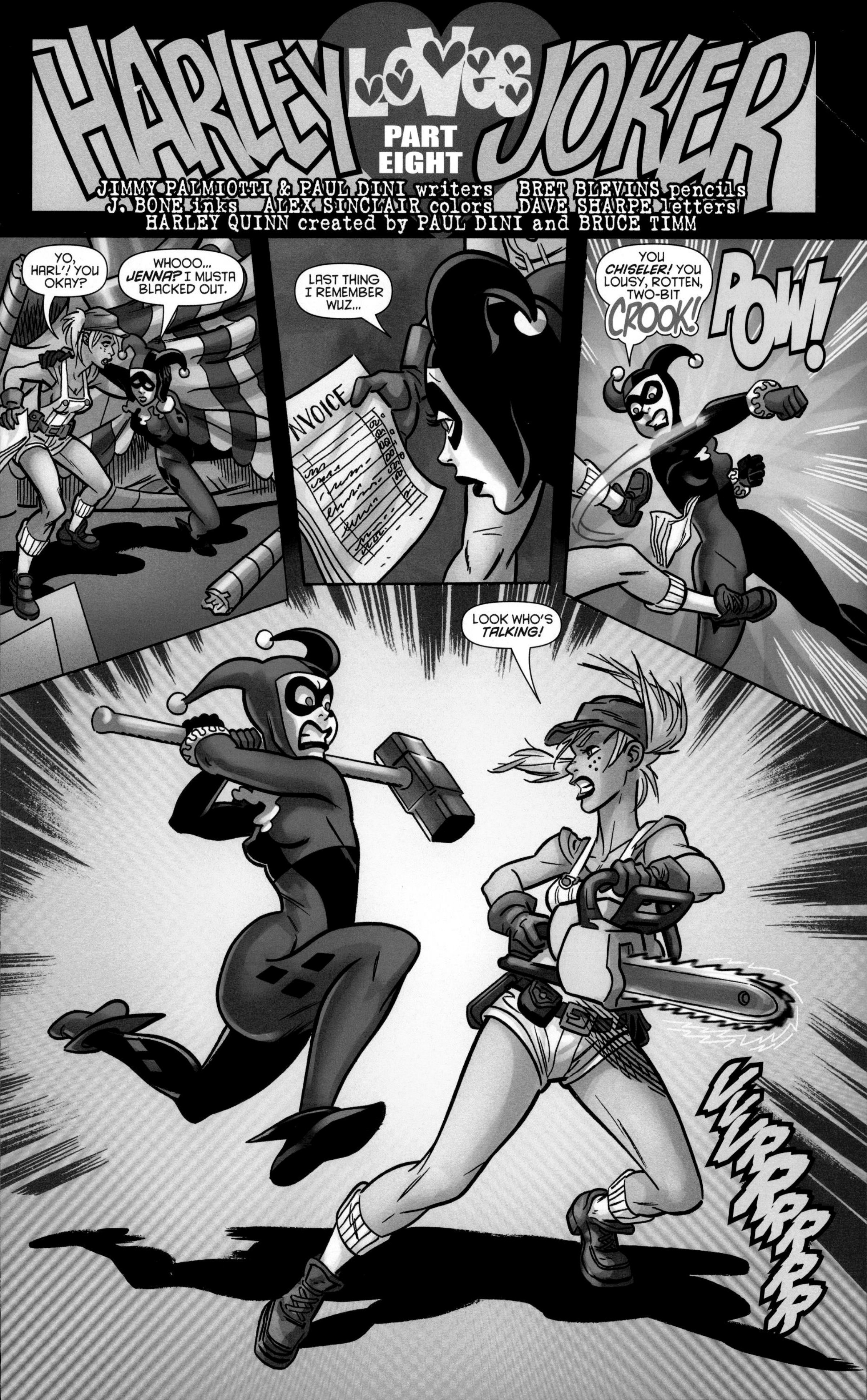
HARLEY LOVES JOKER
PART EIGHT
JIMMY PALMIOTTI & PAUL DINI writers BRET BLEVINS pencils
J. BONE inks ALEX SINCLAIR colors DAVE SHARPE letters
HARLEY QUINN created by PAUL DINI and BRUCE TIMM
YO, HARL'! YOU OKAY?
WHOOO... JENNA? I MUSTA BLACKED OUT.
LAST THING I REMEMBER WUZ...
INVOICE
YOU CHISELER! YOU LOUSY, ROTTEN, TWO-BIT CROOK!
POW!
LOOK WHO'S TALKING!
VVRRRRRRR

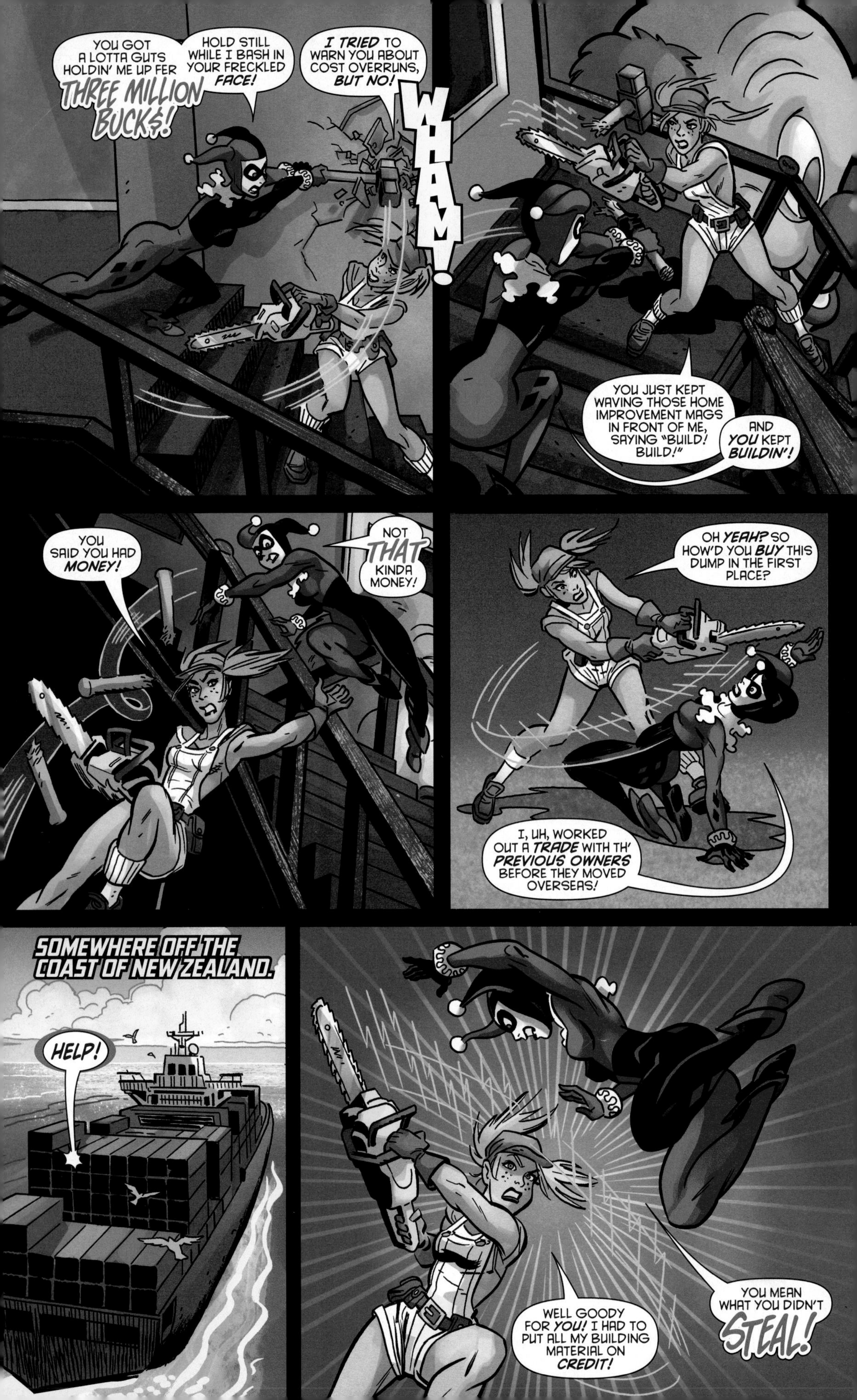
YOU GOT A LOTTA GUTS HOLDIN' ME UP FER THREE MILLION BUCK$!
HOLD STILL WHILE I BASH IN YOUR FRECKLED FACE!
I TRIED TO WARN YOU ABOUT COST OVERRUNS, BUT NO!
WHAM!
YOU JUST KEPT WAVING THOSE HOME IMPROVEMENT MAGS IN FRONT OF ME, SAYING "BUILD! BUILD!"
AND YOU KEPT BUILDIN'!
YOU SAID YOU HAD MONEY!
NOT THAT KINDA MONEY!
OH YEAH? SO HOW'D YOU BUY THIS DUMP IN THE FIRST PLACE?
I, UH, WORKED OUT A TRADE WITH TH' PREVIOUS OWNERS BEFORE THEY MOVED OVERSEAS!
SOMEWHERE OFF THE COAST OF NEW ZEALAND.
HELP!
WELL GOODY FOR YOU! I HAD TO PUT ALL MY BUILDING MATERIAL ON CREDIT!
YOU MEAN WHAT YOU DIDN'T STEAL!

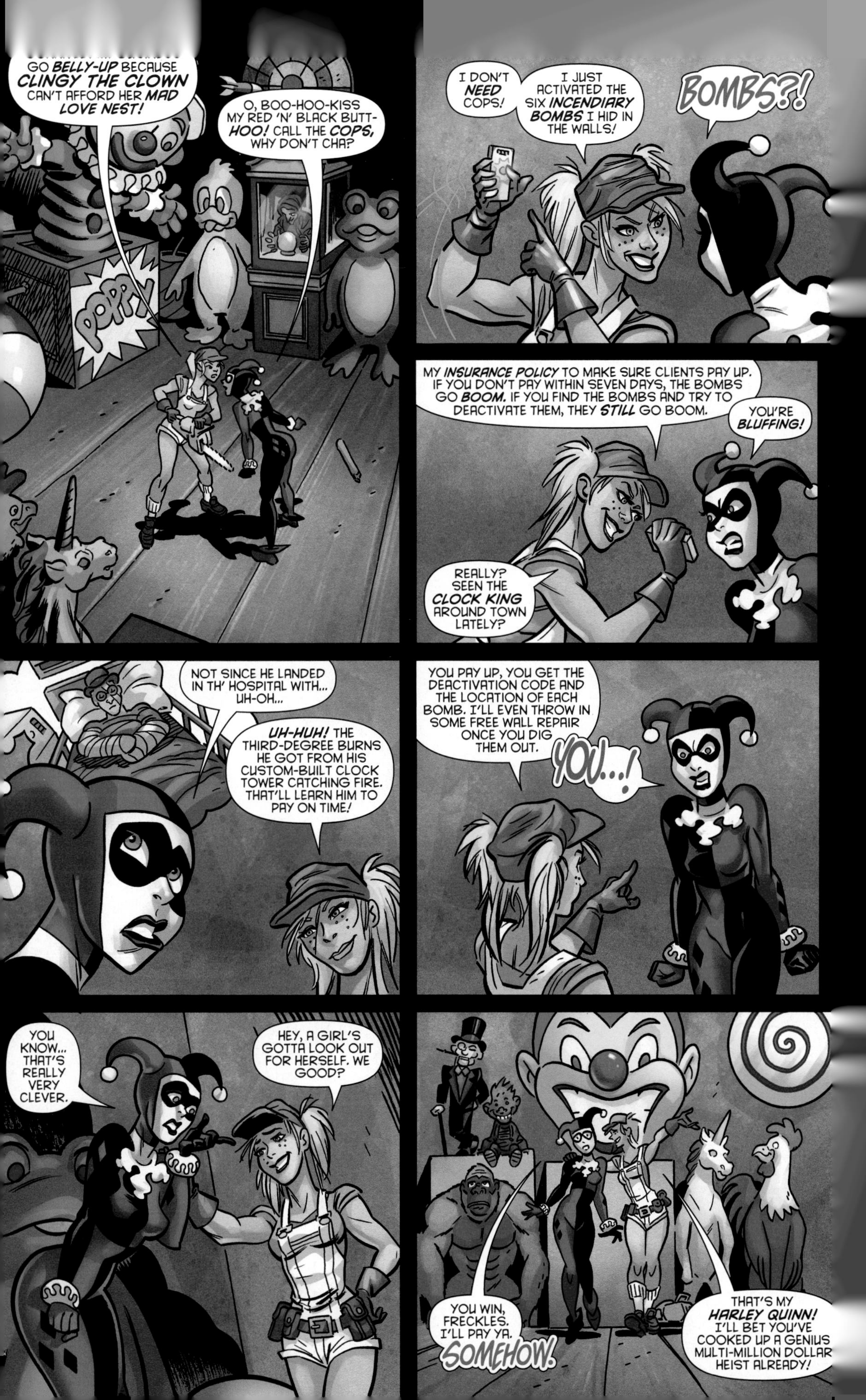

GO BELLY-UP BECAUSE CLINGY THE CLOWN CAN'T AFFORD HER MAD LOVE NEST!
O, BOO-HOO-KISS MY RED 'N' BLACK BUTT-HOO! CALL THE COPS, WHY DON'T CHA?
POPPY
I DON'T NEED COPS!
I JUST ACTIVATED THE SIX INCENDIARY BOMBS I HID IN THE WALLS!
BOMBS?!
MY INSURANCE POLICY TO MAKE SURE CLIENTS PAY UP. IF YOU DON'T PAY WITHIN SEVEN DAYS, THE BOMBS GO BOOM. IF YOU FIND THE BOMBS AND TRY TO DEACTIVATE THEM, THEY STILL GO BOOM.
YOU'RE BLUFFING!
REALLY? SEEN THE CLOCK KING AROUND TOWN LATELY?
NOT SINCE HE LANDED IN TH' HOSPITAL WITH... UH-OH...
UH-HUH! THE THIRD-DEGREE BURNS HE GOT FROM HIS CUSTOM-BUILT CLOCK TOWER CATCHING FIRE. THAT'LL LEARN HIM TO PAY ON TIME!
YOU PAY UP, YOU GET THE DEACTIVATION CODE AND THE LOCATION OF EACH BOMB. I'LL EVEN THROW IN SOME FREE WALL REPAIR ONCE YOU DIG THEM OUT.
YOU...!
YOU KNOW... THAT'S REALLY VERY CLEVER.
HEY, A GIRL'S GOTTA LOOK OUT FOR HERSELF. WE GOOD?
YOU WIN, FRECKLES. I'LL PAY YA.
SOMEHOW.
THAT'S MY HARLEY QUINN! I'LL BET YOU'VE COOKED UP A GENIUS MULTI-MILLION DOLLAR HEIST ALREADY!

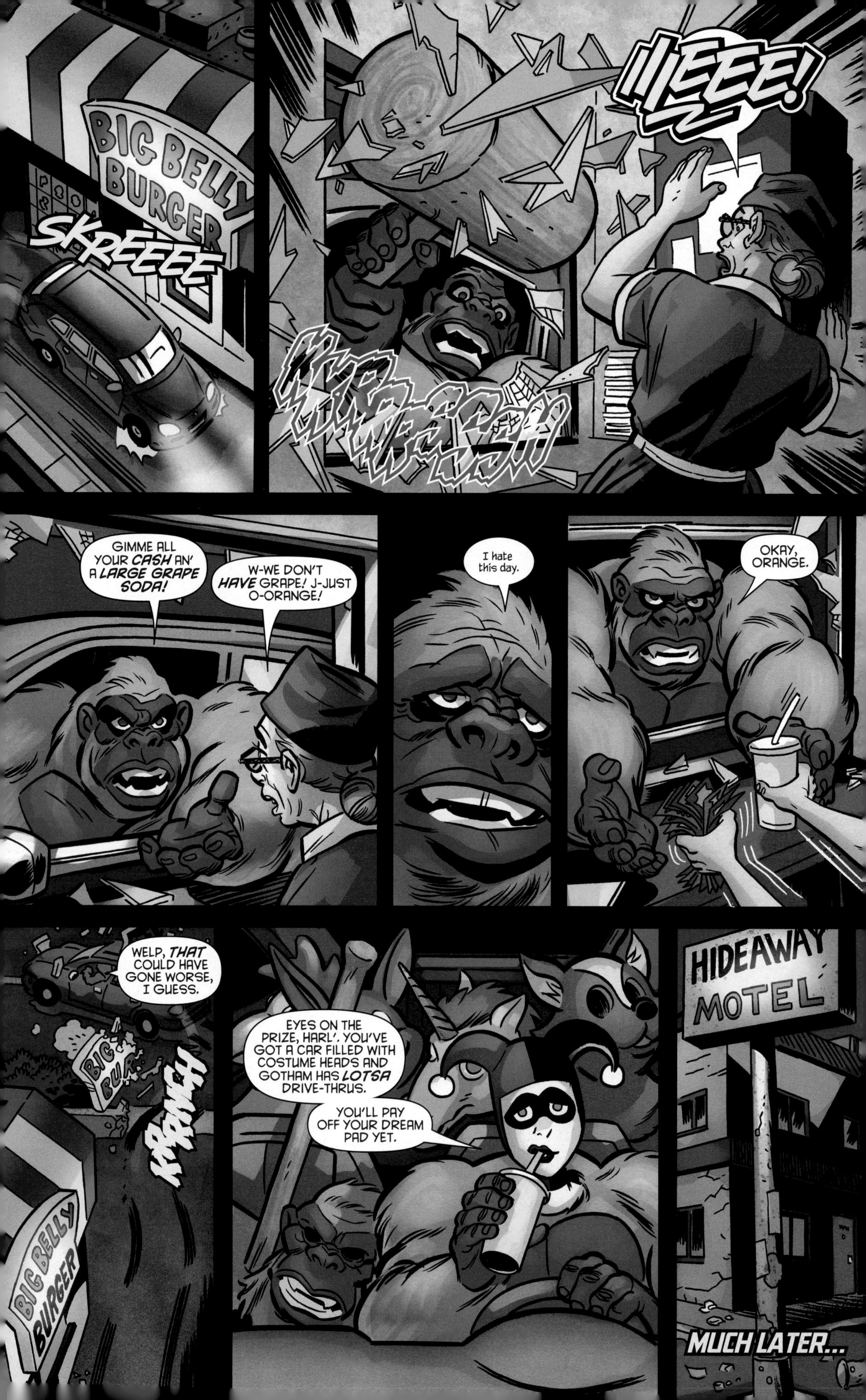
BIG BELLY BURGER
SKREEEEE
EEEE!
GIMME ALL YOUR CASH AN' A LARGE GRAPE SODA!
W-WE DON'T HAVE GRAPE! J-JUST O-ORANGE!
I hate this day.
OKAY, ORANGE.
WELP, THAT COULD HAVE GONE WORSE, I GUESS.
BIG BELLY BURGER
EYES ON THE PRIZE, HARL'. YOU'VE GOT A CAR FILLED WITH COSTUME HEADS AND GOTHAM HAS LOTSA DRIVE-THRUS.
YOU'LL PAY OFF YOUR DREAM PAD YET.
HIDEAWAY MOTEL
MUCH LATER...

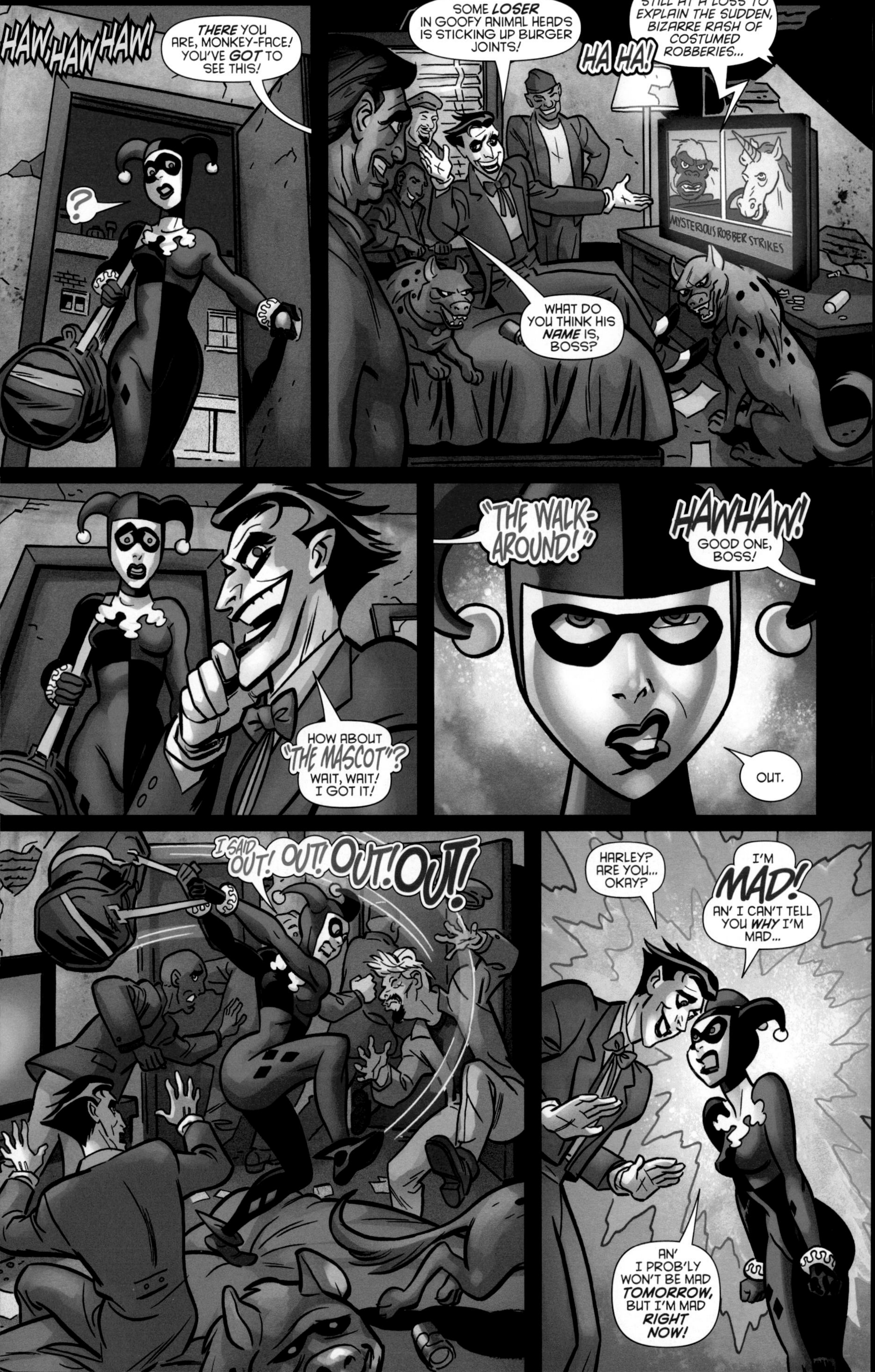
HAW HAW HAW!
THERE YOU ARE, MONKEY-FACE! YOU'VE GOT TO SEE THIS!
?
SOME LOSER IN GOOFY ANIMAL HEADS IS STICKING UP BURGER JOINTS!
HA HA!
POLICE ARE STILL AT A LOSS TO EXPLAIN THE SUDDEN, BIZARRE RASH OF COSTUMED ROBBERIES...
MYSTERIOUS ROBBER STRIKES
WHAT DO YOU THINK HIS NAME IS, BOSS?
HOW ABOUT "THE MASCOT"? WAIT, WAIT! I GOT IT!
"THE WALK-AROUND!"
HAWHAW! GOOD ONE, BOSS!
OUT.
I SAID OUT! OUT! OUT! OUT!
HARLEY? ARE YOU... OKAY?
I'M MAD! AN' I CAN'T TELL YOU WHY I'M MAD...
AN' I PROB'LY WON'T BE MAD TOMORROW, BUT I'M MAD RIGHT NOW!

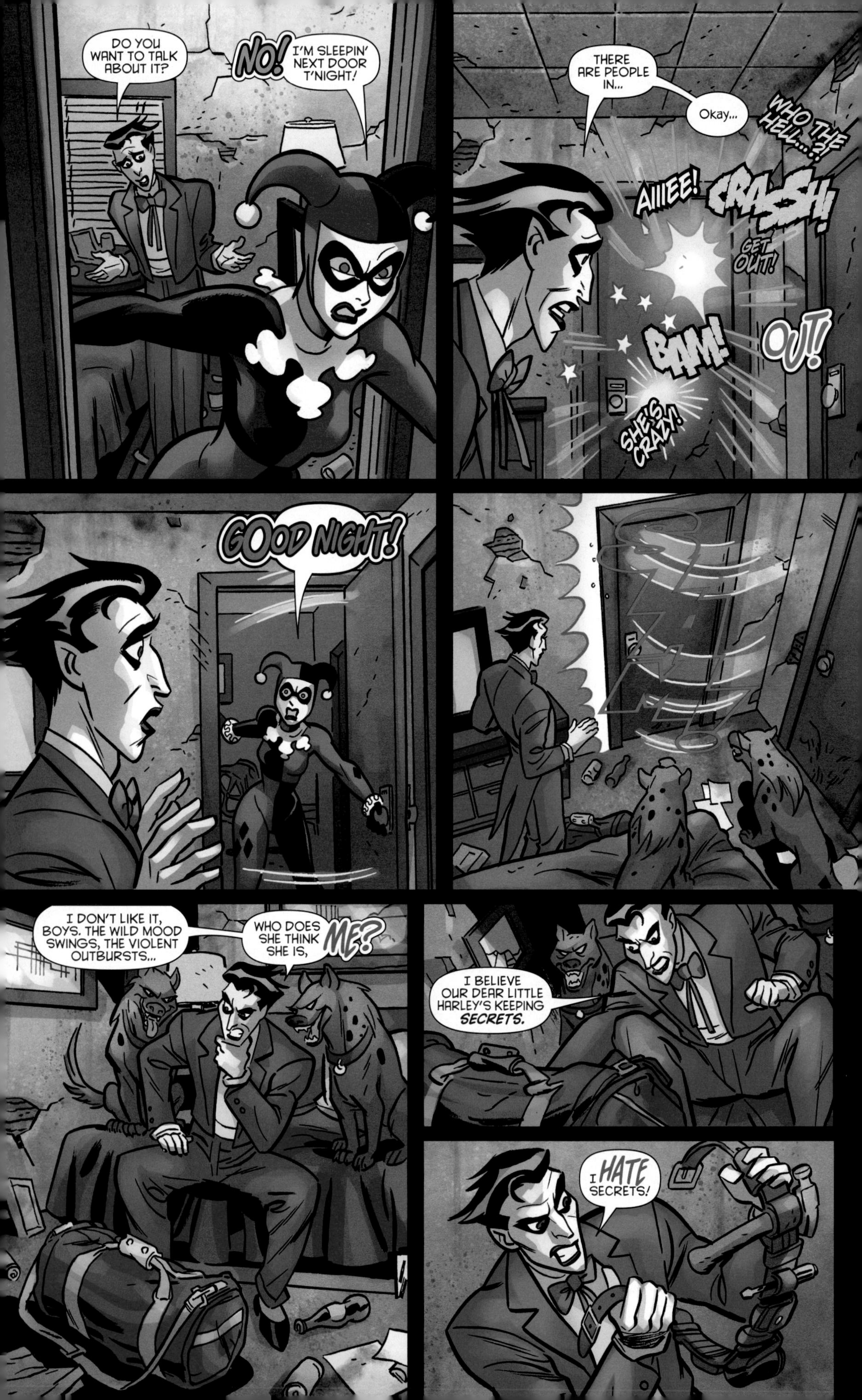
DO YOU WANT TO TALK ABOUT IT?
NO!
I'M SLEEPIN' NEXT DOOR T'NIGHT!
THERE ARE PEOPLE IN...
Okay...
WHO THE HELL...?!
AIIIEE!
CRASH!
GET OUT!
BAM!
OUT!
SHE'S CRAZY!
GOOD NIGHT!
I DON'T LIKE IT, BOYS. THE WILD MOOD SWINGS, THE VIOLENT OUTBURSTS...
WHO DOES SHE THINK SHE IS, ME?
I BELIEVE OUR DEAR LITTLE HARLEY'S KEEPING SECRETS.
I HATE SECRETS!

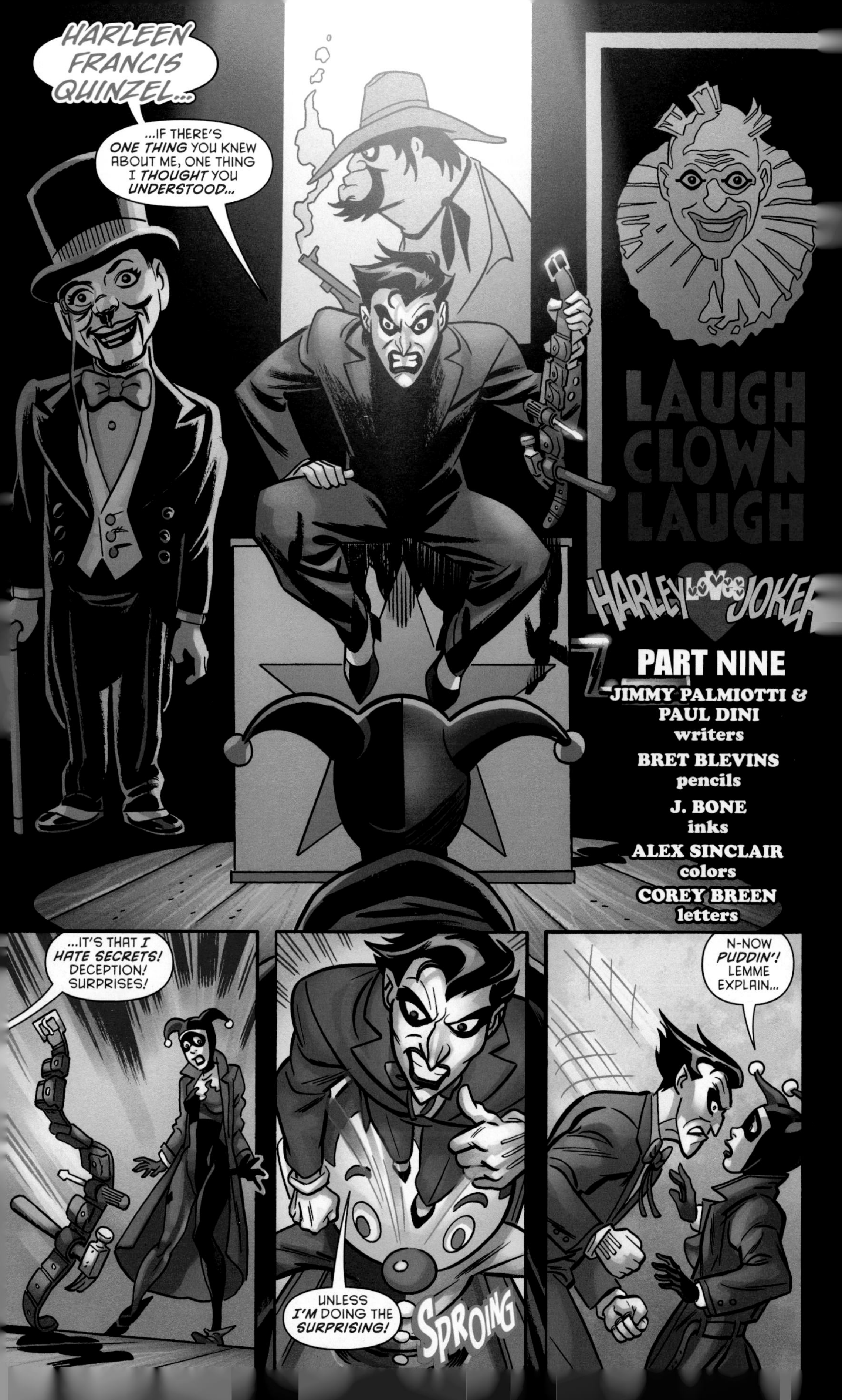
HARLEEN FRANCIS QUINZEL...
...IF THERE'S ONE THING YOU KNEW ABOUT ME, ONE THING I THOUGHT YOU UNDERSTOOD...
LAUGH CLOWN LAUGH
HARLEY LOVES JOKER
PART NINE
JIMMY PALMIOTTI & PAUL DINI writers
BRET BLEVINS pencils
J. BONE inks
ALEX SINCLAIR colors
COREY BREEN letters
...IT'S THAT I HATE SECRETS! DECEPTION! SURPRISES!
UNLESS I'M DOING THE SURPRISING!
SPROING
N-NOW PUDDIN'! LEMME EXPLAIN...

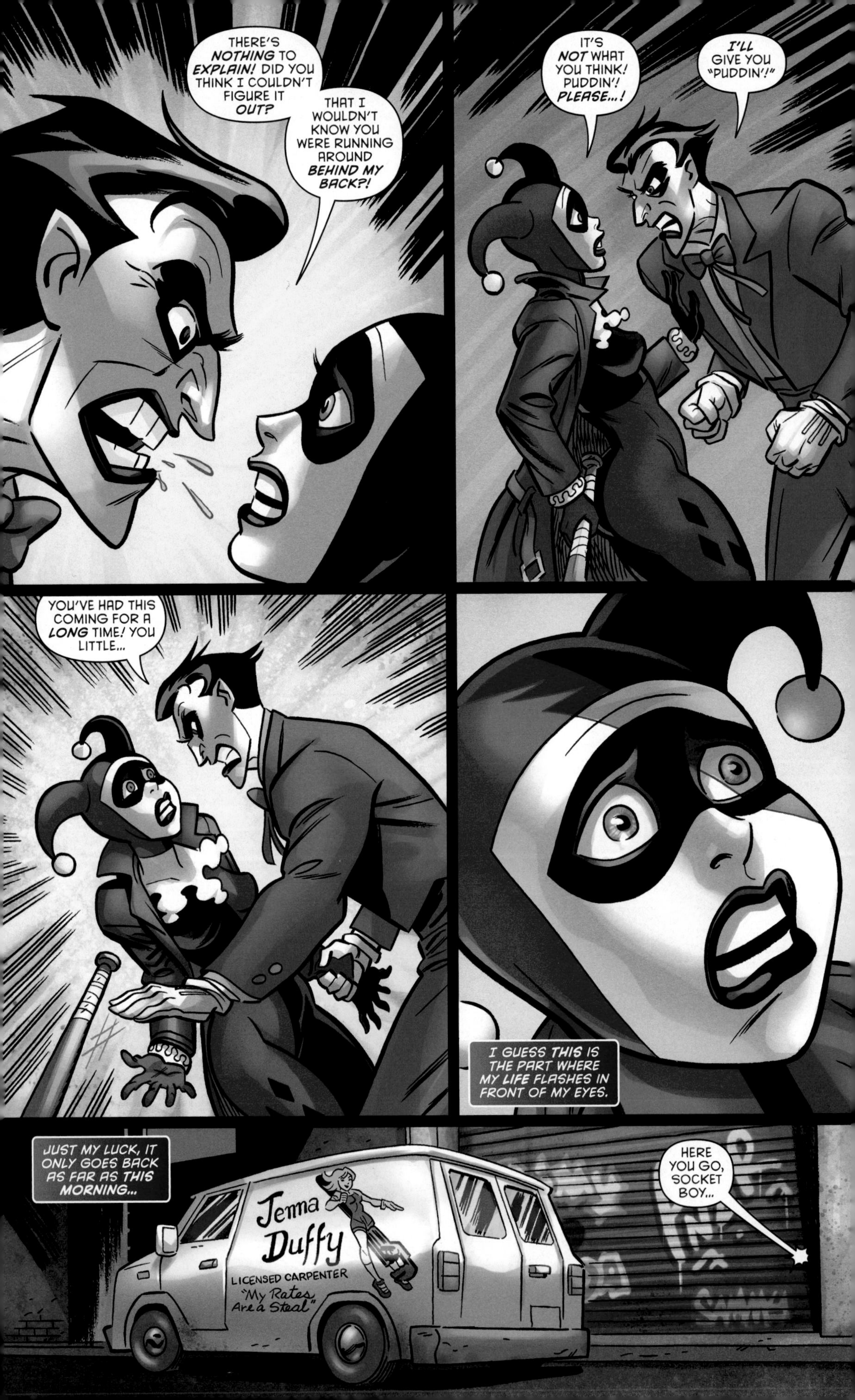

THERE'S NOTHING TO EXPLAIN! DID YOU THINK I COULDN'T FIGURE IT OUT?
THAT I WOULDN'T KNOW YOU WERE RUNNING AROUND BEHIND MY BACK?!
IT'S NOT WHAT YOU THINK! PUDDIN'! PLEASE...!
I'LL GIVE YOU "PUDDIN'!"
YOU'VE HAD THIS COMING FOR A LONG TIME! YOU LITTLE...
I GUESS THIS IS THE PART WHERE MY LIFE FLASHES IN FRONT OF MY EYES.
JUST MY LUCK, IT ONLY GOES BACK AS FAR AS THIS MORNING...
Jenna Duffy
LICENSED CARPENTER
"My Rates Are a Steal"
HERE YOU GO, SOCKET BOY...

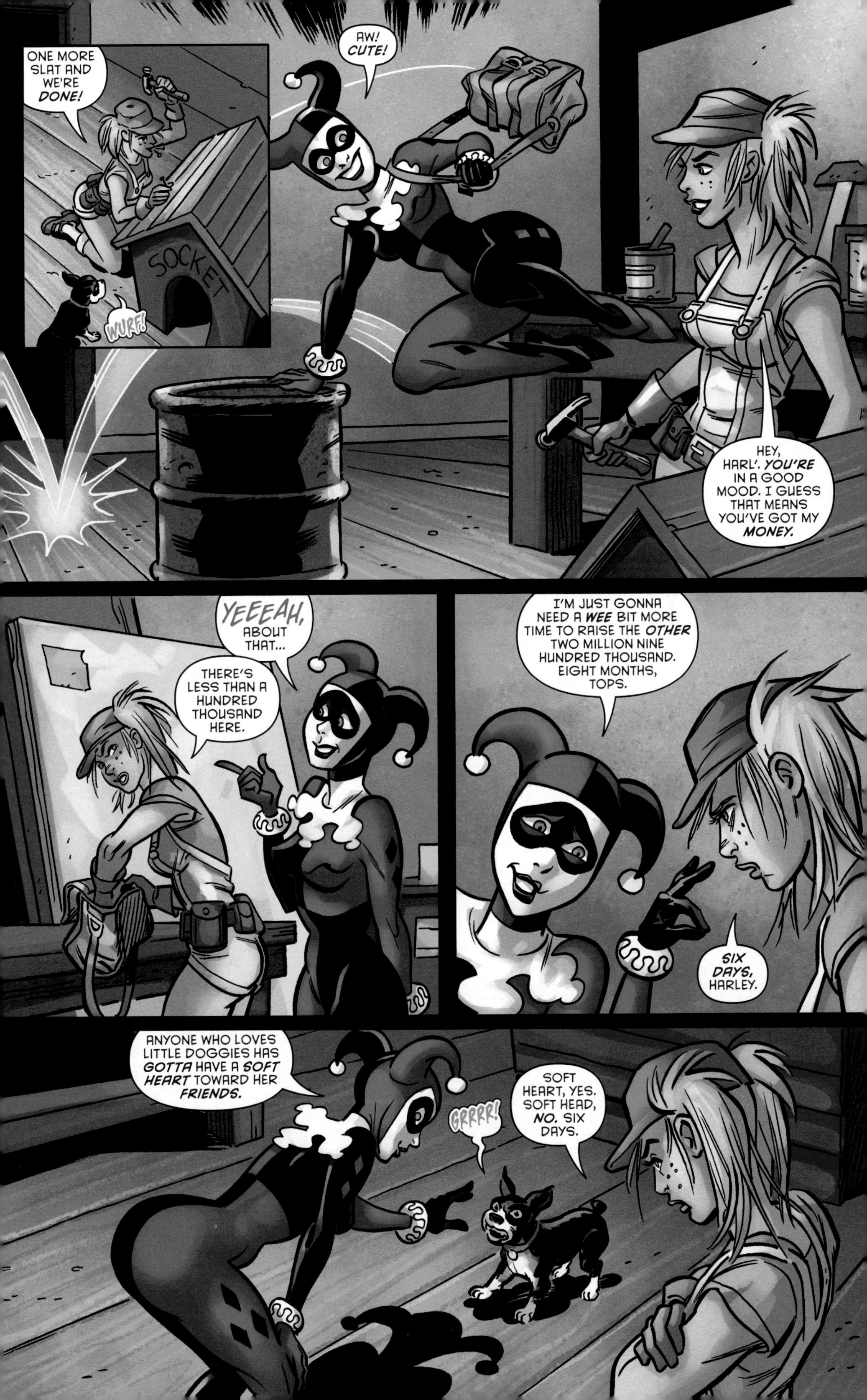
ONE MORE SLAT AND WE'RE DONE!
SOCKET
WURF!
AW! CUTE!
HEY, HARL'. YOU'RE IN A GOOD MOOD. I GUESS THAT MEANS YOU'VE GOT MY MONEY.
YEEEAH, ABOUT THAT...
THERE'S LESS THAN A HUNDRED THOUSAND HERE.
I'M JUST GONNA NEED A WEE BIT MORE TIME TO RAISE THE OTHER TWO MILLION NINE HUNDRED THOUSAND. EIGHT MONTHS, TOPS.
SIX DAYS, HARLEY.
ANYONE WHO LOVES LITTLE DOGGIES HAS GOTTA HAVE A SOFT HEART TOWARD HER FRIENDS.
GRRRR!
SOFT HEART, YES. SOFT HEAD, NO. SIX DAYS.

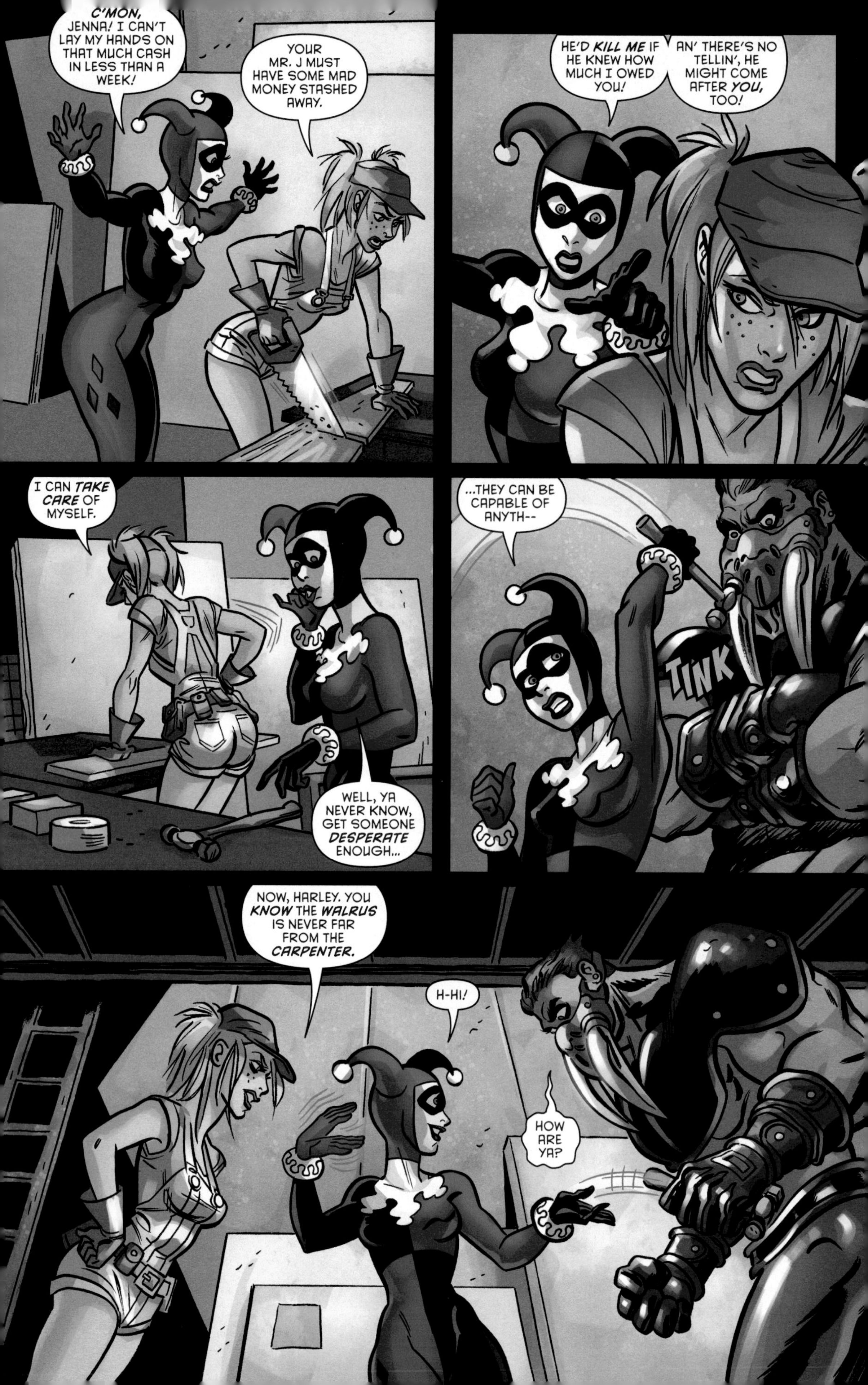
C'MON, JENNA! I CAN'T LAY MY HANDS ON THAT MUCH CASH IN LESS THAN A WEEK!
YOUR MR. J MUST HAVE SOME MAD MONEY STASHED AWAY.
HE'D KILL ME IF HE KNEW HOW MUCH I OWED YOU!
AN' THERE'S NO TELLIN', HE MIGHT COME AFTER YOU, TOO!
I CAN TAKE CARE OF MYSELF.
WELL, YA NEVER KNOW, GET SOMEONE DESPERATE ENOUGH...
...THEY CAN BE CAPABLE OF ANYTH--
TINK
NOW, HARLEY. YOU KNOW THE WALRUS IS NEVER FAR FROM THE CARPENTER.
H-HI!
HOW ARE YA?

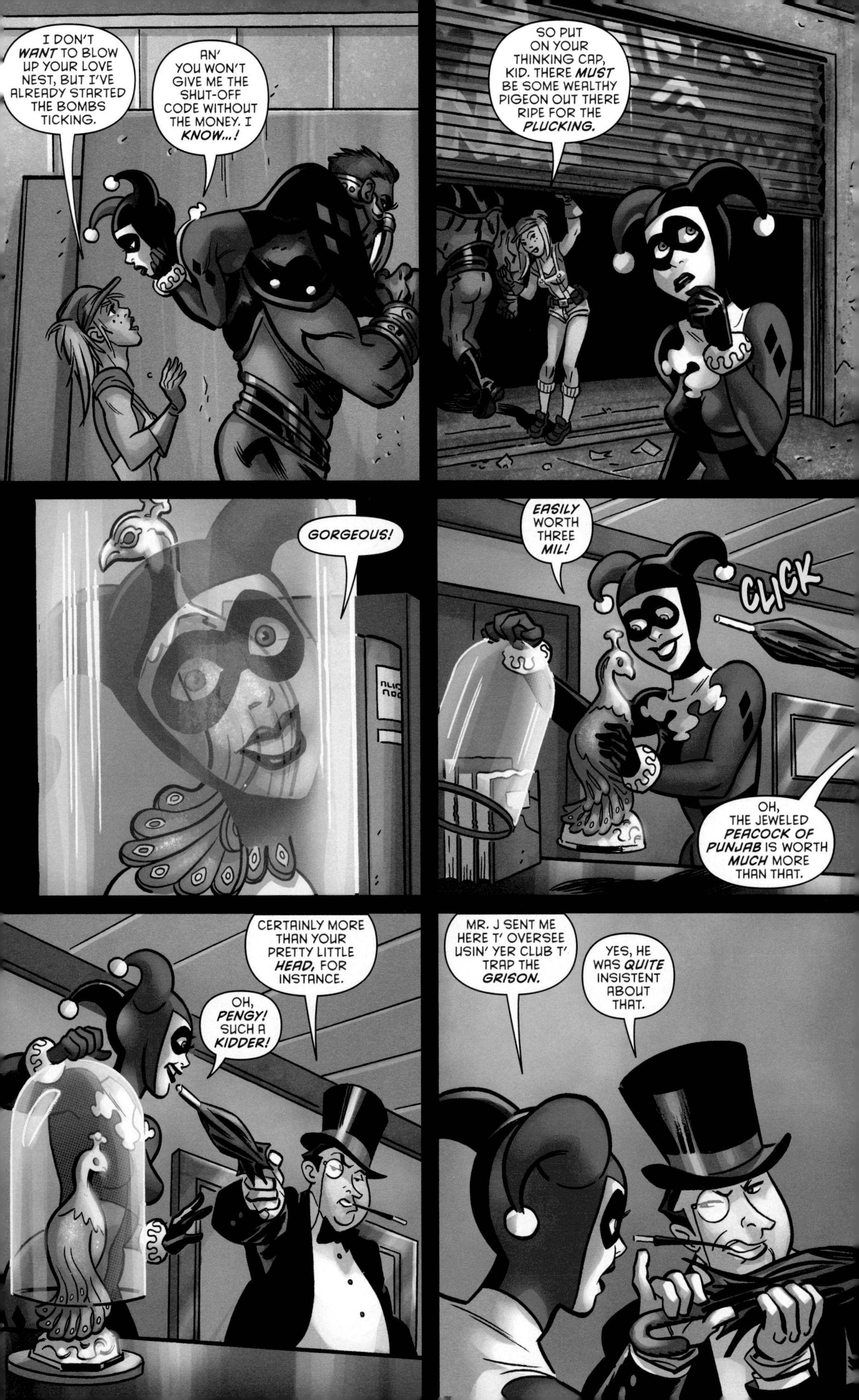
I DON'T *WANT* TO BLOW UP YOUR LOVE NEST, BUT I'VE ALREADY STARTED THE BOMBS TICKING.
AN' YOU WON'T GIVE ME THE SHUT-OFF CODE WITHOUT THE MONEY. I *KNOW...!*
SO PUT ON YOUR THINKING CAP, KID. THERE *MUST* BE SOME WEALTHY PIGEON OUT THERE RIPE FOR THE *PLUCKING.*
GORGEOUS!
EASILY WORTH THREE *MIL!*
CLICK
OH, THE JEWELED *PEACOCK OF PUNJAB* IS WORTH *MUCH* MORE THAN THAT.
CERTAINLY MORE THAN YOUR PRETTY LITTLE *HEAD,* FOR INSTANCE.
OH, *PENGY!* SUCH A *KIDDER!*
MR. J SENT ME HERE T' OVERSEE USIN' YER CLUB T' TRAP THE *GRISON.*
YES, HE WAS *QUITE* INSISTENT ABOUT THAT.

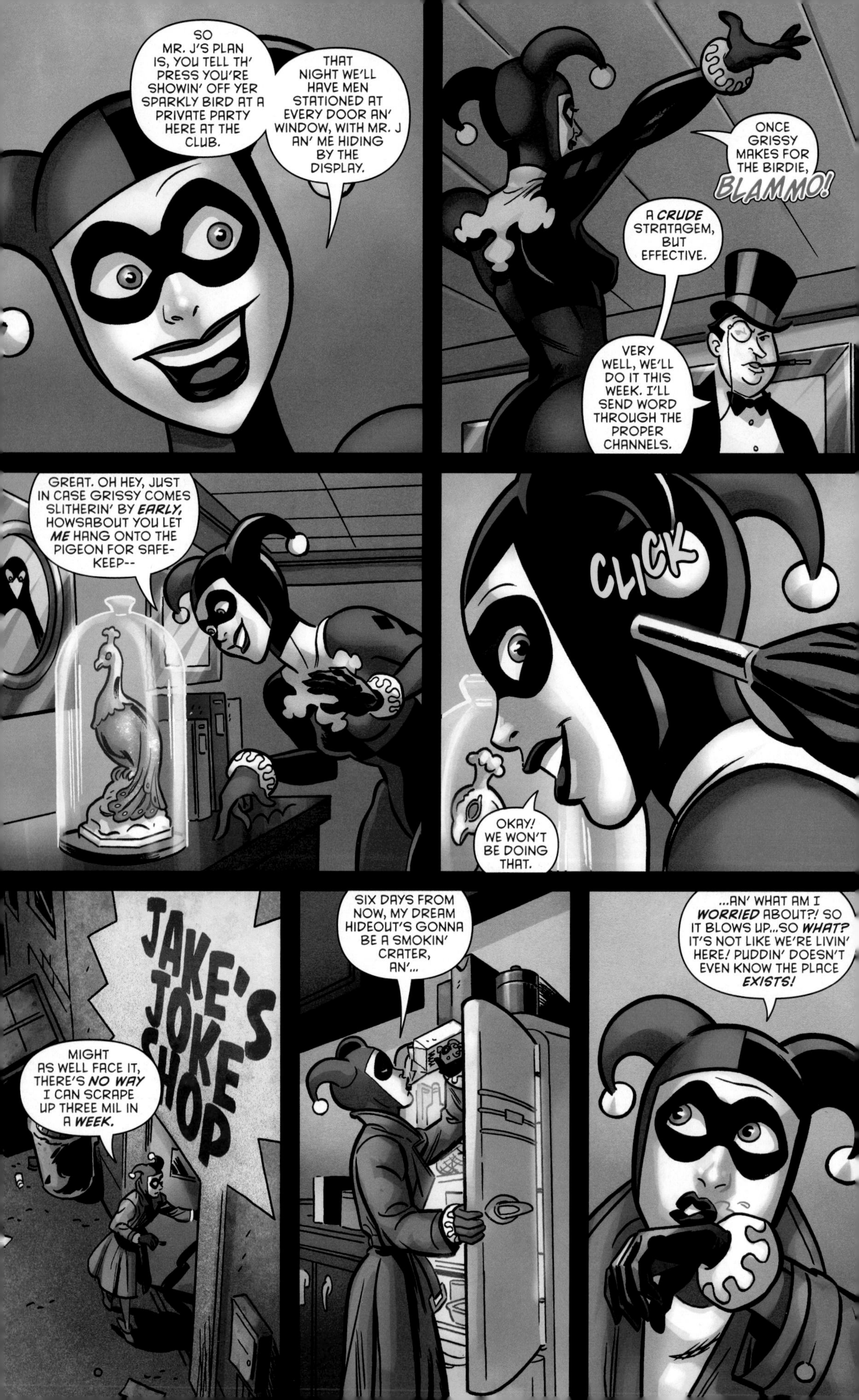
SO MR. J'S PLAN IS, YOU TELL TH' PRESS YOU'RE SHOWIN' OFF YER SPARKLY BIRD AT A PRIVATE PARTY HERE AT THE CLUB.
THAT NIGHT WE'LL HAVE MEN STATIONED AT EVERY DOOR AN' WINDOW, WITH MR. J AN' ME HIDING BY THE DISPLAY.
ONCE GRISSY MAKES FOR THE BIRDIE, BLAMMO!
A CRUDE STRATAGEM, BUT EFFECTIVE.
VERY WELL, WE'LL DO IT THIS WEEK. I'LL SEND WORD THROUGH THE PROPER CHANNELS.
GREAT. OH HEY, JUST IN CASE GRISSY COMES SLITHERIN' BY EARLY, HOWSABOUT YOU LET ME HANG ONTO THE PIGEON FOR SAFE-KEEP--
CLICK
OKAY! WE WON'T BE DOING THAT.
JAKE'S JOKE SHOP
MIGHT AS WELL FACE IT, THERE'S NO WAY I CAN SCRAPE UP THREE MIL IN A WEEK.
SIX DAYS FROM NOW, MY DREAM HIDEOUT'S GONNA BE A SMOKIN' CRATER, AN'...
...AN' WHAT AM I WORRIED ABOUT?! SO IT BLOWS UP...SO WHAT? IT'S NOT LIKE WE'RE LIVIN' HERE! PUDDIN' DOESN'T EVEN KNOW THE PLACE EXISTS!

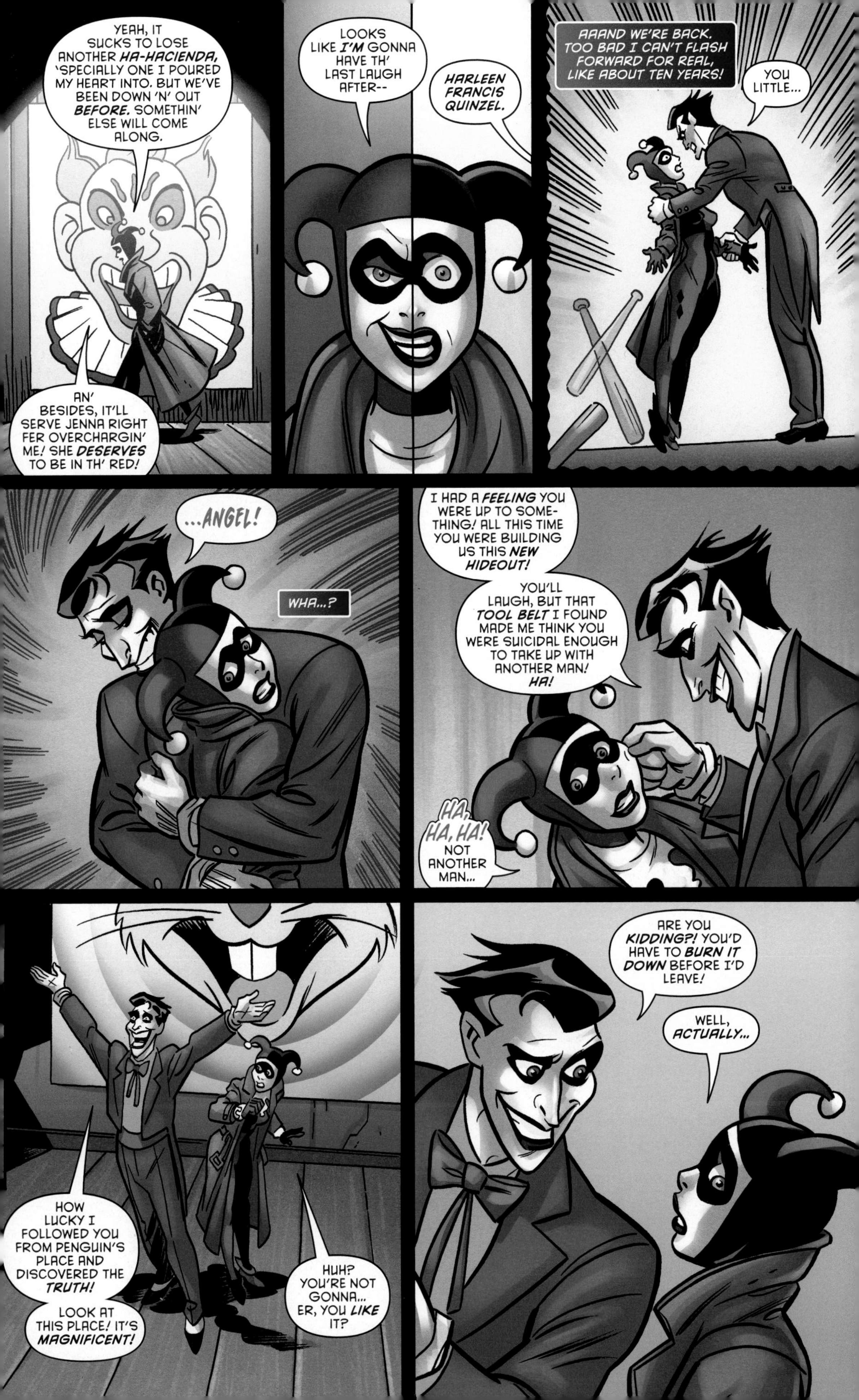
YEAH, IT SUCKS TO LOSE ANOTHER HA-HACIENDA, 'SPECIALLY ONE I POURED MY HEART INTO. BUT WE'VE BEEN DOWN 'N' OUT BEFORE. SOMETHIN' ELSE WILL COME ALONG.
AN' BESIDES, IT'LL SERVE JENNA RIGHT FER OVERCHARGIN' ME! SHE DESERVES TO BE IN TH' RED!
LOOKS LIKE I'M GONNA HAVE TH' LAST LAUGH AFTER--
HARLEEN FRANCIS QUINZEL.
AAAND WE'RE BACK. TOO BAD I CAN'T FLASH FORWARD FOR REAL, LIKE ABOUT TEN YEARS!
YOU LITTLE...
...ANGEL!
WHA...?
I HAD A FEELING YOU WERE UP TO SOME-THING! ALL THIS TIME YOU WERE BUILDING US THIS NEW HIDEOUT!
YOU'LL LAUGH, BUT THAT TOOL BELT I FOUND MADE ME THINK YOU WERE SUICIDAL ENOUGH TO TAKE UP WITH ANOTHER MAN! HA!
HA, HA, HA! NOT ANOTHER MAN...
HOW LUCKY I FOLLOWED YOU FROM PENGUIN'S PLACE AND DISCOVERED THE TRUTH!
LOOK AT THIS PLACE! IT'S MAGNIFICENT!
HUH? YOU'RE NOT GONNA... ER, YOU LIKE IT?
ARE YOU KIDDING?! YOU'D HAVE TO BURN IT DOWN BEFORE I'D LEAVE!
WELL, ACTUALLY...

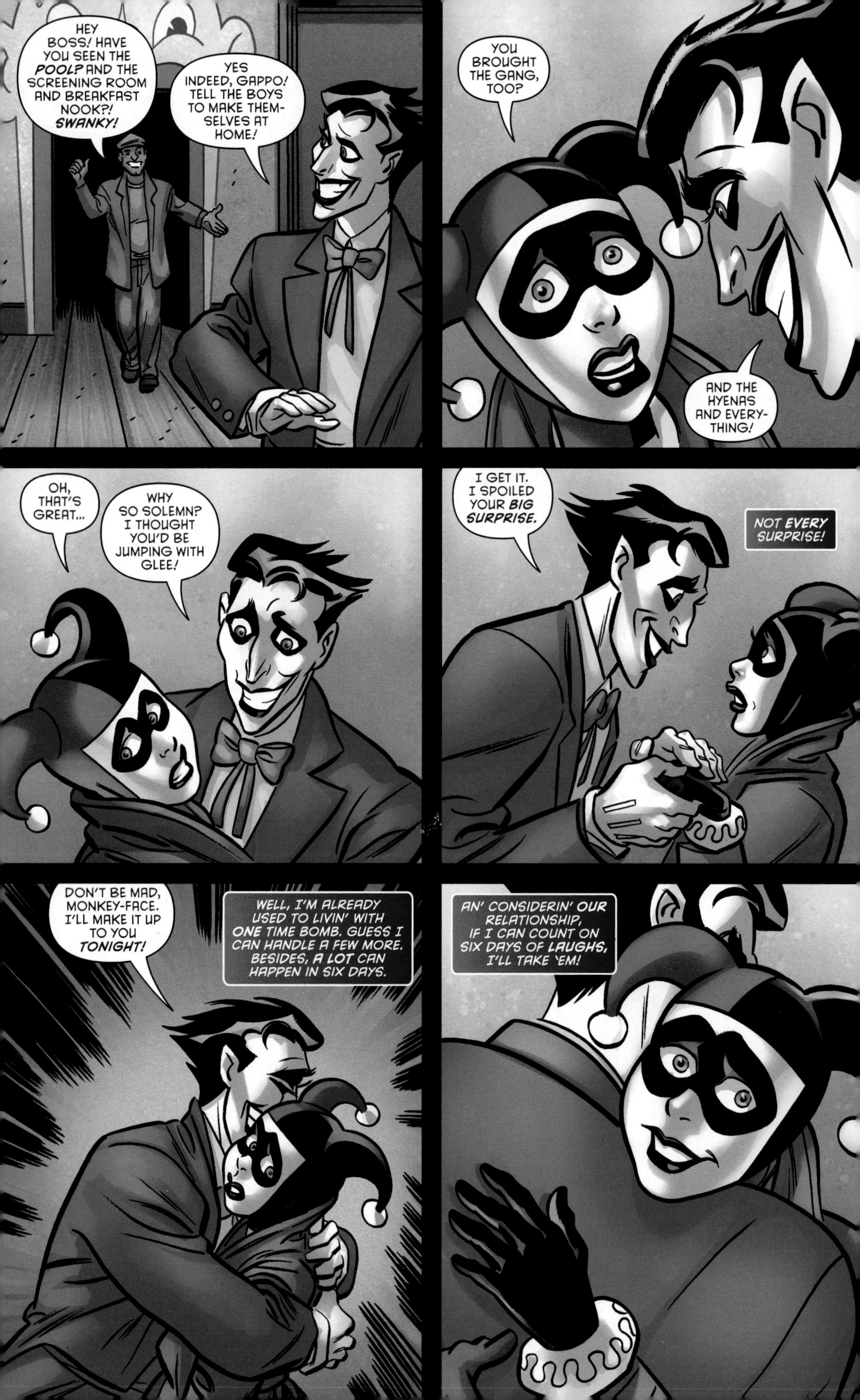
HEY BOSS! HAVE YOU SEEN THE POOL? AND THE SCREENING ROOM AND BREAKFAST NOOK?! SWANKY!
YES INDEED, GAPPO! TELL THE BOYS TO MAKE THEM-SELVES AT HOME!
YOU BROUGHT THE GANG, TOO?
AND THE HYENAS AND EVERY-THING!
OH, THAT'S GREAT...
WHY SO SOLEMN? I THOUGHT YOU'D BE JUMPING WITH GLEE!
I GET IT. I SPOILED YOUR BIG SURPRISE.
NOT EVERY SURPRISE!
DON'T BE MAD, MONKEY-FACE. I'LL MAKE IT UP TO YOU TONIGHT!
WELL, I'M ALREADY USED TO LIVIN' WITH ONE TIME BOMB. GUESS I CAN HANDLE A FEW MORE. BESIDES, A LOT CAN HAPPEN IN SIX DAYS.
AN' CONSIDERIN' OUR RELATIONSHIP, IF I CAN COUNT ON SIX DAYS OF LAUGHS, I'LL TAKE 'EM!

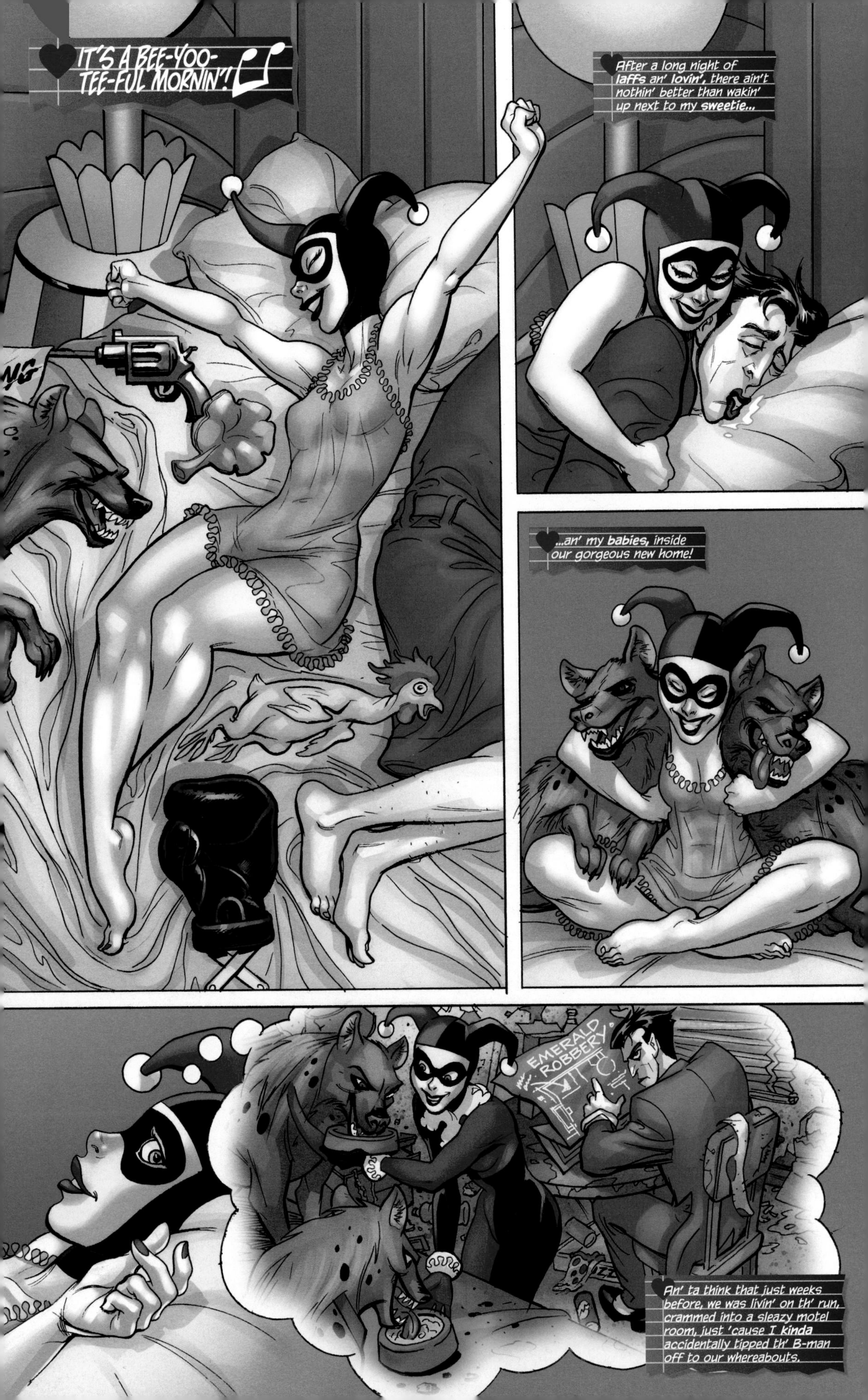
IT'S A BEE-YOO-TEE-FUL MORNIN'!
NG
After a long night of laffs an' lovin', there ain't nothin' better than wakin' up next to my sweetie...
...an' my babies, inside our gorgeous new home!
EMERALD ROBBERY
An' ta think that just weeks before, we was livin' on th' run, crammed into a sleazy motel room, just 'cause I kinda accidentally tipped th' B-man off to our whereabouts.

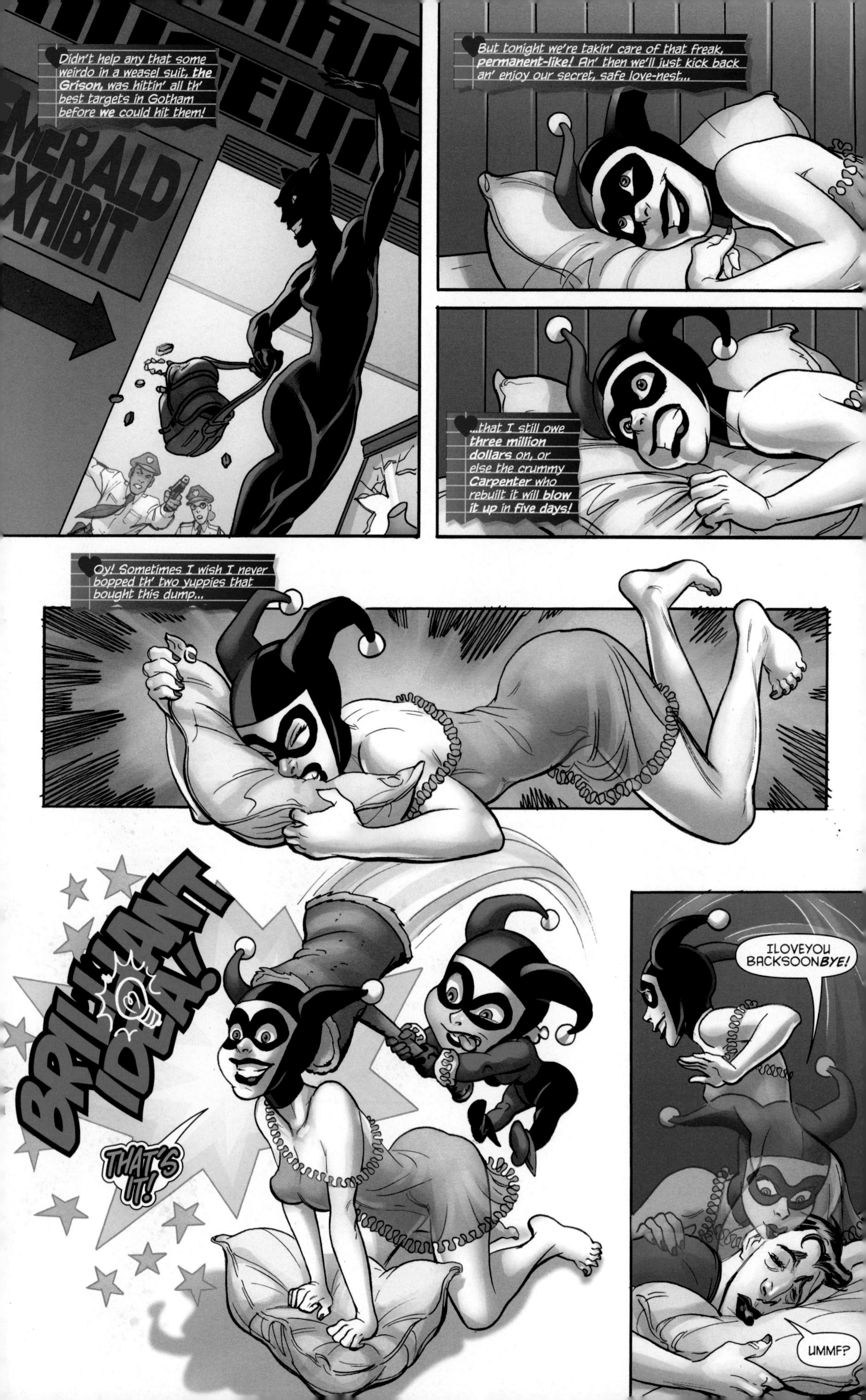

EMERALD EXHIBIT
Didn't help any that some weirdo in a weasel suit, the Grison, was hittin' all th' best targets in Gotham before we could hit them!
But tonight we're takin' care of that freak, permanent-like! An' then we'll just kick back an' enjoy our secret, safe love-nest...
...that I still owe three million dollars on, or else the crummy Carpenter who rebuilt it will blow it up in five days!
Oy! Sometimes I wish I never bopped th' two yuppies that bought this dump...
BRILLIANT IDEA!
THAT'S IT!
ILOVEYOU BACKSOONBYE!
UMMF?

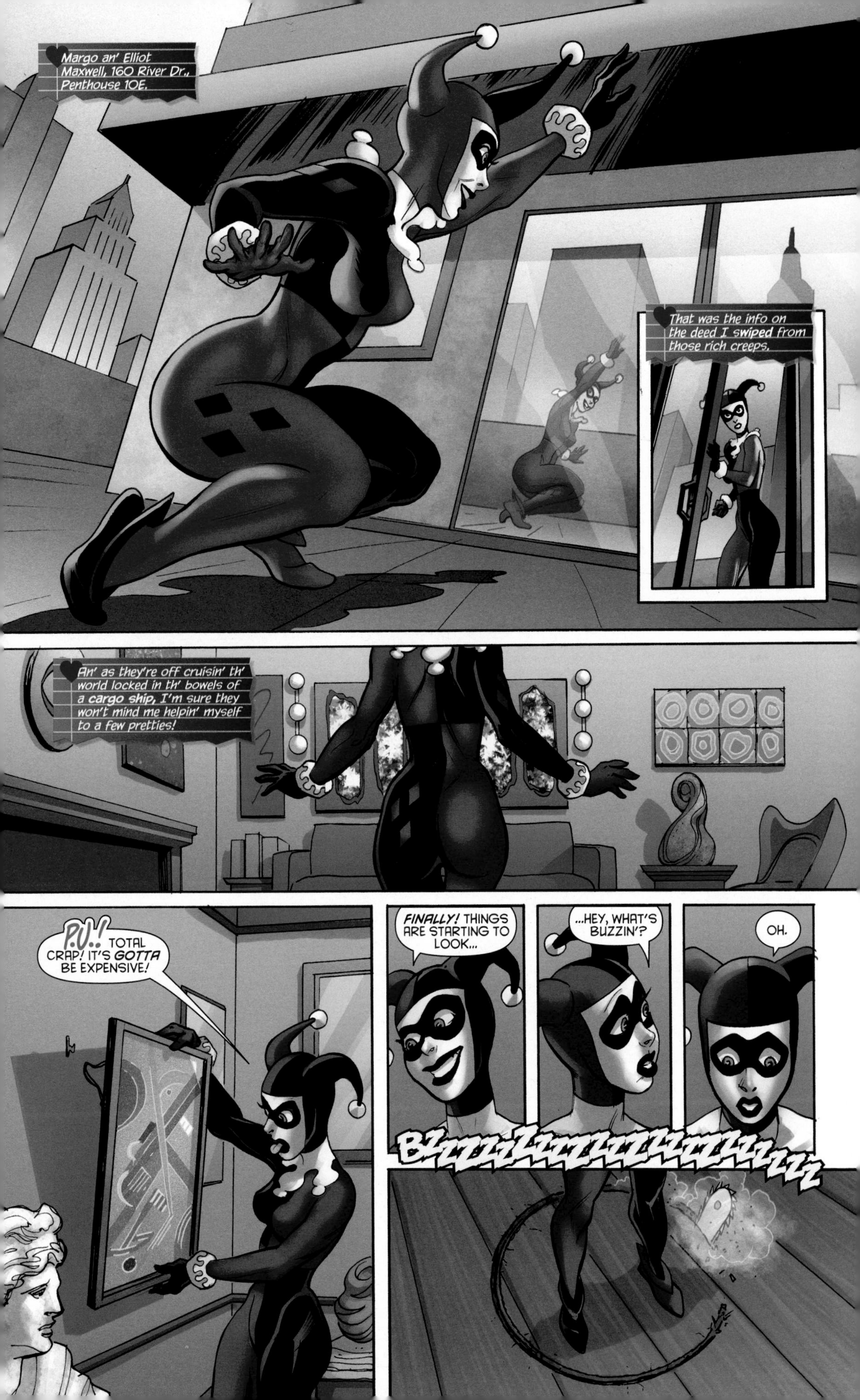
Margo an' Elliot Maxwell, 160 River Dr., Penthouse 10E.
That was the info on the deed I swiped from those rich creeps.
An' as they're off cruisin' th' world locked in th' bowels of a cargo ship, I'm sure they won't mind me helpin' myself to a few pretties!
P.U.! TOTAL CRAP! IT'S GOTTA BE EXPENSIVE!
FINALLY! THINGS ARE STARTING TO LOOK...
...HEY, WHAT'S BUZZIN'?
OH.
BZZZZZZZZZZZZZZZZZZZZZZZZ

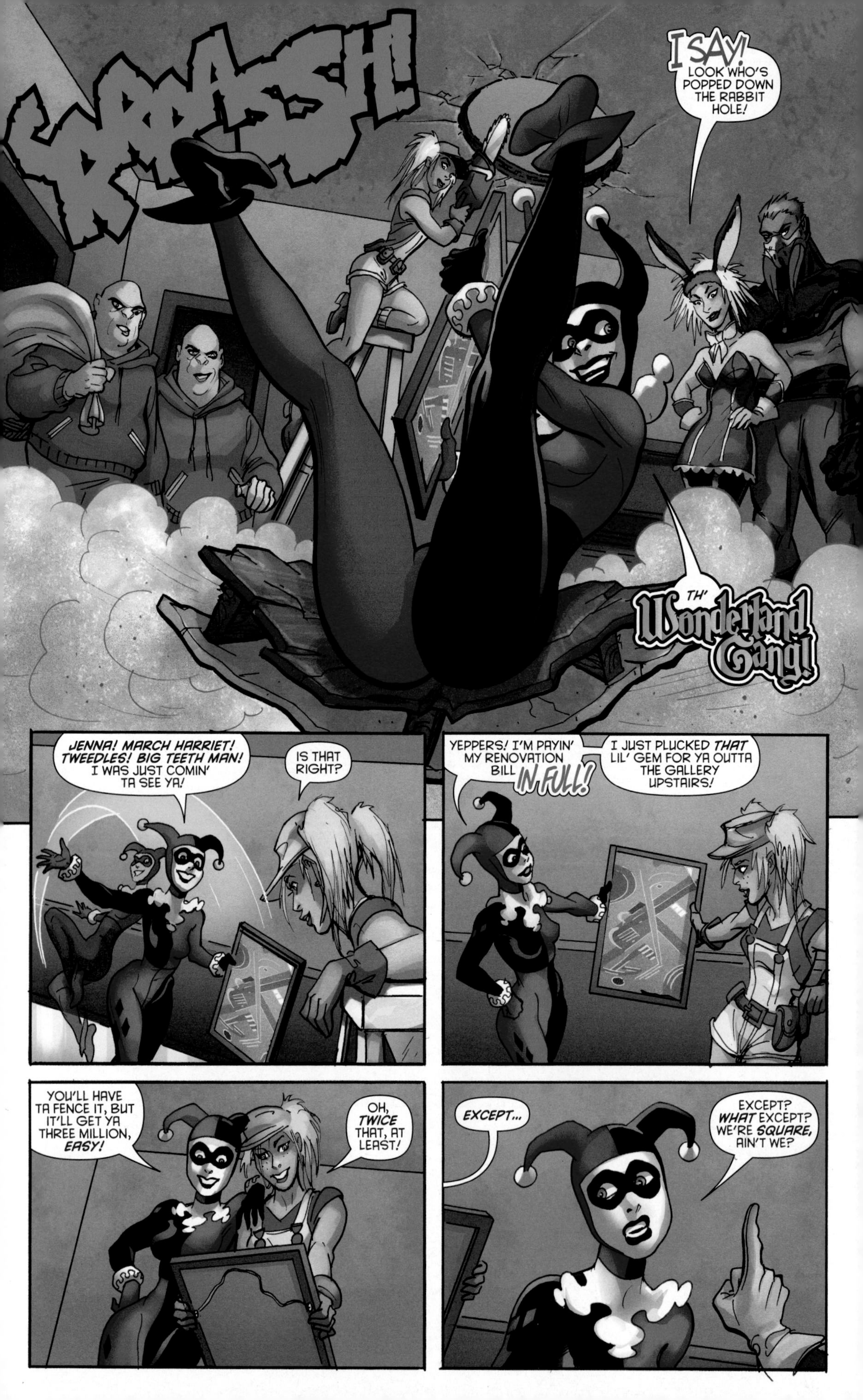
KRRAASH!
I SAY! LOOK WHO'S POPPED DOWN THE RABBIT HOLE!
TH' Wonderland Gang!
JENNA! MARCH HARRIET! TWEEDLES! BIG TEETH MAN! I WAS JUST COMIN' TA SEE YA!
IS THAT RIGHT?
YEPPERS! I'M PAYIN' MY RENOVATION BILL IN FULL!
I JUST PLUCKED THAT LIL' GEM FOR YA OUTTA THE GALLERY UPSTAIRS!
YOU'LL HAVE TA FENCE IT, BUT IT'LL GET YA THREE MILLION, EASY!
OH, TWICE THAT, AT LEAST!
EXCEPT...
EXCEPT? WHAT EXCEPT? WE'RE SQUARE, AIN'T WE?

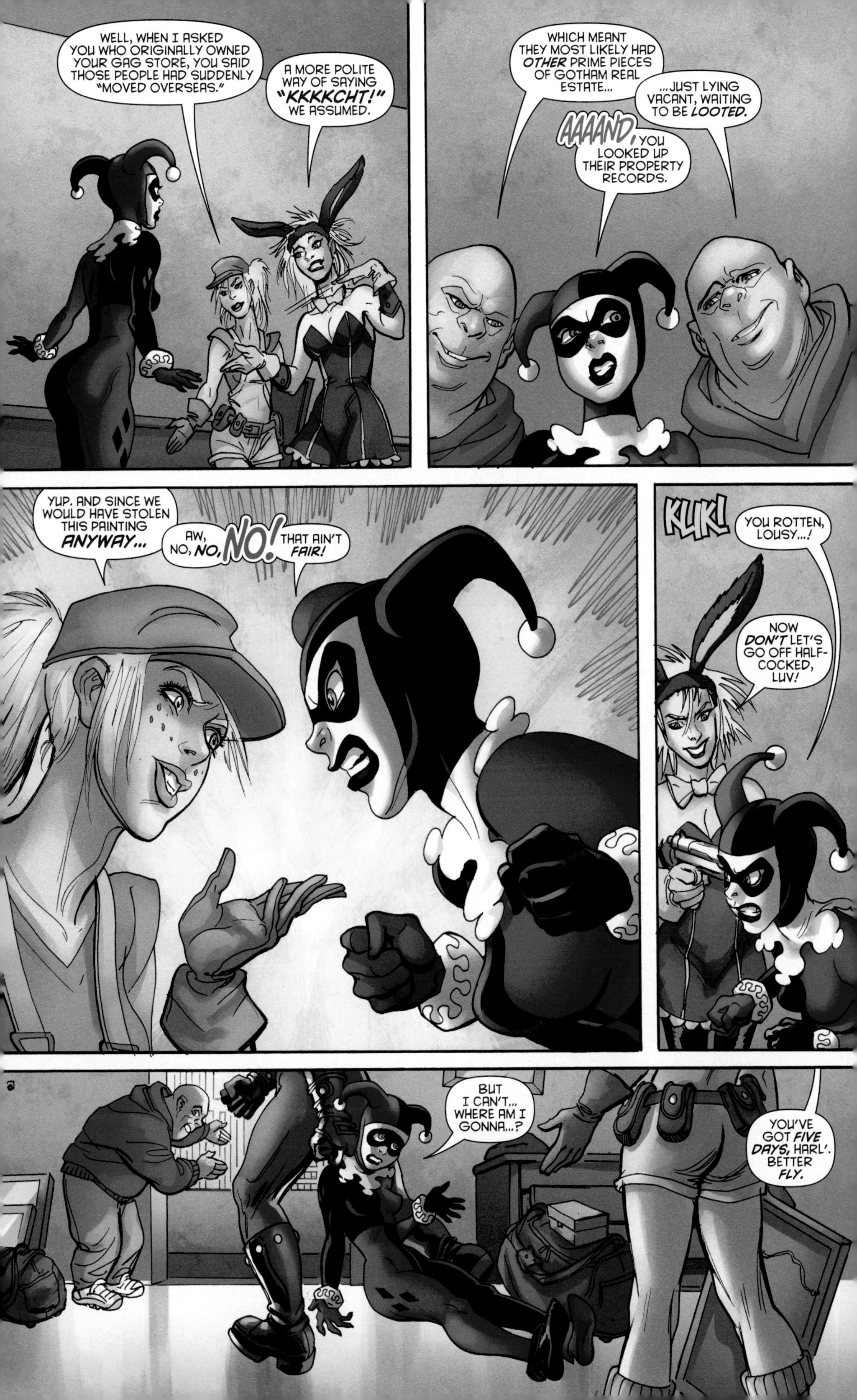
WELL, WHEN I ASKED YOU WHO ORIGINALLY OWNED YOUR GAG STORE, YOU SAID THOSE PEOPLE HAD SUDDENLY "MOVED OVERSEAS."
A MORE POLITE WAY OF SAYING "KKKKCHT!" WE ASSUMED.
WHICH MEANT THEY MOST LIKELY HAD OTHER PRIME PIECES OF GOTHAM REAL ESTATE...
...JUST LYING VACANT, WAITING TO BE LOOTED.
AAAAND, YOU LOOKED UP THEIR PROPERTY RECORDS.
YUP. AND SINCE WE WOULD HAVE STOLEN THIS PAINTING ANYWAY...
AW, NO, NO, NO! THAT AIN'T FAIR!
KLIK!
YOU ROTTEN, LOUSY...!
NOW DON'T LET'S GO OFF HALF-COCKED, LUV!
BUT I CAN'T... WHERE AM I GONNA...?
YOU'VE GOT FIVE DAYS, HARL'. BETTER FLY.

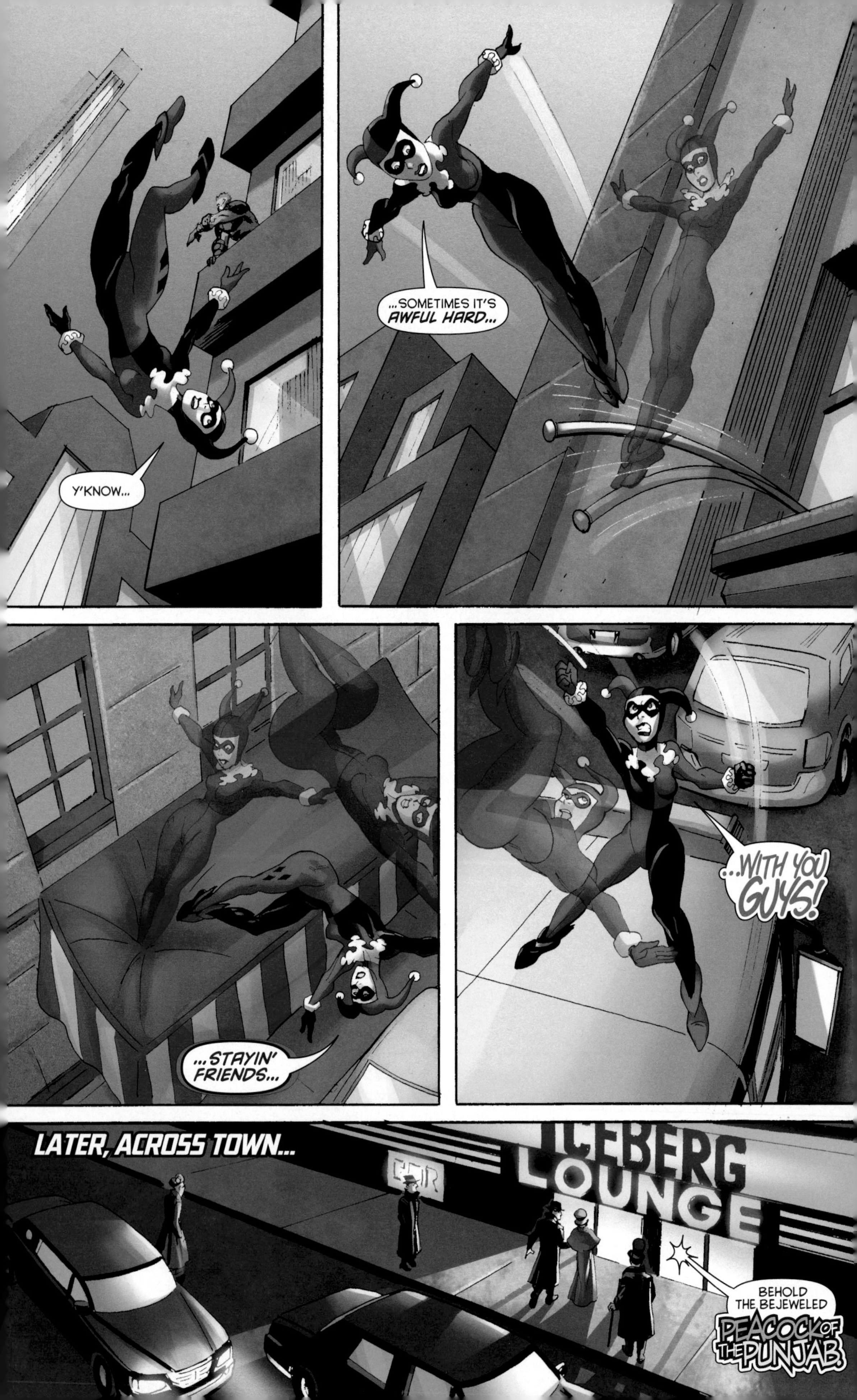

Y'KNOW...
...SOMETIMES IT'S AWFUL HARD...
...STAYIN' FRIENDS...
...WITH YOU GUYS!
LATER, ACROSS TOWN...
ICEBERG LOUNGE
BEHOLD THE BEJEWELED PEACOCK OF THE PUNJAB.

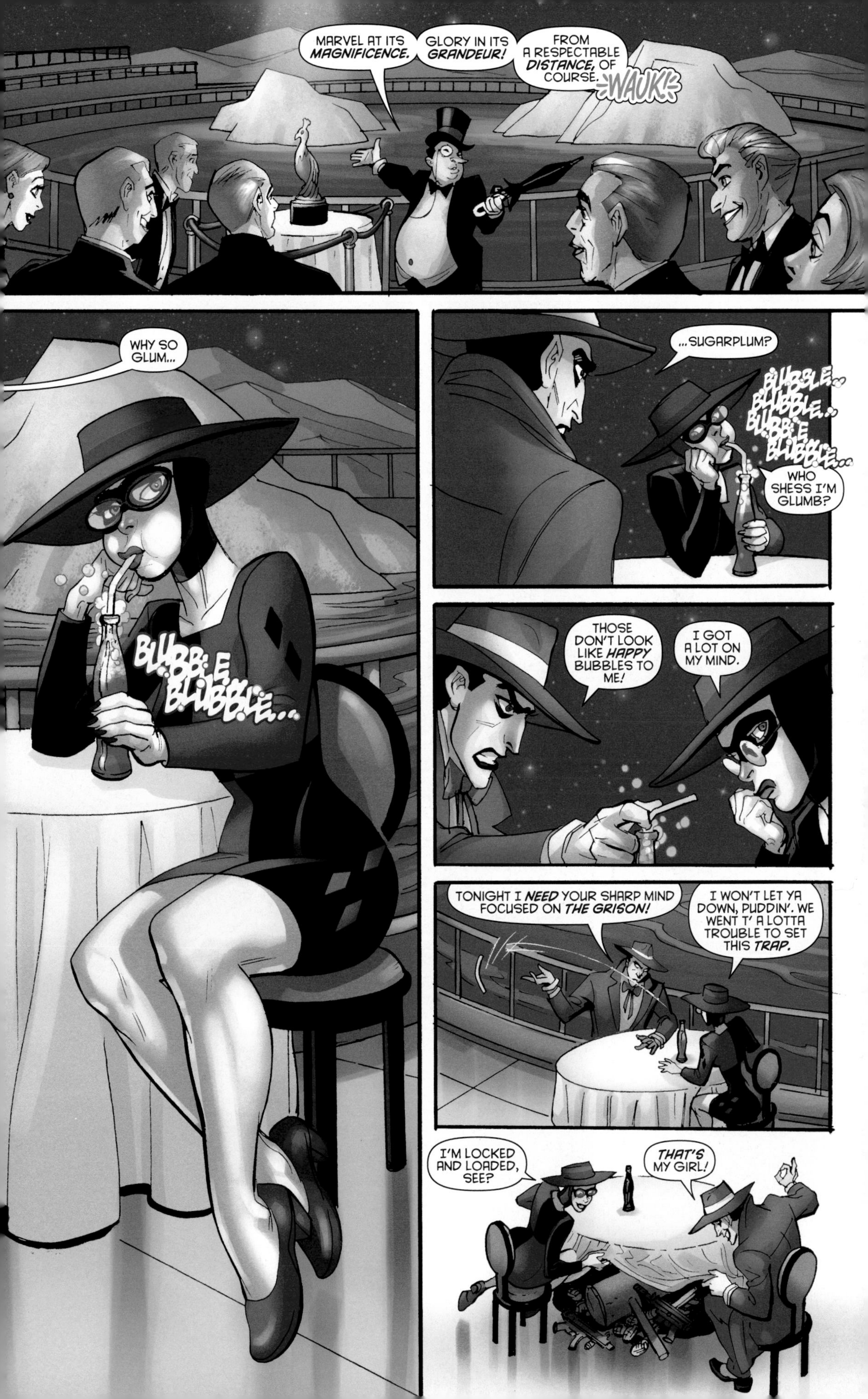

MARVEL AT ITS *MAGNIFICENCE.*
GLORY IN ITS *GRANDEUR!*
FROM A RESPECTABLE *DISTANCE,* OF COURSE.
WAUK!
WHY SO GLUM...
BLUBBLE BLUBBLE...
...SUGARPLUM?
BLUBBLE.. BLUBBLE.. BLUBBLE BLUBBLE...
WHO SHESS I'M GLUMB?
THOSE DON'T LOOK LIKE *HAPPY* BUBBLES TO ME!
I GOT A LOT ON MY MIND.
TONIGHT I *NEED* YOUR SHARP MIND FOCUSED ON *THE GRISON!*
I WON'T LET YA DOWN, PUDDIN'. WE WENT T' A LOTTA TROUBLE TO SET THIS *TRAP.*
I'M LOCKED AND LOADED, SEE?
THAT'S MY GIRL!

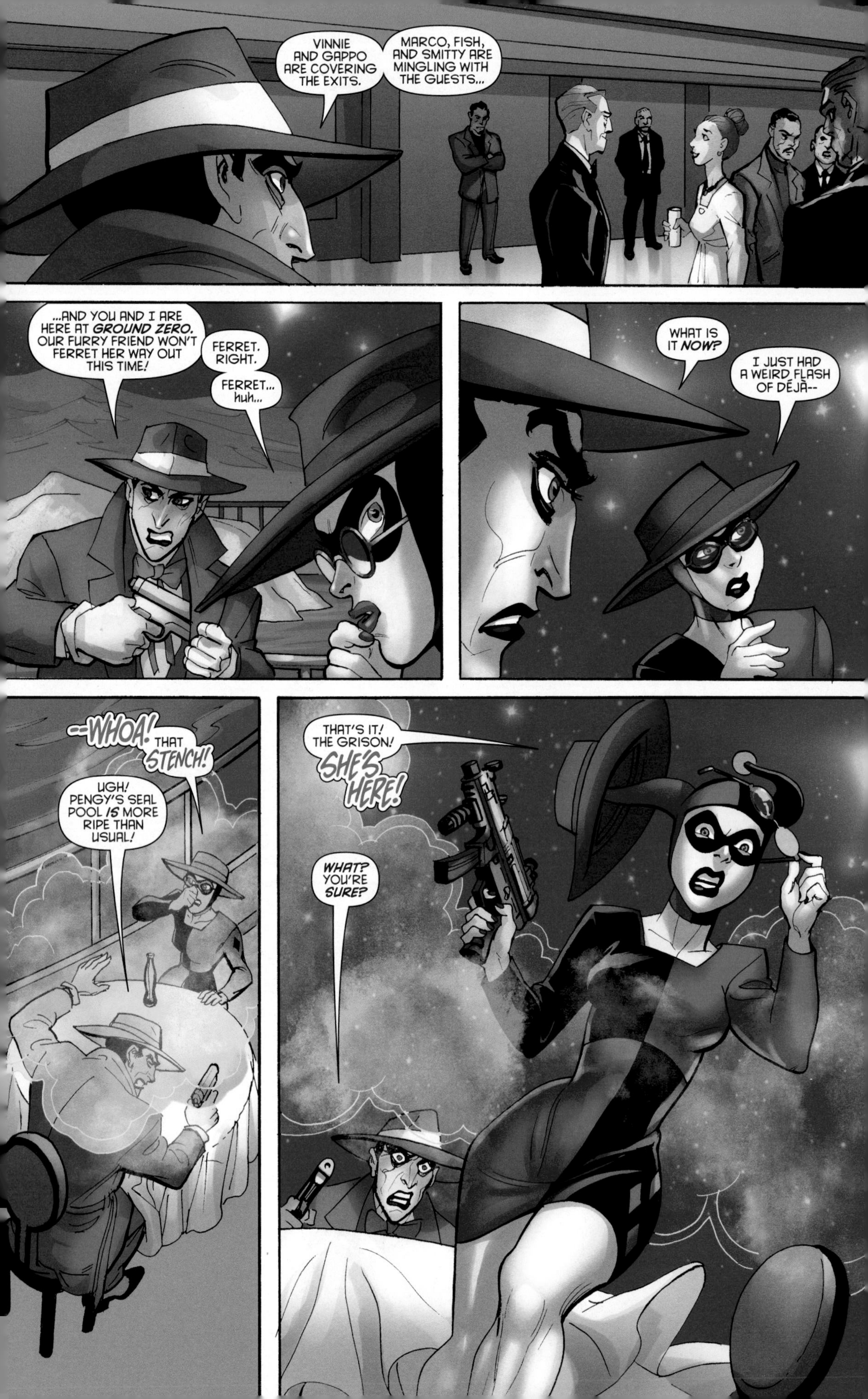
VINNIE AND GAPPO ARE COVERING THE EXITS.
MARCO, FISH, AND SMITTY ARE MINGLING WITH THE GUESTS...
...AND YOU AND I ARE HERE AT GROUND ZERO. OUR FURRY FRIEND WON'T FERRET HER WAY OUT THIS TIME!
FERRET. RIGHT.
FERRET... HUH...
WHAT IS IT NOW?
I JUST HAD A WEIRD FLASH OF DÉJÀ--
--WHOA! THAT STENCH!
UGH! PENGY'S SEAL POOL IS MORE RIPE THAN USUAL!
THAT'S IT! THE GRISON! SHE'S HERE!
WHAT? YOU'RE SURE?

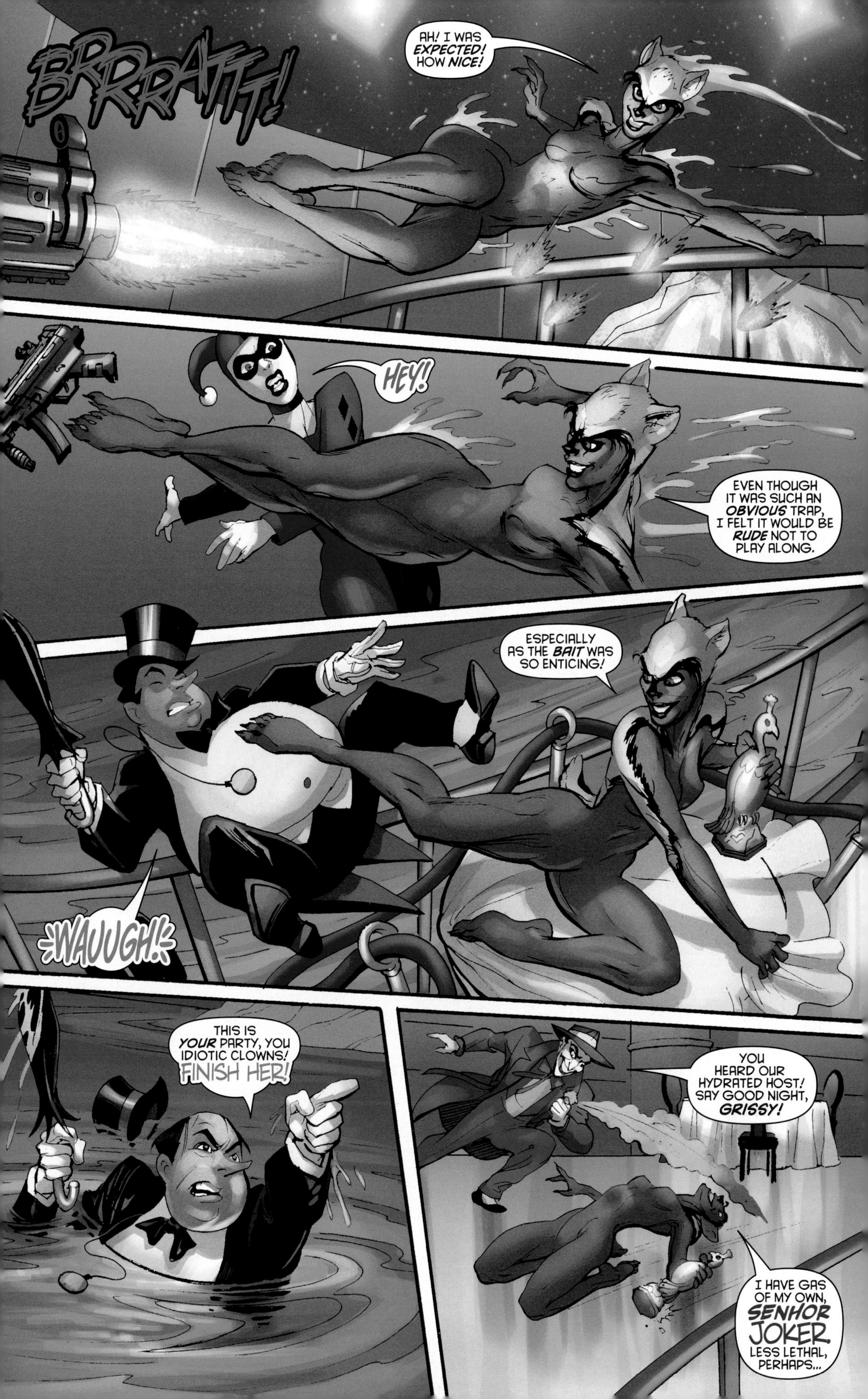
BRRRATTT!
AH! I WAS EXPECTED! HOW NICE!
HEY!
EVEN THOUGH IT WAS SUCH AN OBVIOUS TRAP, I FELT IT WOULD BE RUDE NOT TO PLAY ALONG.
ESPECIALLY AS THE BAIT WAS SO ENTICING!
WAUUGH!
THIS IS YOUR PARTY, YOU IDIOTIC CLOWNS! FINISH HER!
YOU HEARD OUR HYDRATED HOST! SAY GOOD NIGHT, GRISSY!
I HAVE GAS OF MY OWN, SENHOR JOKER. LESS LETHAL, PERHAPS...

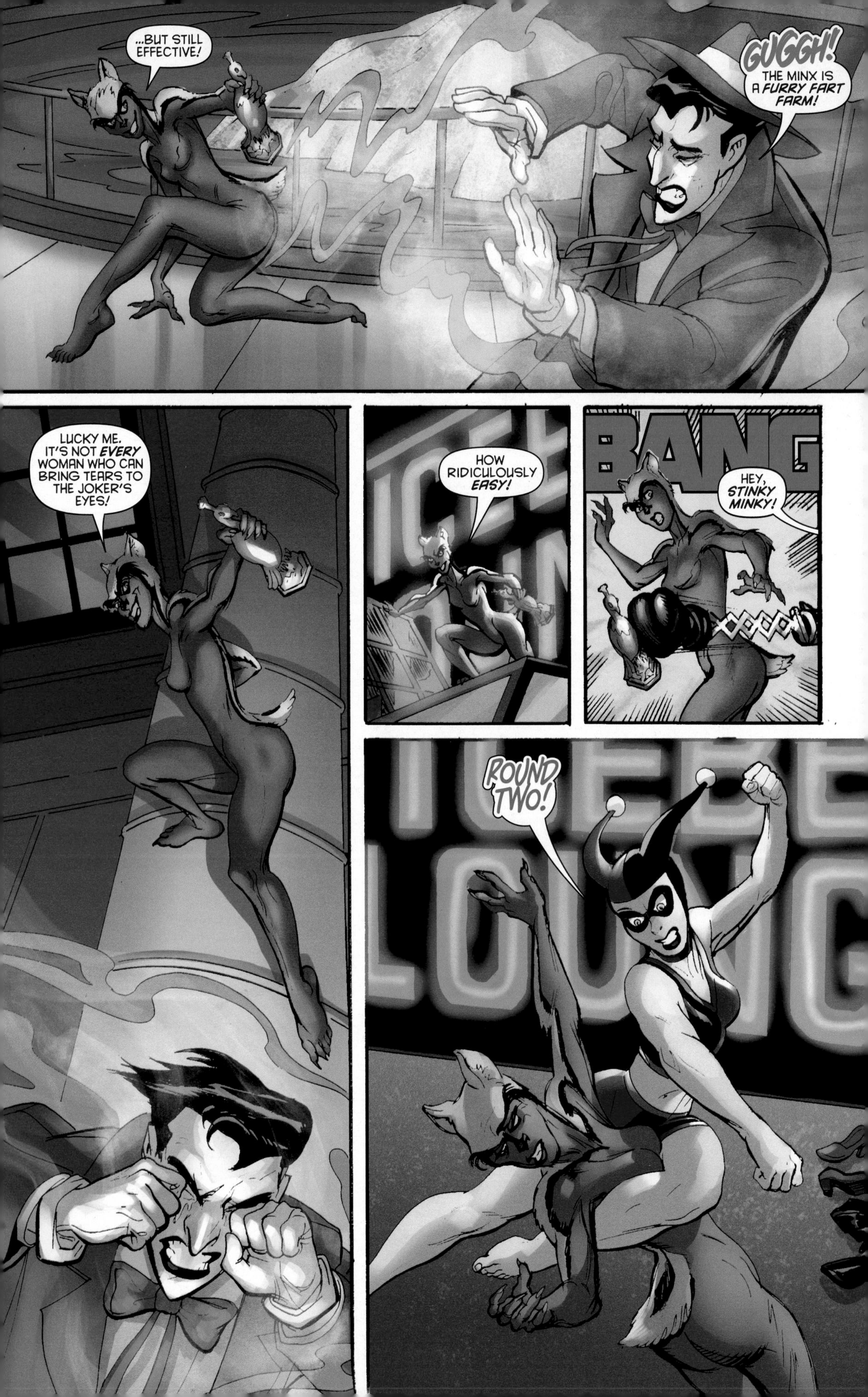

...BUT STILL EFFECTIVE!
GUGGH! THE MINX IS A FURRY FART FARM!
LUCKY ME. IT'S NOT EVERY WOMAN WHO CAN BRING TEARS TO THE JOKER'S EYES!
HOW RIDICULOUSLY EASY!
BANG
HEY, STINKY MINKY!
ROUND TWO!

I DON'T KNOW *HOW*...

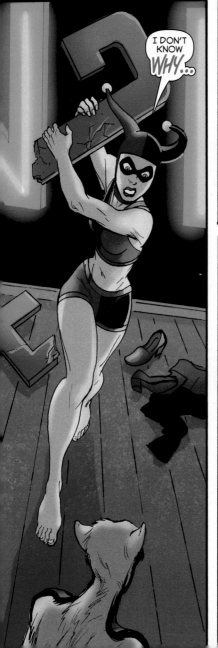

I DON'T KNOW *WHY*...

ALL I KNOW IS, AFTER ALL THESE *YEARS*...

IT'S REALLY *YOU*, AIN'T IT...

...GABRIELA MATIAS?!

I'M DELIGHTED YOU *REMEMBER* ME, AMIGA.

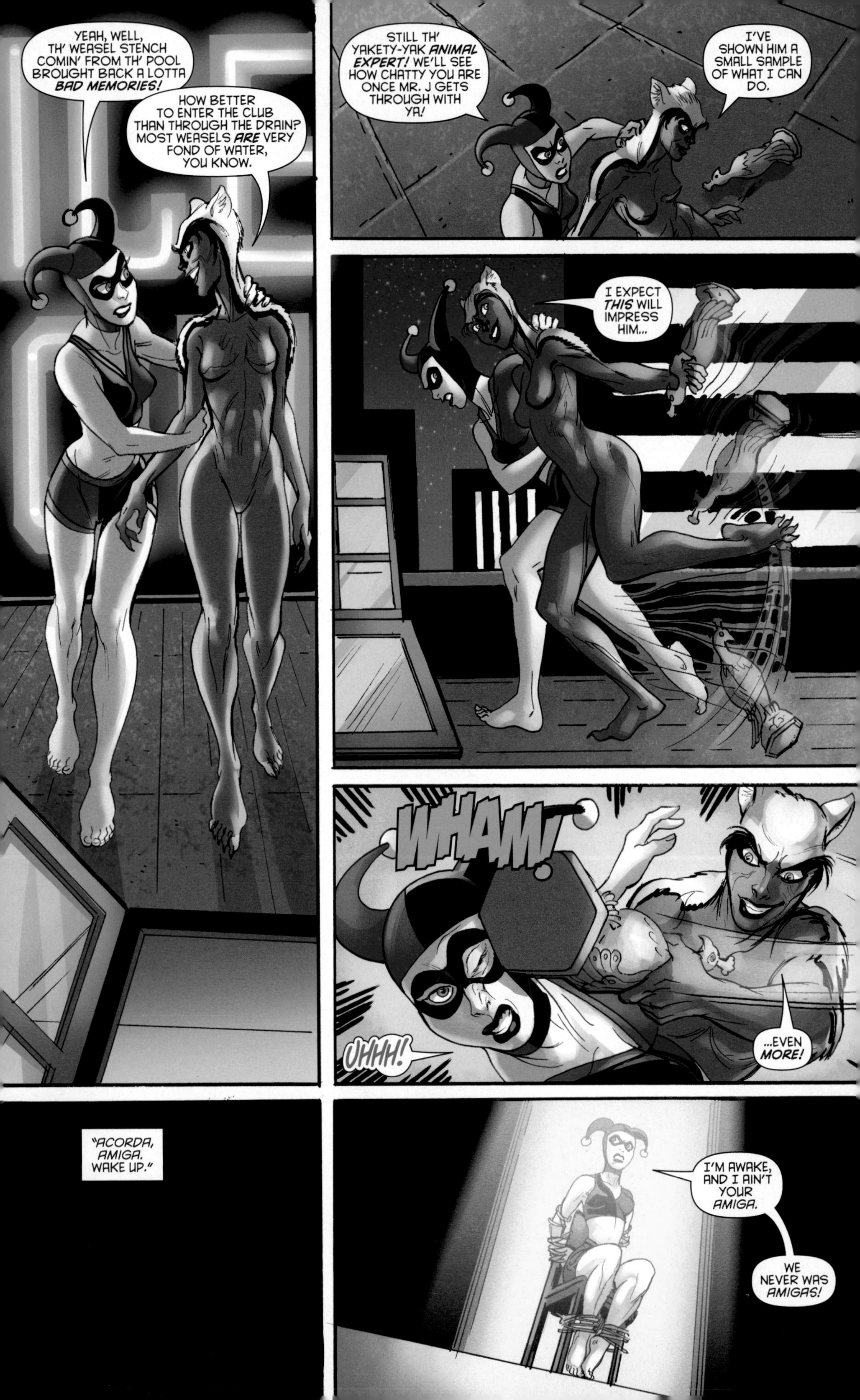
YEAH, WELL, TH' WEASEL STENCH COMIN' FROM TH' POOL BROUGHT BACK A LOTTA BAD MEMORIES!
HOW BETTER TO ENTER THE CLUB THAN THROUGH THE DRAIN? MOST WEASELS ARE VERY FOND OF WATER, YOU KNOW.
STILL TH' YAKETY-YAK ANIMAL EXPERT! WE'LL SEE HOW CHATTY YOU ARE ONCE MR. J GETS THROUGH WITH YA!
I'VE SHOWN HIM A SMALL SAMPLE OF WHAT I CAN DO.
I EXPECT THIS WILL IMPRESS HIM...
WHAM!
UHHH!
...EVEN MORE!
"ACORDA, AMIGA. WAKE UP."
I'M AWAKE, AND I AIN'T YOUR AMIGA.
WE NEVER WAS AMIGAS!

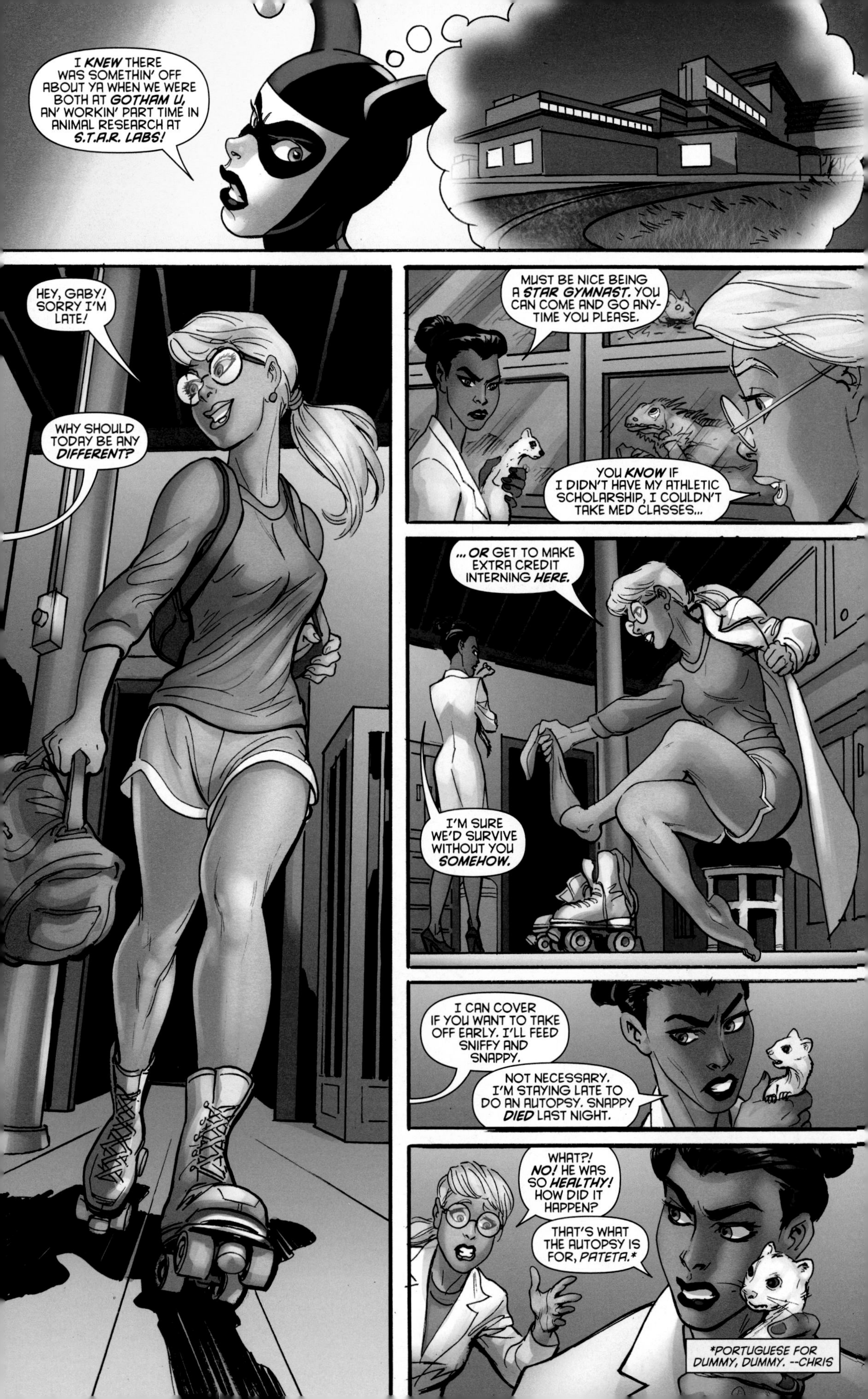
I KNEW THERE WAS SOMETHIN' OFF ABOUT YA WHEN WE WERE BOTH AT GOTHAM U, AN' WORKIN' PART TIME IN ANIMAL RESEARCH AT S.T.A.R. LABS!
HEY, GABY! SORRY I'M LATE!
WHY SHOULD TODAY BE ANY DIFFERENT?
MUST BE NICE BEING A STAR GYMNAST. YOU CAN COME AND GO ANY-TIME YOU PLEASE.
YOU KNOW IF I DIDN'T HAVE MY ATHLETIC SCHOLARSHIP, I COULDN'T TAKE MED CLASSES...
...OR GET TO MAKE EXTRA CREDIT INTERNING HERE.
I'M SURE WE'D SURVIVE WITHOUT YOU SOMEHOW.
I CAN COVER IF YOU WANT TO TAKE OFF EARLY. I'LL FEED SNIFFY AND SNAPPY.
NOT NECESSARY. I'M STAYING LATE TO DO AN AUTOPSY. SNAPPY DIED LAST NIGHT.
WHAT?! NO! HE WAS SO HEALTHY! HOW DID IT HAPPEN?
THAT'S WHAT THE AUTOPSY IS FOR, PATETA.*
*PORTUGUESE FOR DUMMY, DUMMY. --CHRIS

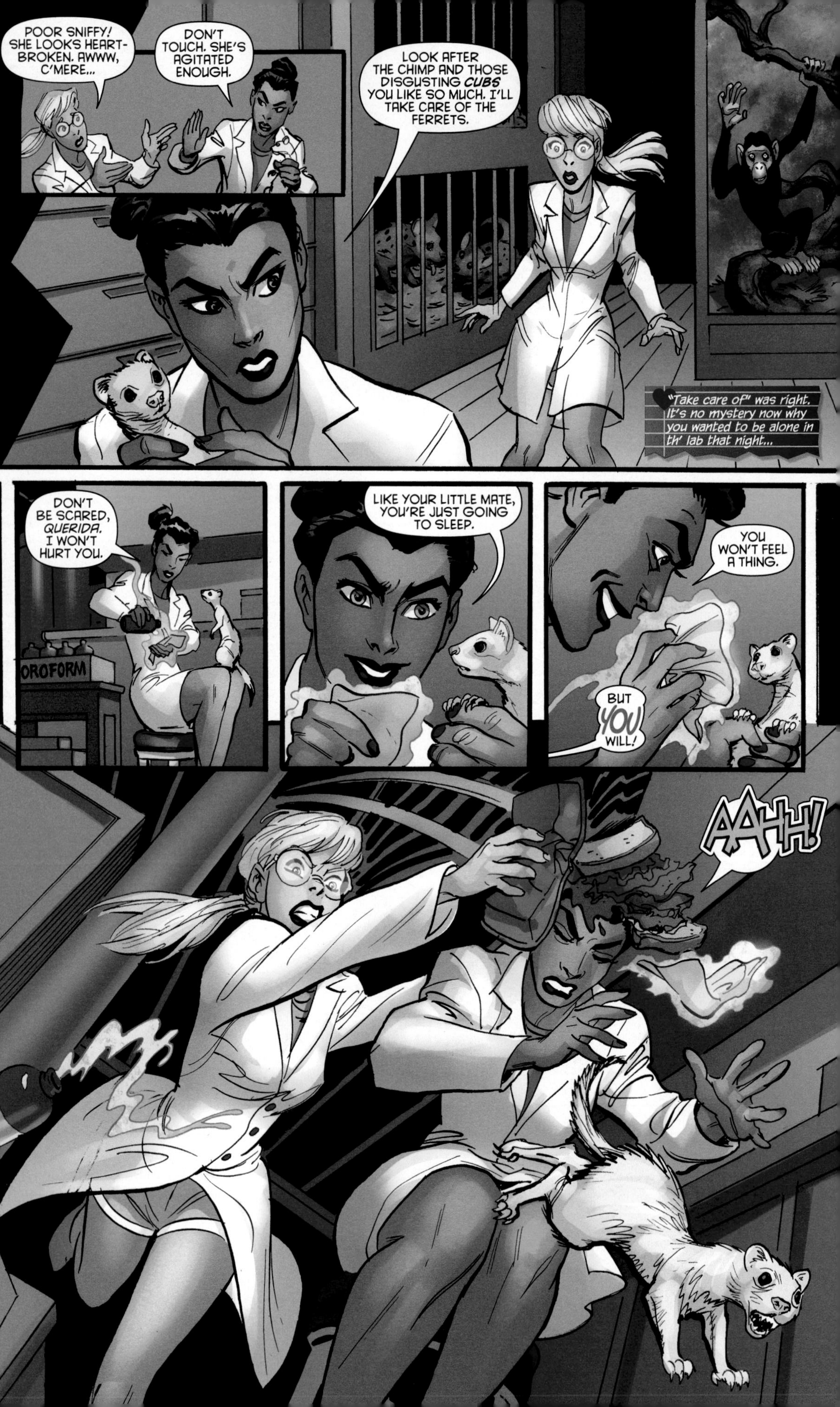
POOR SNIFFY! SHE LOOKS HEART-BROKEN. AWWW, C'MERE...
DON'T TOUCH. SHE'S AGITATED ENOUGH.
LOOK AFTER THE CHIMP AND THOSE DISGUSTING *CUBS* YOU LIKE SO MUCH. I'LL TAKE CARE OF THE FERRETS.
"Take care of" was right. It's no mystery now why you wanted to be alone in th' lab that night...
DON'T BE SCARED, *QUERIDA*. I WON'T HURT YOU.
OROFORM
LIKE YOUR LITTLE MATE, YOU'RE JUST GOING TO SLEEP.
YOU WON'T FEEL A THING.
BUT *YOU* WILL!
AAHH!

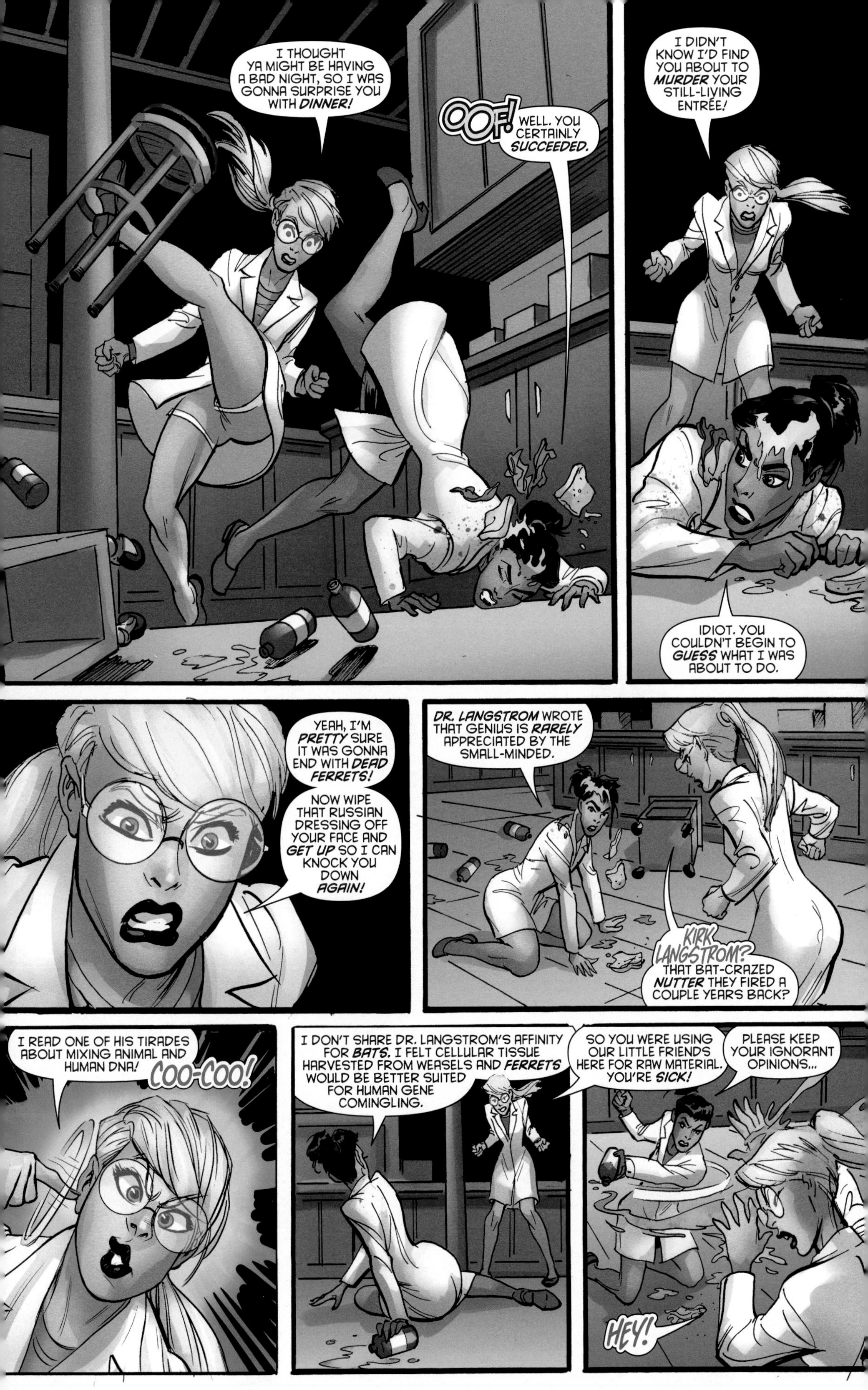
I THOUGHT YA MIGHT BE HAVING A BAD NIGHT, SO I WAS GONNA SURPRISE YOU WITH DINNER!
OOF!
WELL. YOU CERTAINLY SUCCEEDED.
I DIDN'T KNOW I'D FIND YOU ABOUT TO MURDER YOUR STILL-LIVING ENTRÉE!
IDIOT. YOU COULDN'T BEGIN TO GUESS WHAT I WAS ABOUT TO DO.
YEAH, I'M PRETTY SURE IT WAS GONNA END WITH DEAD FERRETS!
NOW WIPE THAT RUSSIAN DRESSING OFF YOUR FACE AND GET UP SO I CAN KNOCK YOU DOWN AGAIN!
DR. LANGSTROM WROTE THAT GENIUS IS RARELY APPRECIATED BY THE SMALL-MINDED.
KIRK LANGSTROM? THAT BAT-CRAZED NUTTER THEY FIRED A COUPLE YEARS BACK?
I READ ONE OF HIS TIRADES ABOUT MIXING ANIMAL AND HUMAN DNA!
COO-COO!
I DON'T SHARE DR. LANGSTROM'S AFFINITY FOR BATS. I FELT CELLULAR TISSUE HARVESTED FROM WEASELS AND FERRETS WOULD BE BETTER SUITED FOR HUMAN GENE COMINGLING.
SO YOU WERE USING OUR LITTLE FRIENDS HERE FOR RAW MATERIAL. YOU'RE SICK!
PLEASE KEEP YOUR IGNORANT OPINIONS...
HEY!

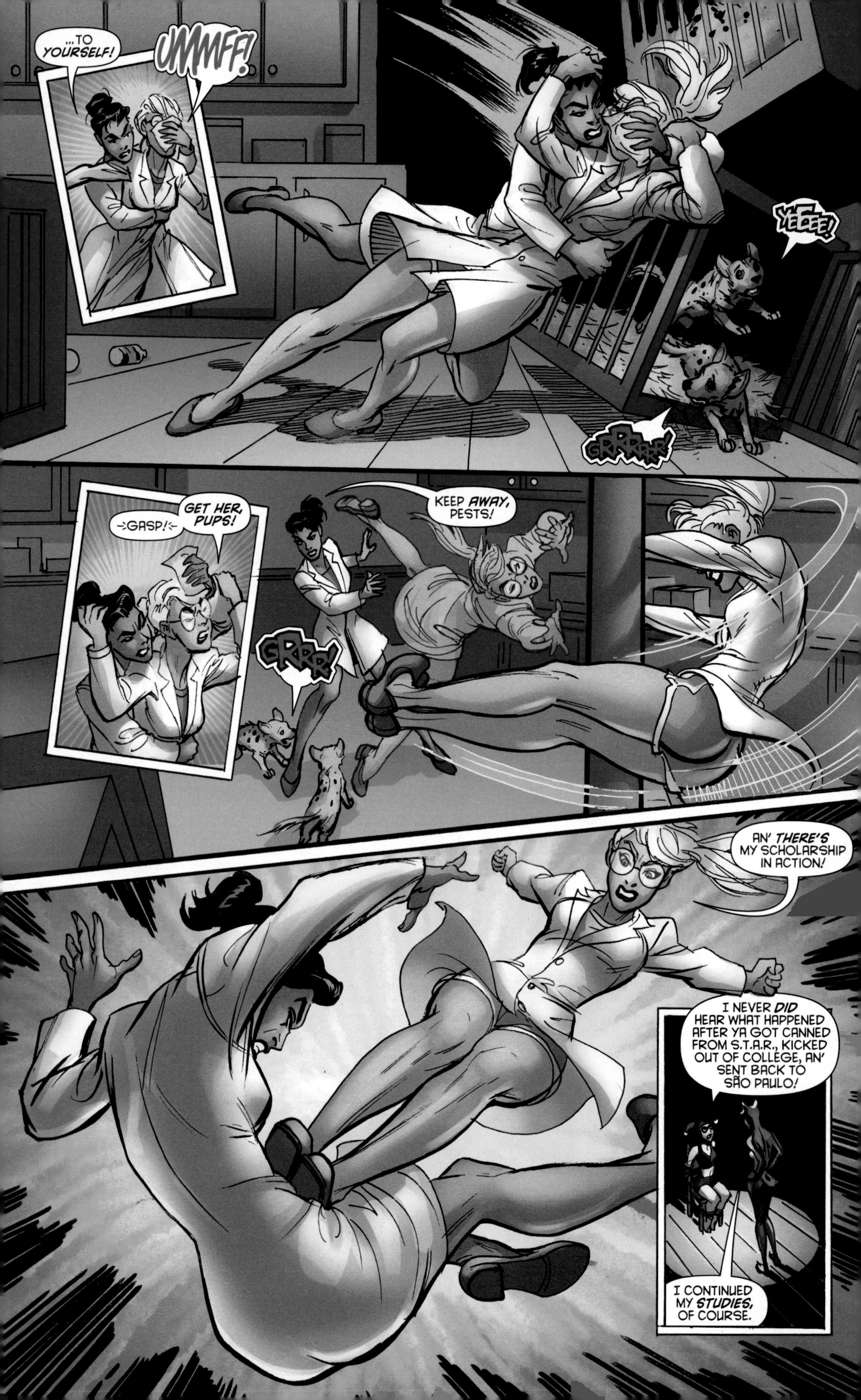
...TO YOURSELF!
UMMFF!
YEEEE!
GRRRRRR!
-GASP!-
GET HER, PUPS!
KEEP AWAY, PESTS!
GRRR!
AN' THERE'S MY SCHOLARSHIP IN ACTION!
I NEVER DID HEAR WHAT HAPPENED AFTER YA GOT CANNED FROM S.T.A.R., KICKED OUT OF COLLEGE, AN' SENT BACK TO SÃO PAULO!
I CONTINUED MY STUDIES, OF COURSE.

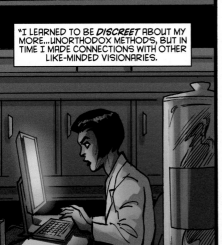

"I LEARNED TO BE *DISCREET* ABOUT MY MORE...UNORTHODOX METHODS, BUT IN TIME I MADE CONNECTIONS WITH OTHER LIKE-MINDED VISIONARIES.

"MY GREATEST INFLUENCE WAS *DR. EMILE DORIAN.* HIS ADVANCES IN GENETIC MANIPULATION DWARFED ANYTHING PIONEERED BY LANGSTROM.

"AT THE BEHEST OF DORIAN'S GIFTED YOUNG ASSISTANT *ABEL CUVIER,* I JOINED THEM AT THEIR PRIVATE RESEARCH FACILITY.

"THEY WERE INTRIGUED WITH MY DESIRE TO CREATE A HYBRID BETWEEN A HUMAN AND A MEMBER OF THE MUSTELID FAMILY.

"NATURALLY I VOLUNTEERED AS THE TEST SUBJECT.

"I CHOSE A CREATURE NATIVE TO MY COUNTRY, KNOWN FOR ITS SPEED, AGILITY AND CUNNING.

"AND THUS, *THE GRISON* WAS BORN!"

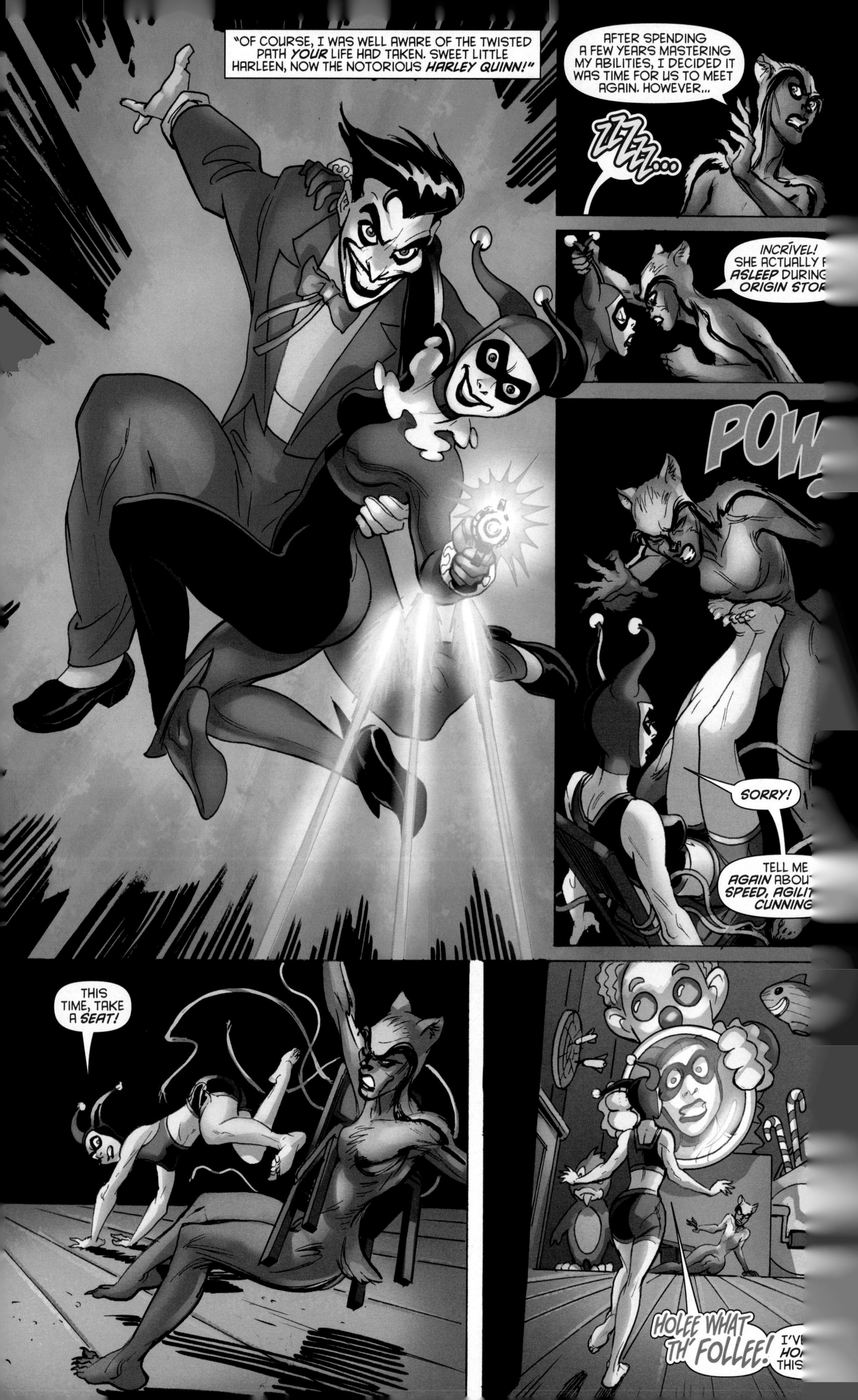
"OF COURSE, I WAS WELL AWARE OF THE TWISTED PATH *YOUR* LIFE HAD TAKEN. SWEET LITTLE HARLEEN, NOW THE NOTORIOUS *HARLEY QUINN!*"
AFTER SPENDING A FEW YEARS MASTERING MY ABILITIES, I DECIDED IT WAS TIME FOR US TO MEET AGAIN. HOWEVER...
ZZZZZ...
INCRÍVEL! SHE ACTUALLY F *ASLEEP* DURING *ORIGIN STOR*
POW
SORRY!
TELL ME *AGAIN* ABOUT *SPEED, AGILIT CUNNING*
THIS TIME, TAKE A *SEAT!*
HOLEE WHAT TH' FOLLEE!

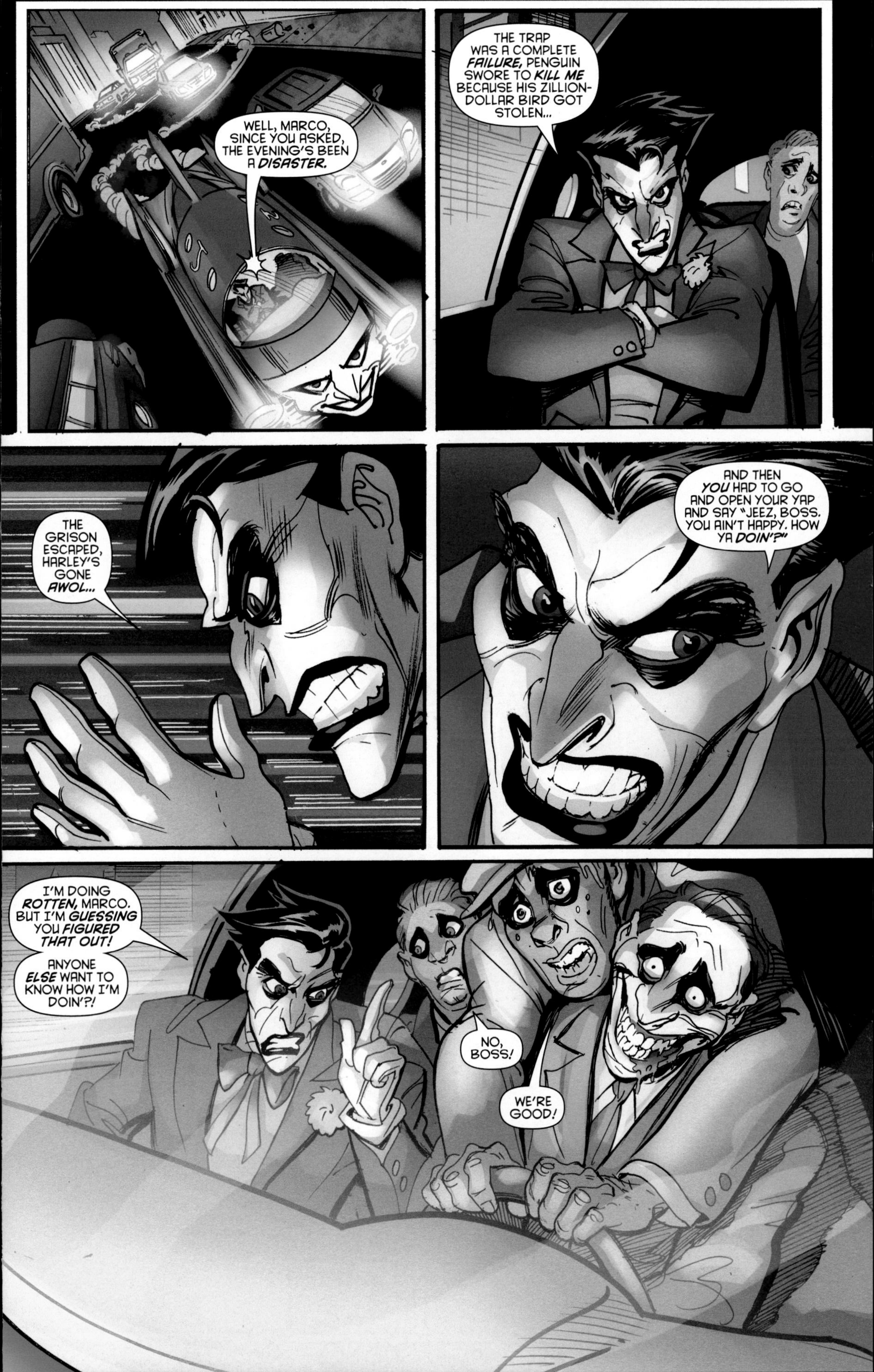

WELL, MARCO, SINCE YOU ASKED, THE EVENING'S BEEN A *DISASTER.*
THE TRAP WAS A COMPLETE *FAILURE,* PENGUIN SWORE TO *KILL ME* BECAUSE HIS ZILLION-DOLLAR BIRD GOT STOLEN...
THE GRISON ESCAPED, HARLEY'S GONE *AWOL...*
AND THEN *YOU* HAD TO GO AND OPEN YOUR YAP AND SAY "JEEZ, BOSS. YOU AIN'T HAPPY. HOW YA *DOIN'?"*
I'M DOING *ROTTEN,* MARCO. BUT I'M *GUESSING* YOU *FIGURED THAT OUT!*
ANYONE *ELSE* WANT TO KNOW HOW I'M DOIN'?!
NO, BOSS!
WE'RE GOOD!

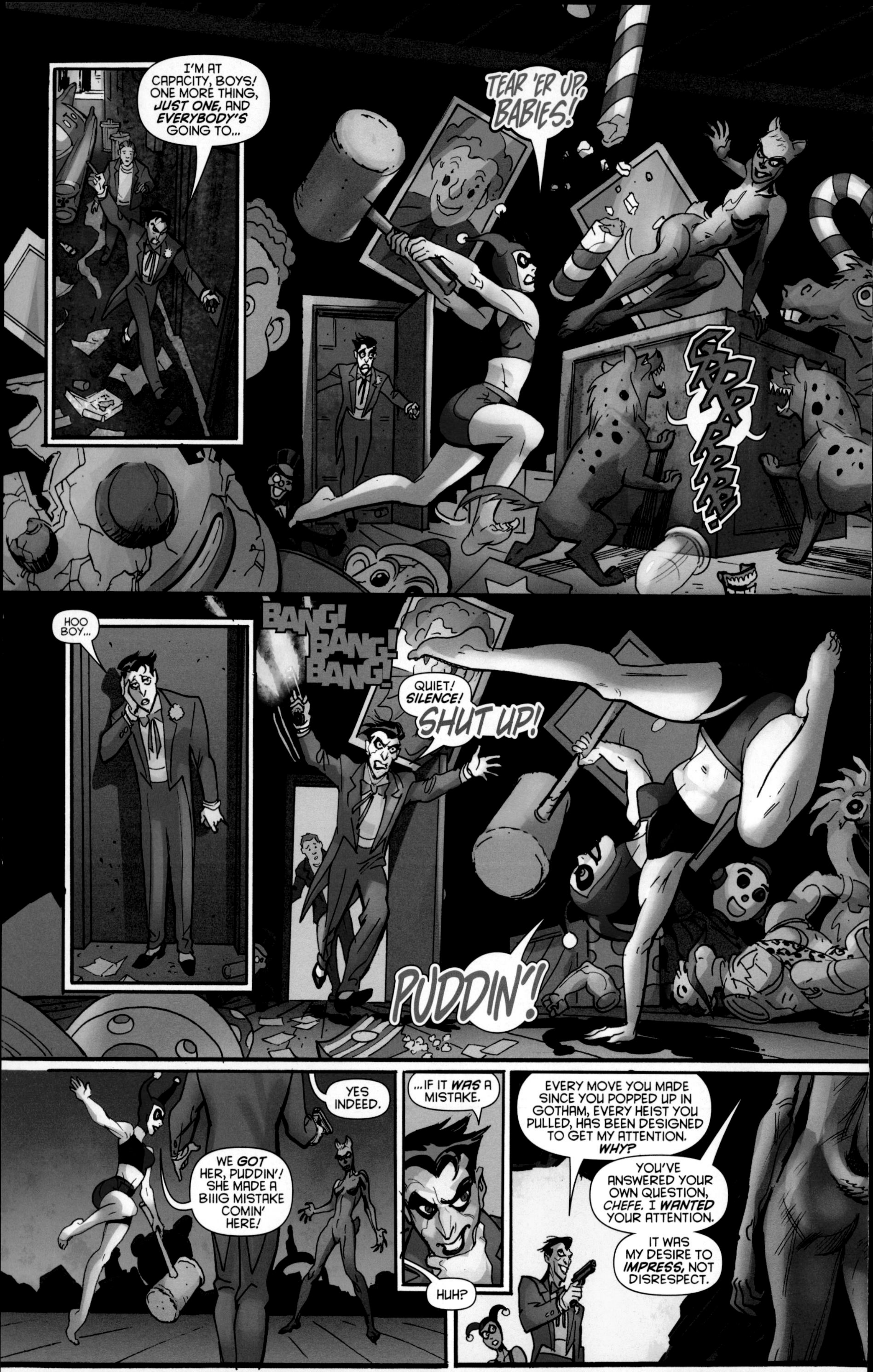
I'M AT CAPACITY, BOYS! ONE MORE THING, JUST ONE, AND EVERYBODY'S GOING TO...
TEAR 'ER UP, BABIES!
GRRRRR!
HOO BOY...
BANG! BANG! BANG!
QUIET! SILENCE! SHUT UP!
PUDDIN'!
WE GOT HER, PUDDIN'! SHE MADE A BIIIG MISTAKE COMIN' HERE!
YES INDEED.
...IF IT WAS A MISTAKE.
HUH?
EVERY MOVE YOU MADE SINCE YOU POPPED UP IN GOTHAM, EVERY HEIST YOU PULLED, HAS BEEN DESIGNED TO GET MY ATTENTION. WHY?
YOU'VE ANSWERED YOUR OWN QUESTION, CHEFE. I WANTED YOUR ATTENTION.
IT WAS MY DESIRE TO IMPRESS, NOT DISRESPECT.

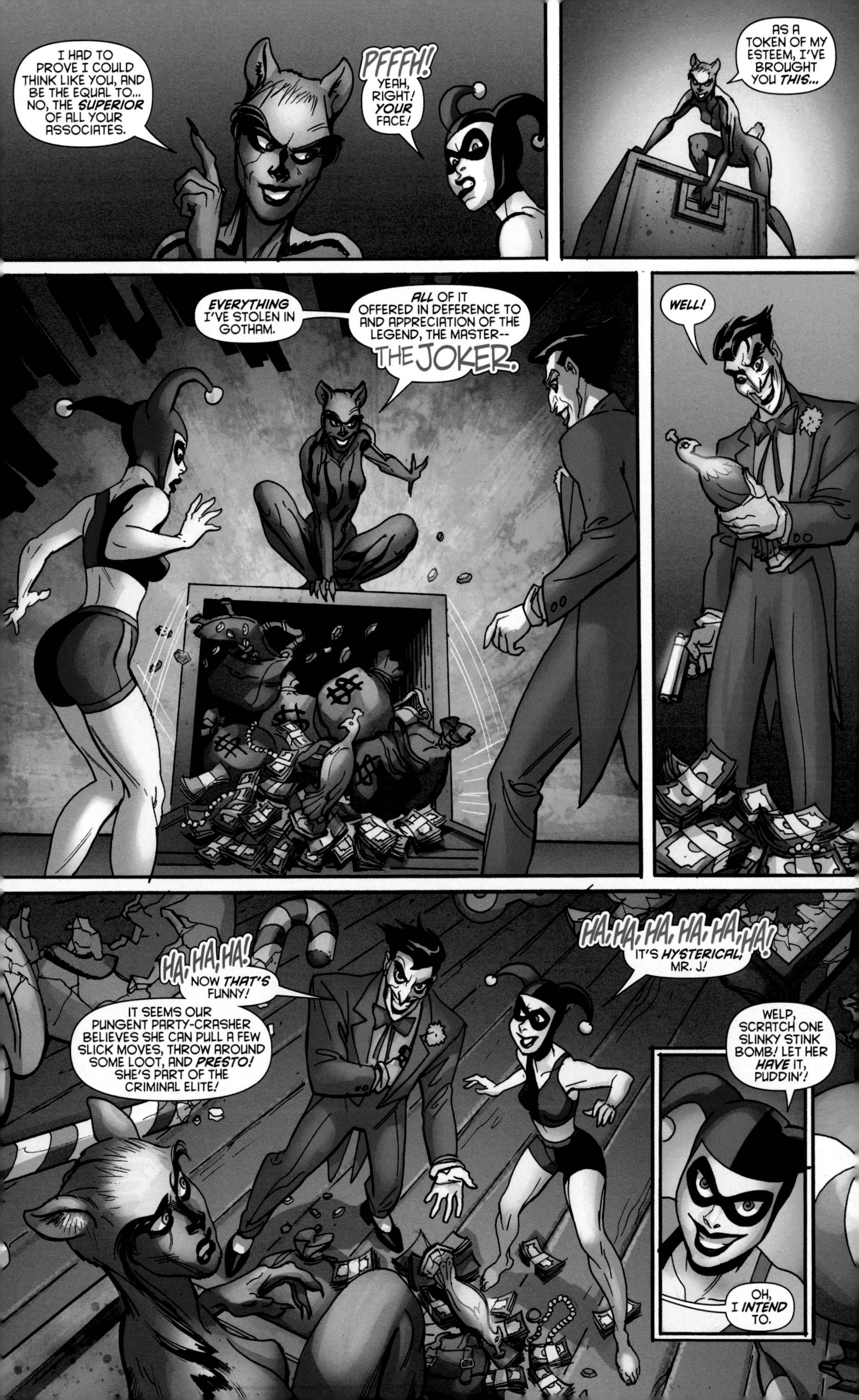

I HAD TO PROVE I COULD THINK LIKE YOU, AND BE THE EQUAL TO... NO, THE SUPERIOR OF ALL YOUR ASSOCIATES.
PFFFH!
YEAH, RIGHT! YOUR FACE!
AS A TOKEN OF MY ESTEEM, I'VE BROUGHT YOU THIS...
EVERYTHING I'VE STOLEN IN GOTHAM.
ALL OF IT OFFERED IN DEFERENCE TO AND APPRECIATION OF THE LEGEND, THE MASTER--
THE JOKER.
WELL!
HA, HA, HA!
NOW THAT'S FUNNY!
IT SEEMS OUR PUNGENT PARTY-CRASHER BELIEVES SHE CAN PULL A FEW SLICK MOVES, THROW AROUND SOME LOOT, AND PRESTO! SHE'S PART OF THE CRIMINAL ELITE!
HA, HA, HA, HA, HA, HA!
IT'S HYSTERICAL, MR. J!
WELP, SCRATCH ONE SLINKY STINK BOMB! LET HER HAVE IT, PUDDIN'!
OH, I INTEND TO.

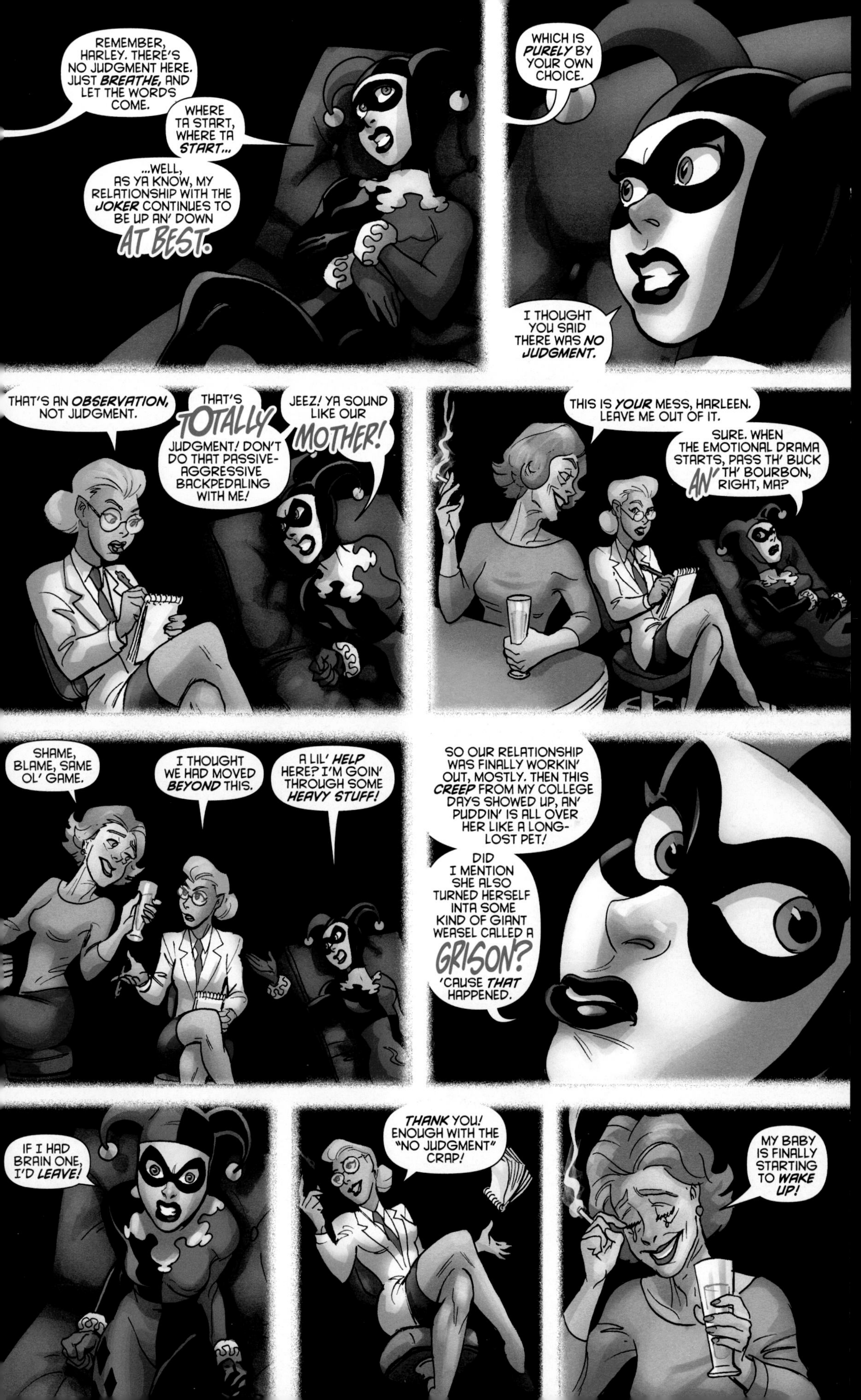
REMEMBER, HARLEY. THERE'S NO JUDGMENT HERE. JUST *BREATHE,* AND LET THE WORDS COME.
WHERE TA START, WHERE TA *START...*
...WELL, AS YA KNOW, MY RELATIONSHIP WITH THE *JOKER* CONTINUES TO BE UP AN' DOWN AT BEST.
WHICH IS *PURELY* BY YOUR OWN CHOICE.
I THOUGHT YOU SAID THERE WAS *NO JUDGMENT.*
THAT'S AN *OBSERVATION,* NOT JUDGMENT.
THAT'S TOTALLY JUDGMENT! DON'T DO THAT PASSIVE-AGGRESSIVE BACKPEDALING WITH ME!
JEEZ! YA SOUND LIKE OUR MOTHER!
THIS IS *YOUR* MESS, HARLEEN. LEAVE ME OUT OF IT.
SURE. WHEN THE EMOTIONAL DRAMA STARTS, PASS TH' BUCK AN' TH' BOURBON, RIGHT, MA?
SHAME, BLAME, SAME OL' GAME.
I THOUGHT WE HAD MOVED *BEYOND* THIS.
A LIL' *HELP* HERE? I'M GOIN' THROUGH SOME *HEAVY STUFF!*
SO OUR RELATIONSHIP WAS FINALLY WORKIN' OUT, MOSTLY. THEN THIS *CREEP* FROM MY COLLEGE DAYS SHOWED UP, AN' PUDDIN' IS ALL OVER HER LIKE A LONG-LOST PET!
DID I MENTION SHE ALSO TURNED HERSELF INTA SOME KIND OF GIANT WEASEL CALLED A GRISON? 'CAUSE *THAT* HAPPENED.
IF I HAD BRAIN ONE, I'D *LEAVE!*
THANK YOU! ENOUGH WITH THE "NO JUDGMENT" CRAP!
MY BABY IS FINALLY STARTING TO *WAKE UP!*

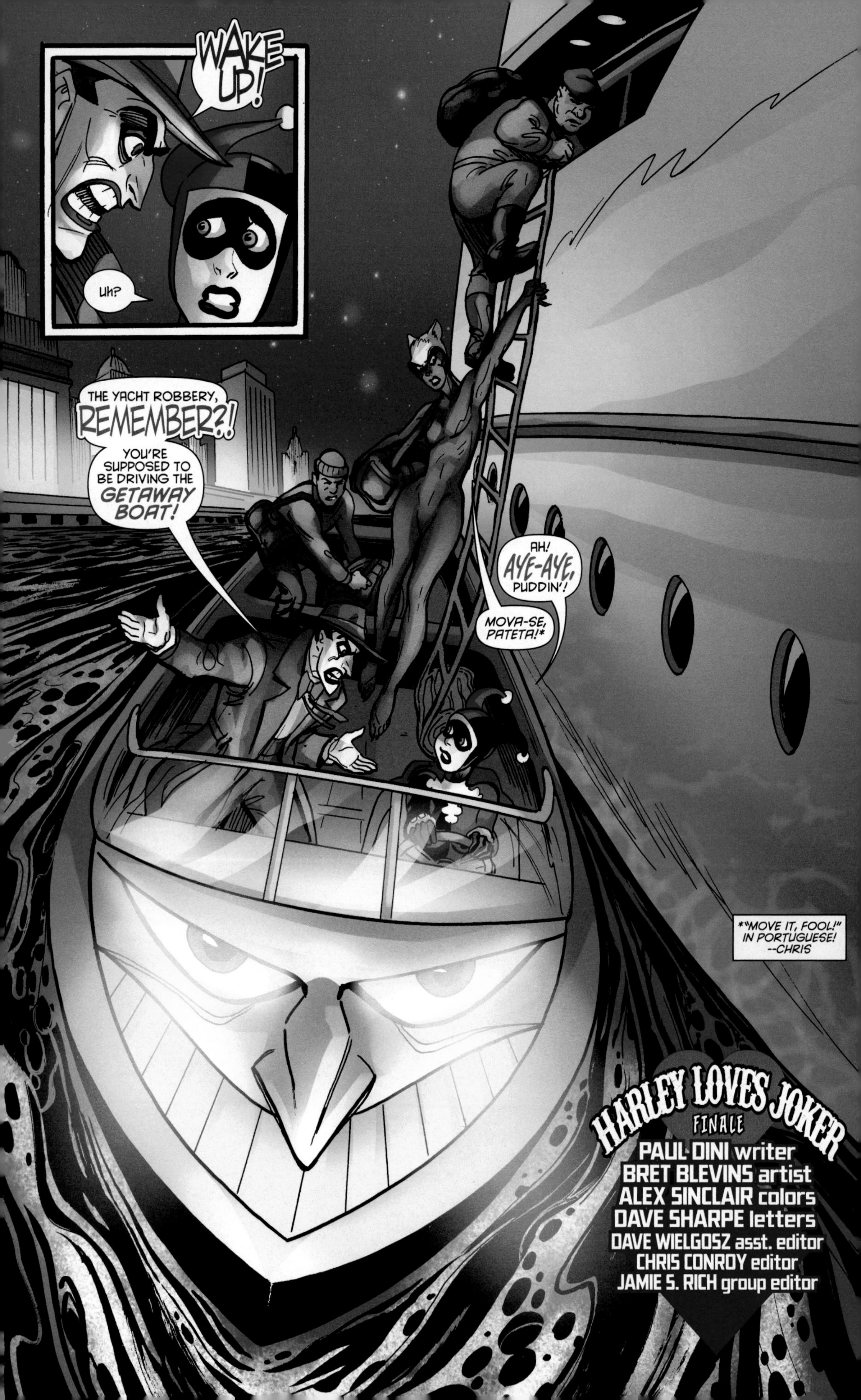
WAKE UP!
Uh?
THE YACHT ROBBERY, REMEMBER?!
YOU'RE SUPPOSED TO BE DRIVING THE GETAWAY BOAT!
AH! AYE-AYE, PUDDIN'!
MOVA-SE, PATETA!*
*"MOVE IT, FOOL!" IN PORTUGUESE! --CHRIS
HARLEY LOVES JOKER
FINALE
PAUL DINI writer
BRET BLEVINS artist
ALEX SINCLAIR colors
DAVE SHARPE letters
DAVE WIELGOSZ asst. editor
CHRIS CONROY editor
JAMIE S. RICH group editor

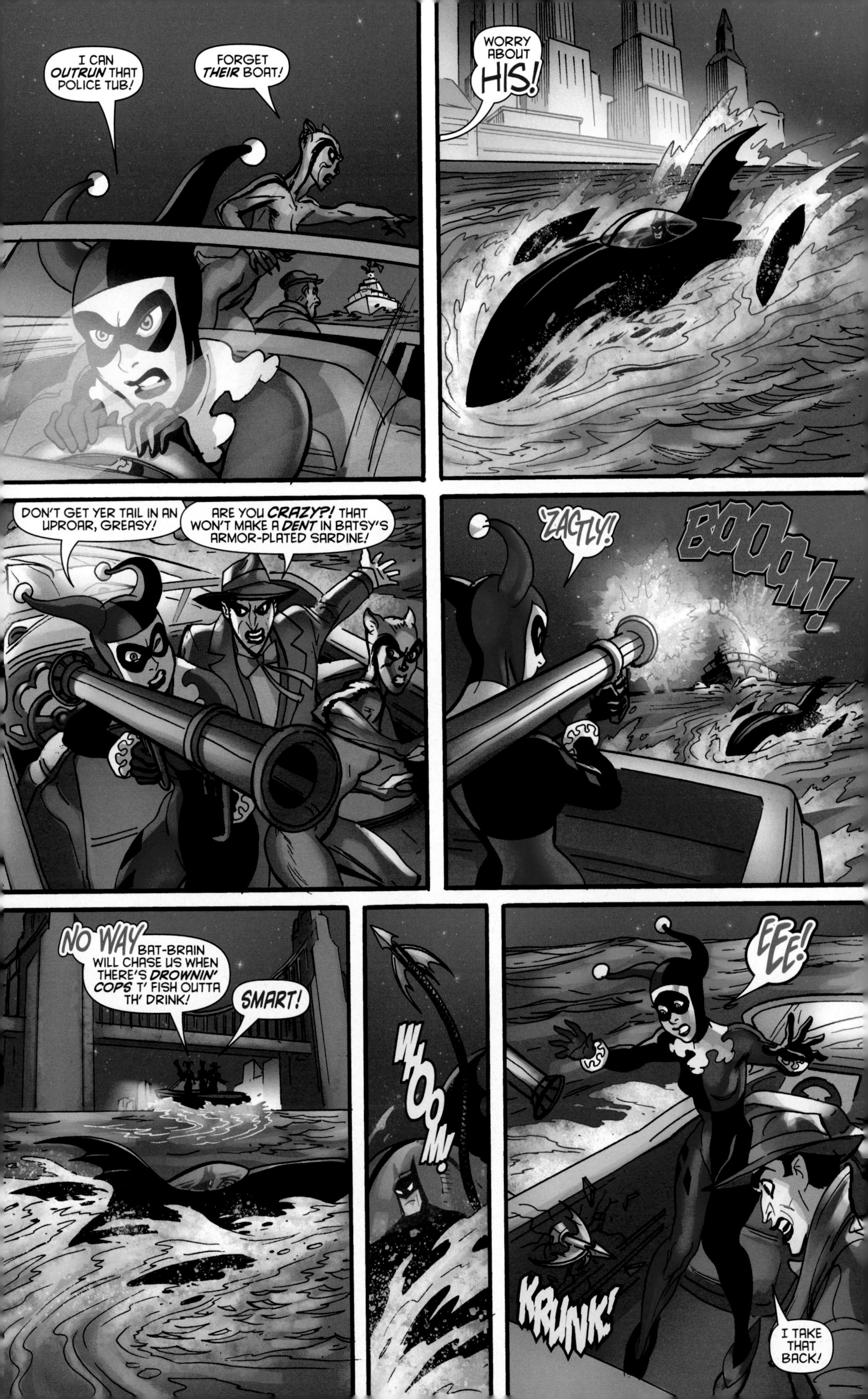
I CAN OUTRUN THAT POLICE TUB!
FORGET THEIR BOAT!
WORRY ABOUT HIS!
DON'T GET YER TAIL IN AN UPROAR, GREASY!
ARE YOU CRAZY?! THAT WON'T MAKE A DENT IN BATSY'S ARMOR-PLATED SARDINE!
'ZACTLY!
BOOOOM!
NO WAY BAT-BRAIN WILL CHASE US WHEN THERE'S DROWNIN' COPS T' FISH OUTTA TH' DRINK!
SMART!
WHOOOM!
EEE!
KRUNK!
I TAKE THAT BACK!

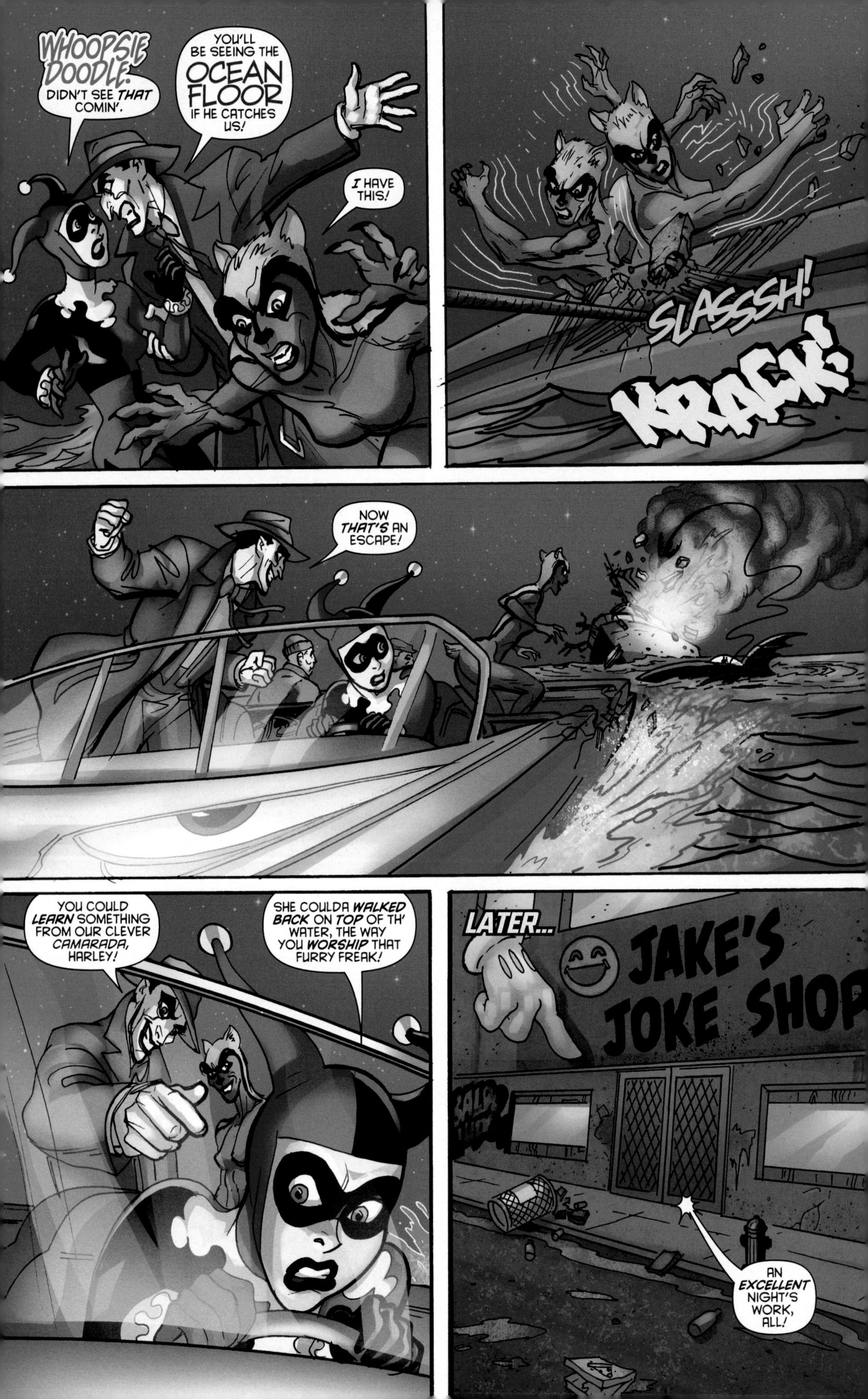
WHOOPSIE DOODLE. DIDN'T SEE THAT COMIN'.
YOU'LL BE SEEING THE OCEAN FLOOR IF HE CATCHES US!
I HAVE THIS!
SLASSSH!
KRACK!
NOW THAT'S AN ESCAPE!
YOU COULD LEARN SOMETHING FROM OUR CLEVER CAMARADA, HARLEY!
SHE COULDA WALKED BACK ON TOP OF TH' WATER, THE WAY YOU WORSHIP THAT FURRY FREAK!
LATER...
JAKE'S JOKE SHOP
AN EXCELLENT NIGHT'S WORK, ALL!

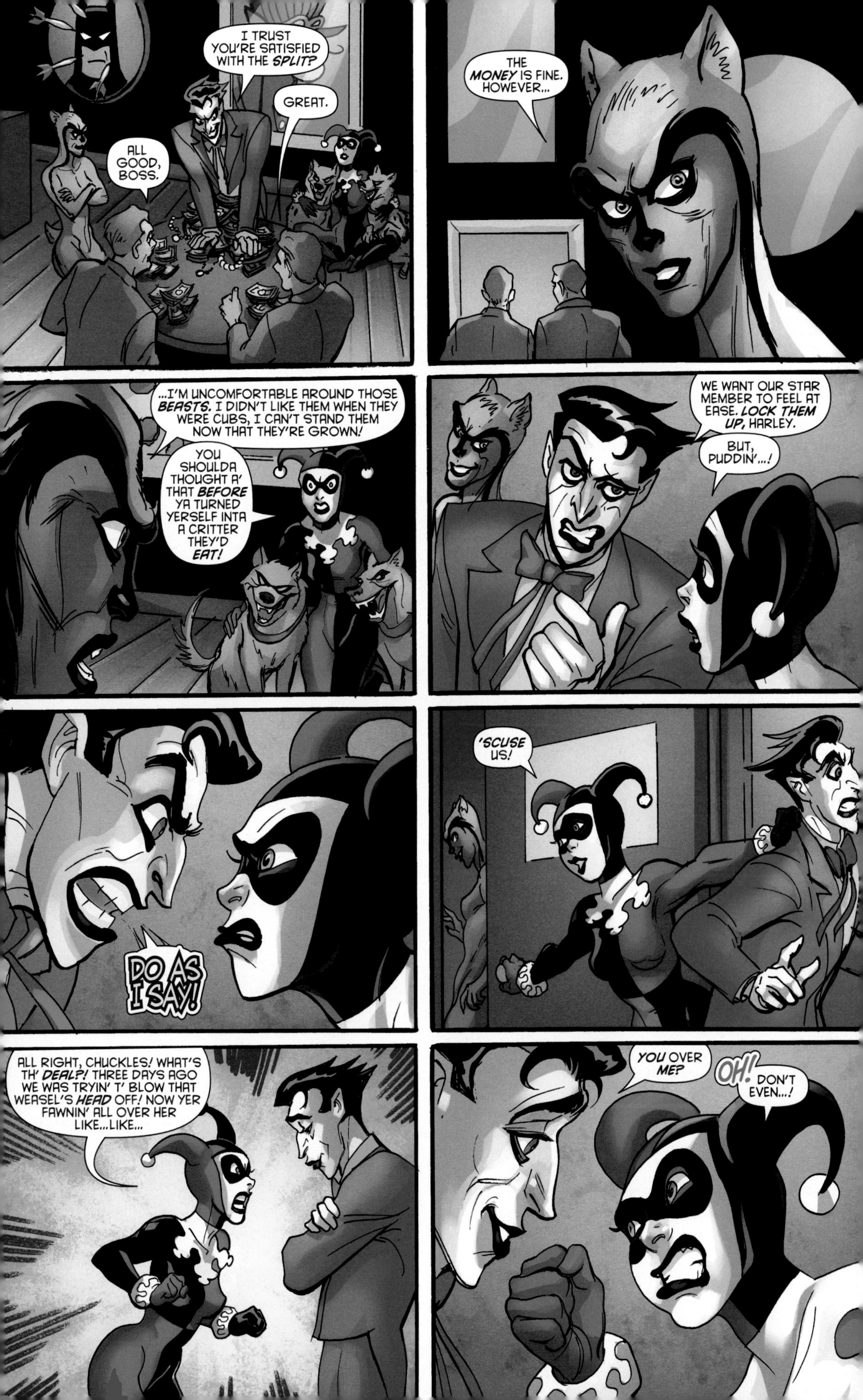
I TRUST YOU'RE SATISFIED WITH THE *SPLIT?*
GREAT.
ALL GOOD, BOSS.
THE *MONEY* IS FINE. HOWEVER...
...I'M UNCOMFORTABLE AROUND THOSE *BEASTS.* I DIDN'T LIKE THEM WHEN THEY WERE CUBS, I CAN'T STAND THEM NOW THAT THEY'RE GROWN!
YOU SHOULDA THOUGHT A' THAT *BEFORE* YA TURNED YERSELF INTA A CRITTER THEY'D *EAT!*
WE WANT OUR STAR MEMBER TO FEEL AT EASE. *LOCK THEM UP,* HARLEY.
BUT, PUDDIN'...!
DO AS I SAY!
'SCUSE US!
ALL RIGHT, CHUCKLES! WHAT'S TH' *DEAL?!* THREE DAYS AGO WE WAS TRYIN' T' BLOW THAT WEASEL'S *HEAD* OFF! NOW YER FAWNIN' ALL OVER HER LIKE...LIKE...
YOU OVER *ME?*
OH! DON'T EVEN...!

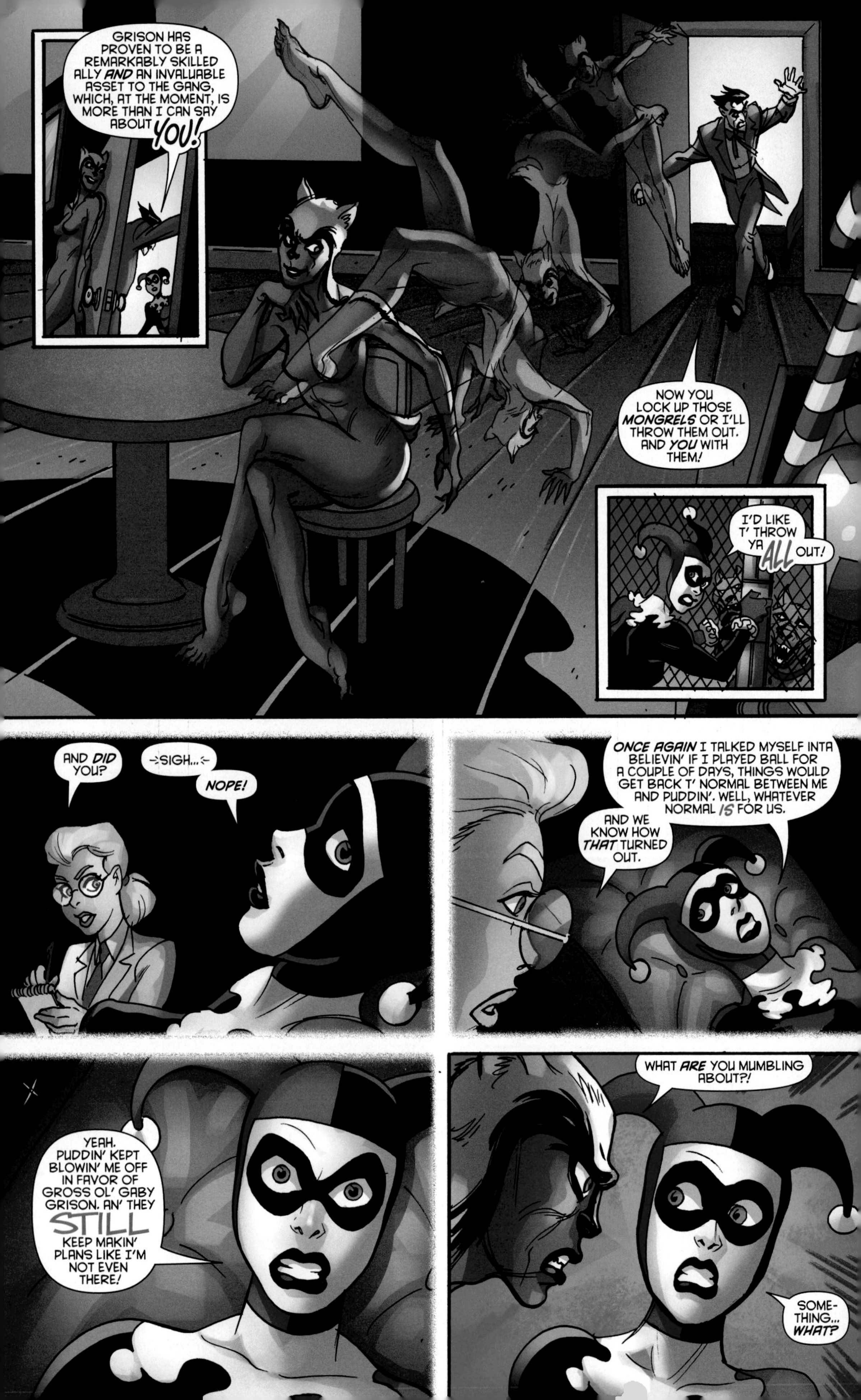
GRISON HAS PROVEN TO BE A REMARKABLY SKILLED ALLY AND AN INVALUABLE ASSET TO THE GANG, WHICH, AT THE MOMENT, IS MORE THAN I CAN SAY ABOUT YOU!
NOW YOU LOCK UP THOSE MONGRELS OR I'LL THROW THEM OUT. AND YOU WITH THEM!
I'D LIKE T' THROW YA ALL OUT!
AND DID YOU?
SIGH...
NOPE!
ONCE AGAIN I TALKED MYSELF INTA BELIEVIN' IF I PLAYED BALL FOR A COUPLE OF DAYS, THINGS WOULD GET BACK T' NORMAL BETWEEN ME AND PUDDIN'. WELL, WHATEVER NORMAL IS FOR US.
AND WE KNOW HOW THAT TURNED OUT.
YEAH. PUDDIN' KEPT BLOWIN' ME OFF IN FAVOR OF GROSS OL' GABY GRISON. AN' THEY STILL KEEP MAKIN' PLANS LIKE I'M NOT EVEN THERE!
WHAT ARE YOU MUMBLING ABOUT?!
SOME-THING... WHAT?

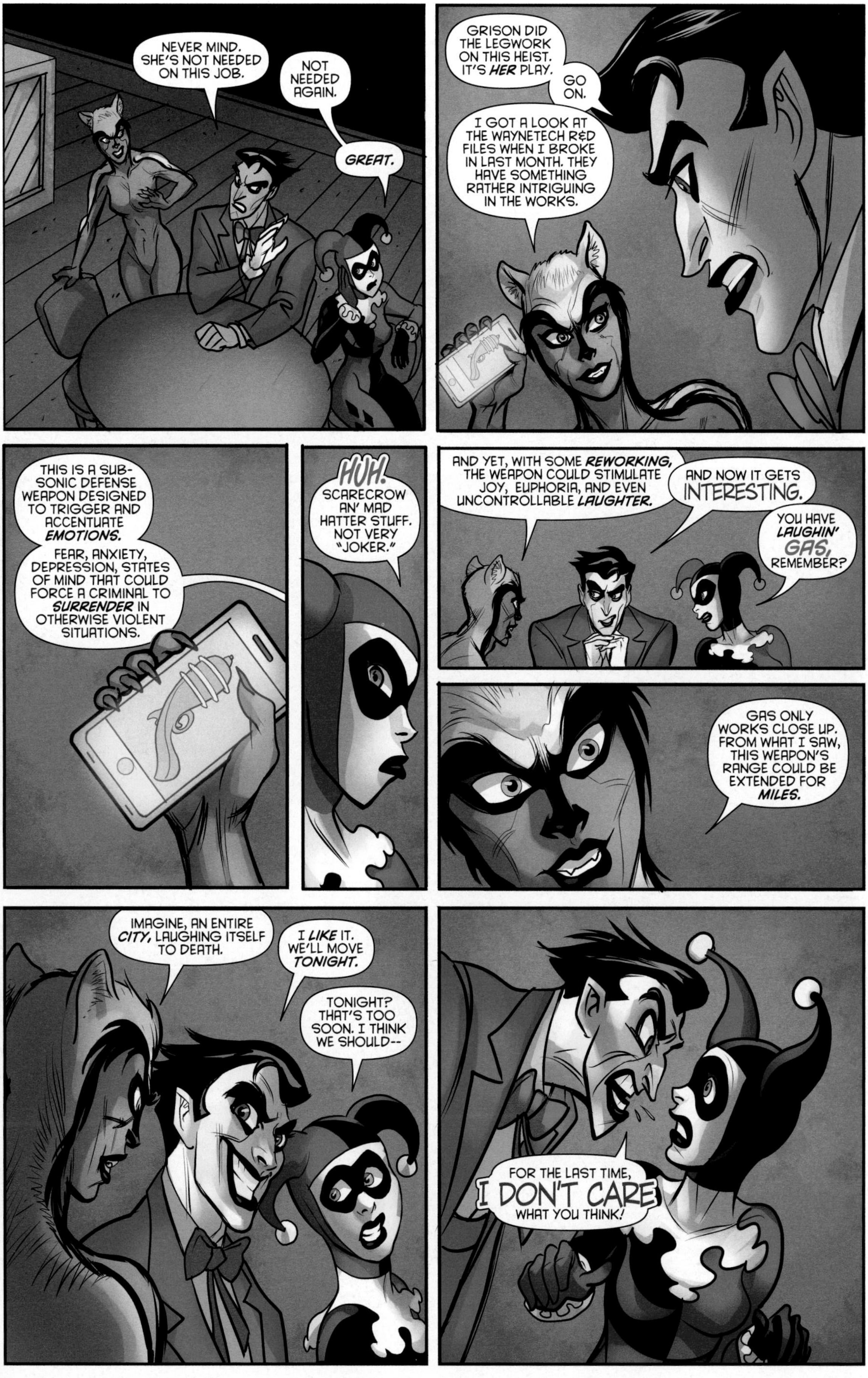
NEVER MIND. SHE'S NOT NEEDED ON THIS JOB.
NOT NEEDED AGAIN.
GREAT.
GRISON DID THE LEGWORK ON THIS HEIST. IT'S HER PLAY.
GO ON.
I GOT A LOOK AT THE WAYNETECH R&D FILES WHEN I BROKE IN LAST MONTH. THEY HAVE SOMETHING RATHER INTRIGUING IN THE WORKS.
THIS IS A SUB-SONIC DEFENSE WEAPON DESIGNED TO TRIGGER AND ACCENTUATE EMOTIONS.
FEAR, ANXIETY, DEPRESSION, STATES OF MIND THAT COULD FORCE A CRIMINAL TO SURRENDER IN OTHERWISE VIOLENT SITUATIONS.
HUH!
SCARECROW AN' MAD HATTER STUFF. NOT VERY "JOKER."
AND YET, WITH SOME REWORKING, THE WEAPON COULD STIMULATE JOY, EUPHORIA, AND EVEN UNCONTROLLABLE LAUGHTER.
AND NOW IT GETS INTERESTING.
YOU HAVE LAUGHIN' GAS, REMEMBER?
GAS ONLY WORKS CLOSE UP. FROM WHAT I SAW, THIS WEAPON'S RANGE COULD BE EXTENDED FOR MILES.
IMAGINE, AN ENTIRE CITY, LAUGHING ITSELF TO DEATH.
I LIKE IT. WE'LL MOVE TONIGHT.
TONIGHT? THAT'S TOO SOON. I THINK WE SHOULD--
FOR THE LAST TIME, I DON'T CARE WHAT YOU THINK!

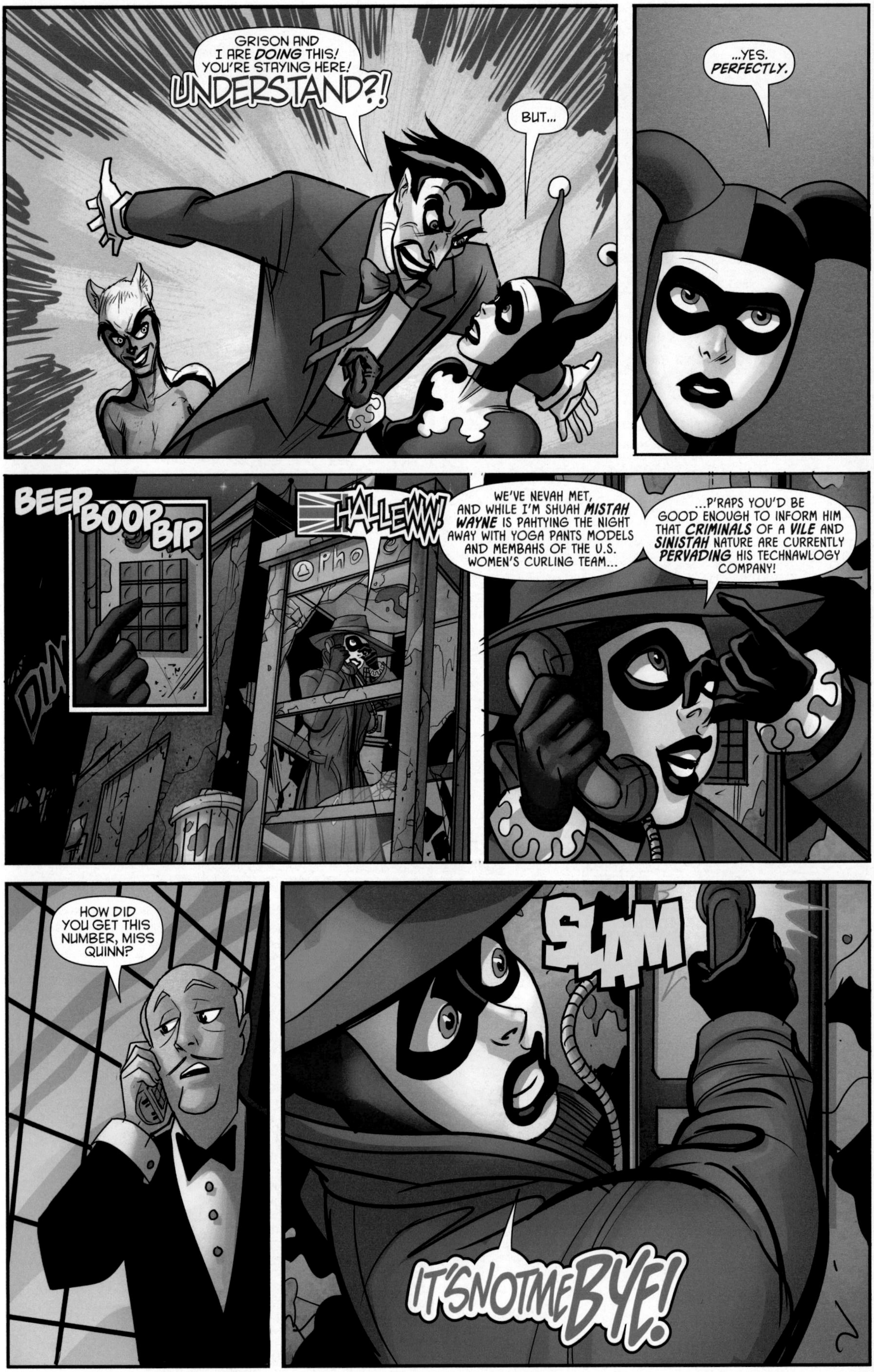
GRISON AND I ARE DOING THIS! YOU'RE STAYING HERE! UNDERSTAND?!
BUT...
...YES. PERFECTLY.
BEEP BOOP BIP
HALLEWW!
WE'VE NEVAH MET, AND WHILE I'M SHUAH MISTAH WAYNE IS PAHTYING THE NIGHT AWAY WITH YOGA PANTS MODELS AND MEMBAHS OF THE U.S. WOMEN'S CURLING TEAM...
...P'RAPS YOU'D BE GOOD ENOUGH TO INFORM HIM THAT CRIMINALS OF A VILE AND SINISTAH NATURE ARE CURRENTLY PERVADING HIS TECHNAWLOGY COMPANY!
HOW DID YOU GET THIS NUMBER, MISS QUINN?
SLAM
IT'SNOTMEBYE!

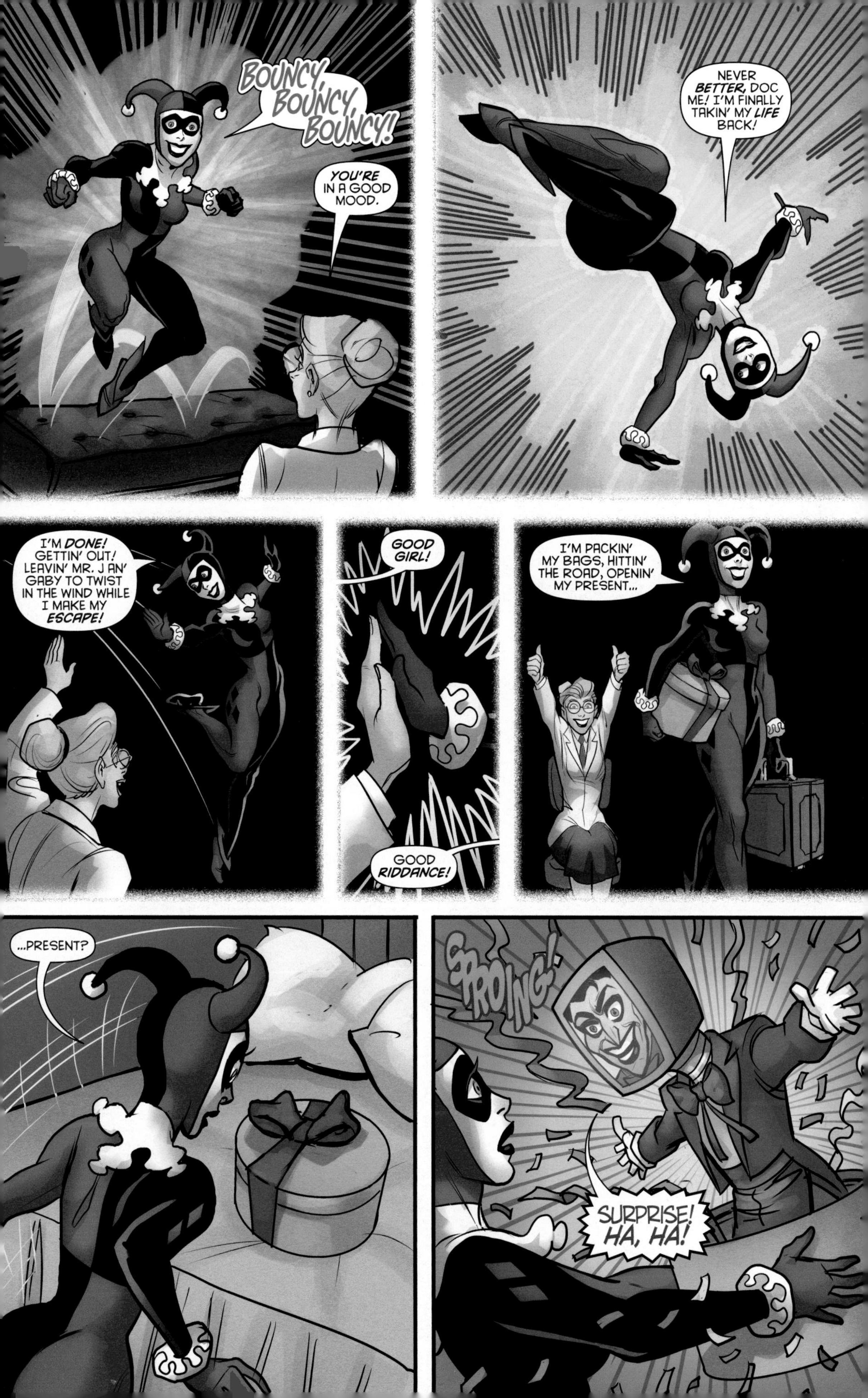
BOUNCY, BOUNCY, BOUNCY!
YOU'RE IN A GOOD MOOD.
NEVER BETTER, DOC ME! I'M FINALLY TAKIN' MY LIFE BACK!
I'M DONE! GETTIN' OUT! LEAVIN' MR. J AN' GABY TO TWIST IN THE WIND WHILE I MAKE MY ESCAPE!
GOOD GIRL!
GOOD RIDDANCE!
I'M PACKIN' MY BAGS, HITTIN' THE ROAD, OPENIN' MY PRESENT...
...PRESENT?
SPROING!
SURPRISE! HA, HA!

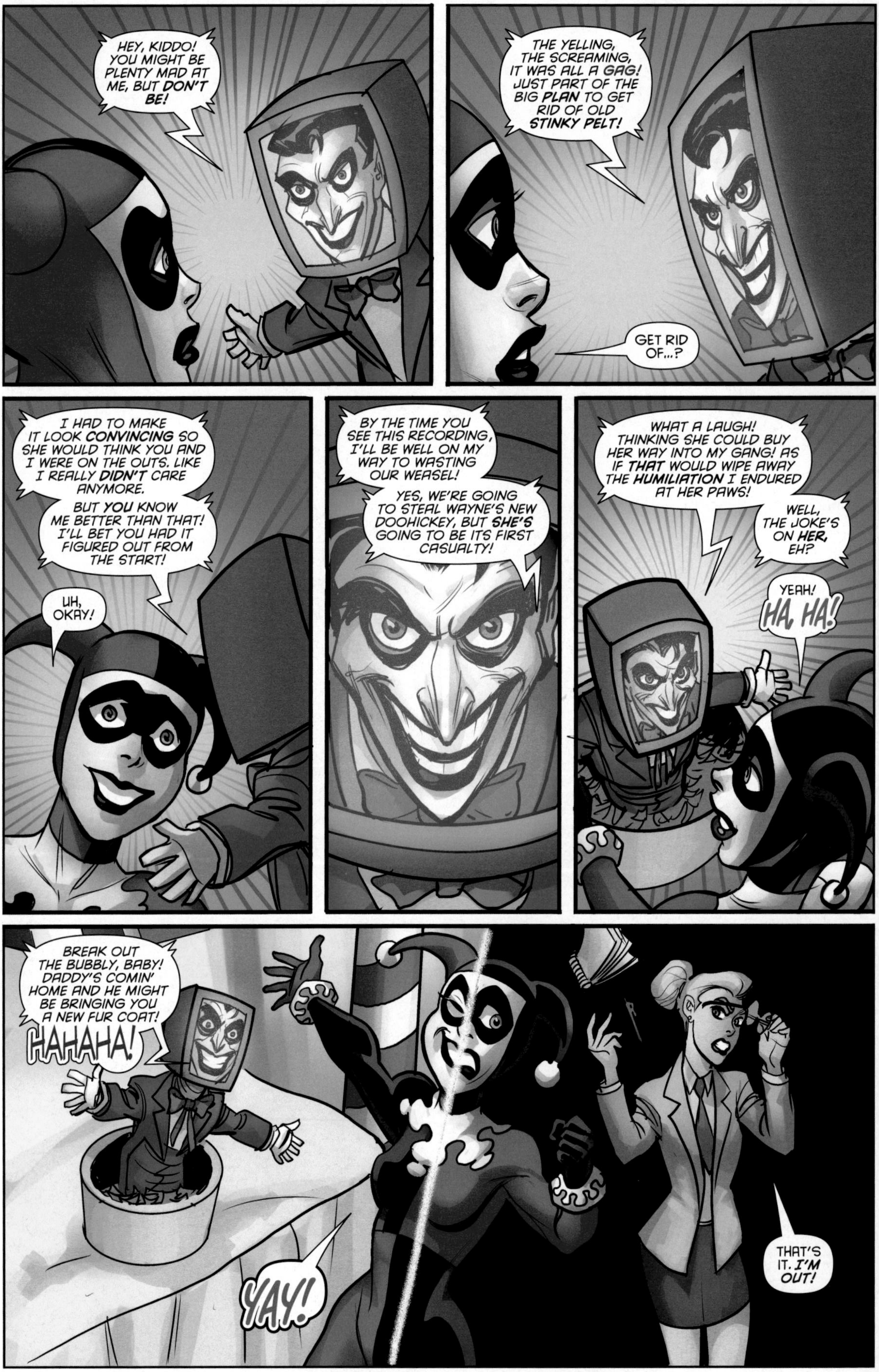
HEY, KIDDO! YOU MIGHT BE PLENTY MAD AT ME, BUT **DON'T BE!**
THE YELLING, THE SCREAMING, IT WAS ALL A **GAG!** JUST PART OF THE BIG **PLAN** TO GET RID OF OLD **STINKY PELT!**
GET RID OF...?
I HAD TO MAKE IT LOOK **CONVINCING** SO SHE WOULD THINK YOU AND I WERE ON THE OUTS. LIKE I REALLY **DIDN'T** CARE ANYMORE.
BUT **YOU** KNOW ME BETTER THAN THAT! I'LL BET YOU HAD IT FIGURED OUT FROM THE START!
UH, OKAY!
BY THE TIME YOU SEE THIS RECORDING, I'LL BE WELL ON MY WAY TO WASTING OUR WEASEL!
YES, WE'RE GOING TO STEAL WAYNE'S NEW DOOHICKEY, BUT **SHE'S** GOING TO BE ITS FIRST CASUALTY!
WHAT A LAUGH! THINKING SHE COULD BUY HER WAY INTO MY GANG! AS IF **THAT** WOULD WIPE AWAY THE **HUMILIATION** I ENDURED AT HER PAWS!
WELL, THE JOKE'S ON **HER,** EH?
YEAH! HA, HA!
BREAK OUT THE BUBBLY, BABY! DADDY'S COMIN' HOME AND HE MIGHT BE BRINGING YOU A NEW FUR COAT!
HAHAHA!
YAY!
THAT'S IT. **I'M OUT!**

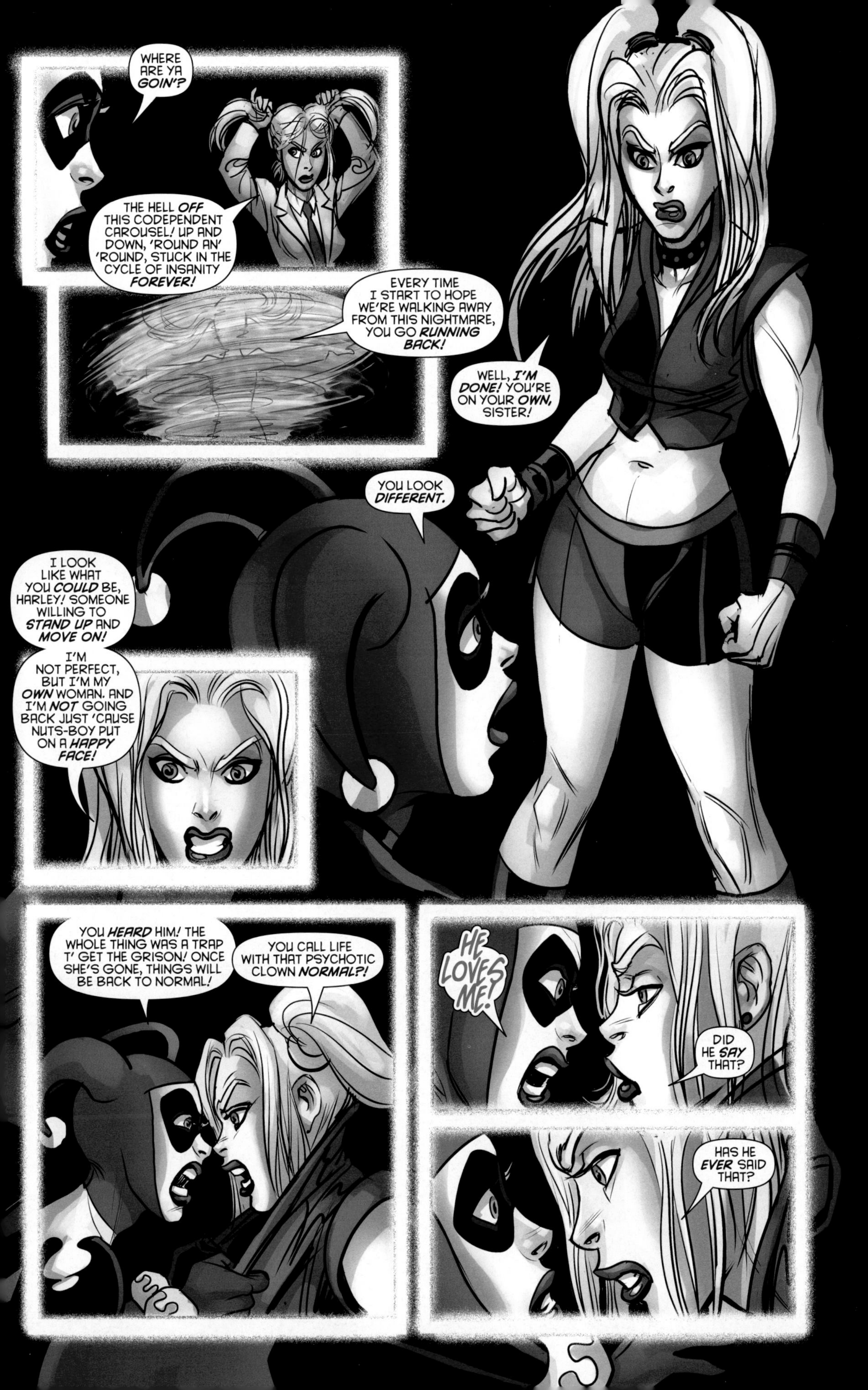
WHERE ARE YA GOIN'?
THE HELL OFF THIS CODEPENDENT CAROUSEL! UP AND DOWN, 'ROUND AN' 'ROUND, STUCK IN THE CYCLE OF INSANITY FOREVER!
EVERY TIME I START TO HOPE WE'RE WALKING AWAY FROM THIS NIGHTMARE, YOU GO RUNNING BACK!
WELL, I'M DONE! YOU'RE ON YOUR OWN, SISTER!
YOU LOOK DIFFERENT.
I LOOK LIKE WHAT YOU COULD BE, HARLEY! SOMEONE WILLING TO STAND UP AND MOVE ON!
I'M NOT PERFECT, BUT I'M MY OWN WOMAN. AND I'M NOT GOING BACK JUST 'CAUSE NUTS-BOY PUT ON A HAPPY FACE!
YOU HEARD HIM! THE WHOLE THING WAS A TRAP T' GET THE GRISON! ONCE SHE'S GONE, THINGS WILL BE BACK TO NORMAL!
YOU CALL LIFE WITH THAT PSYCHOTIC CLOWN NORMAL?!
HE LOVES ME!
DID HE SAY THAT?
HAS HE EVER SAID THAT?

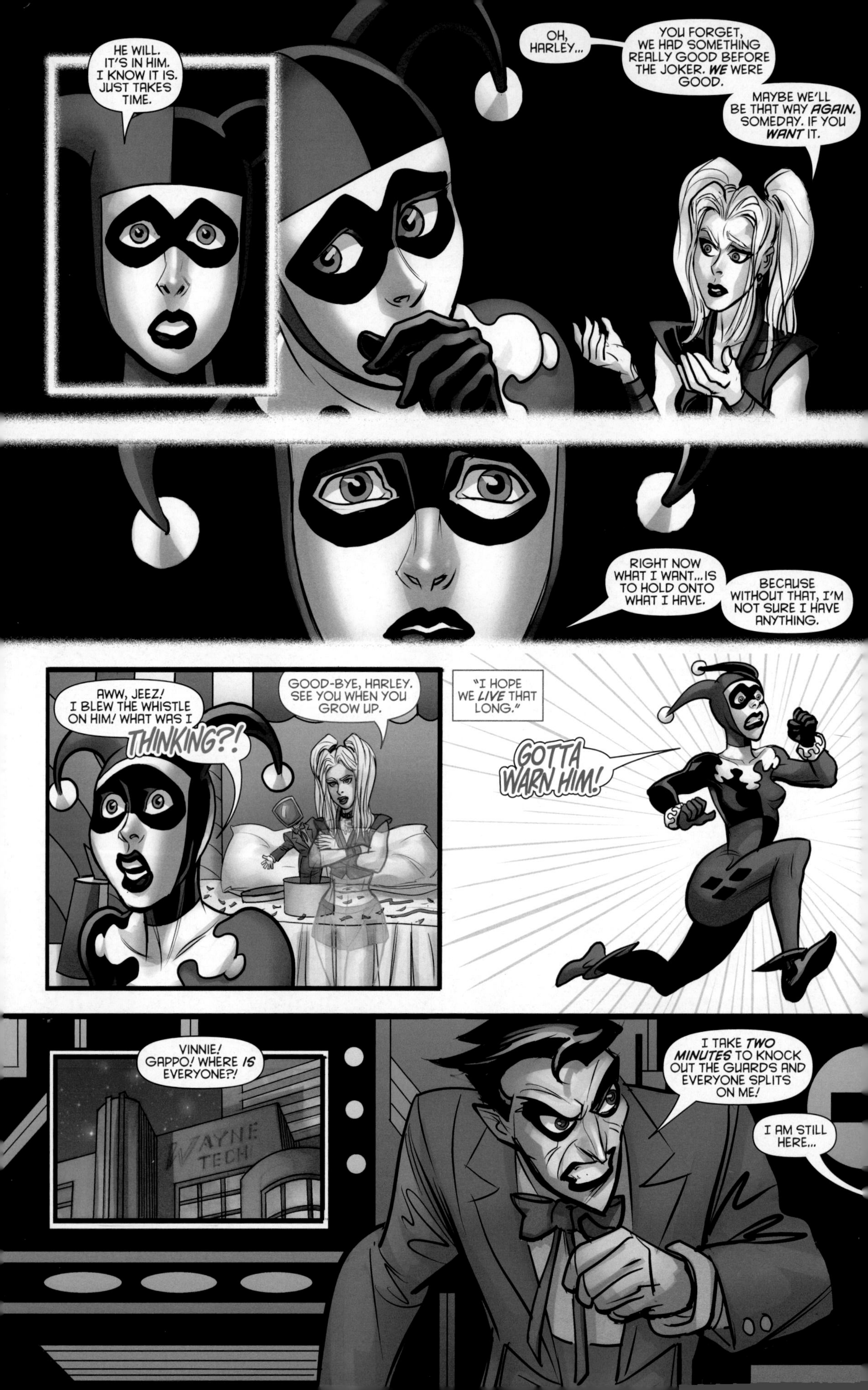

HE WILL. IT'S IN HIM. I KNOW IT IS. JUST TAKES TIME.
OH, HARLEY...
YOU FORGET, WE HAD SOMETHING REALLY GOOD BEFORE THE JOKER. WE WERE GOOD.
MAYBE WE'LL BE THAT WAY AGAIN. SOMEDAY. IF YOU WANT IT.
RIGHT NOW WHAT I WANT... IS TO HOLD ONTO WHAT I HAVE.
BECAUSE WITHOUT THAT, I'M NOT SURE I HAVE ANYTHING.
AWW, JEEZ! I BLEW THE WHISTLE ON HIM! WHAT WAS I THINKING?!
GOOD-BYE, HARLEY. SEE YOU WHEN YOU GROW UP.
"I HOPE WE LIVE THAT LONG."
GOTTA WARN HIM!
VINNIE! GAPPO! WHERE IS EVERYONE?!
WAYNE TECH
I TAKE TWO MINUTES TO KNOCK OUT THE GUARDS AND EVERYONE SPLITS ON ME!
I AM STILL HERE...

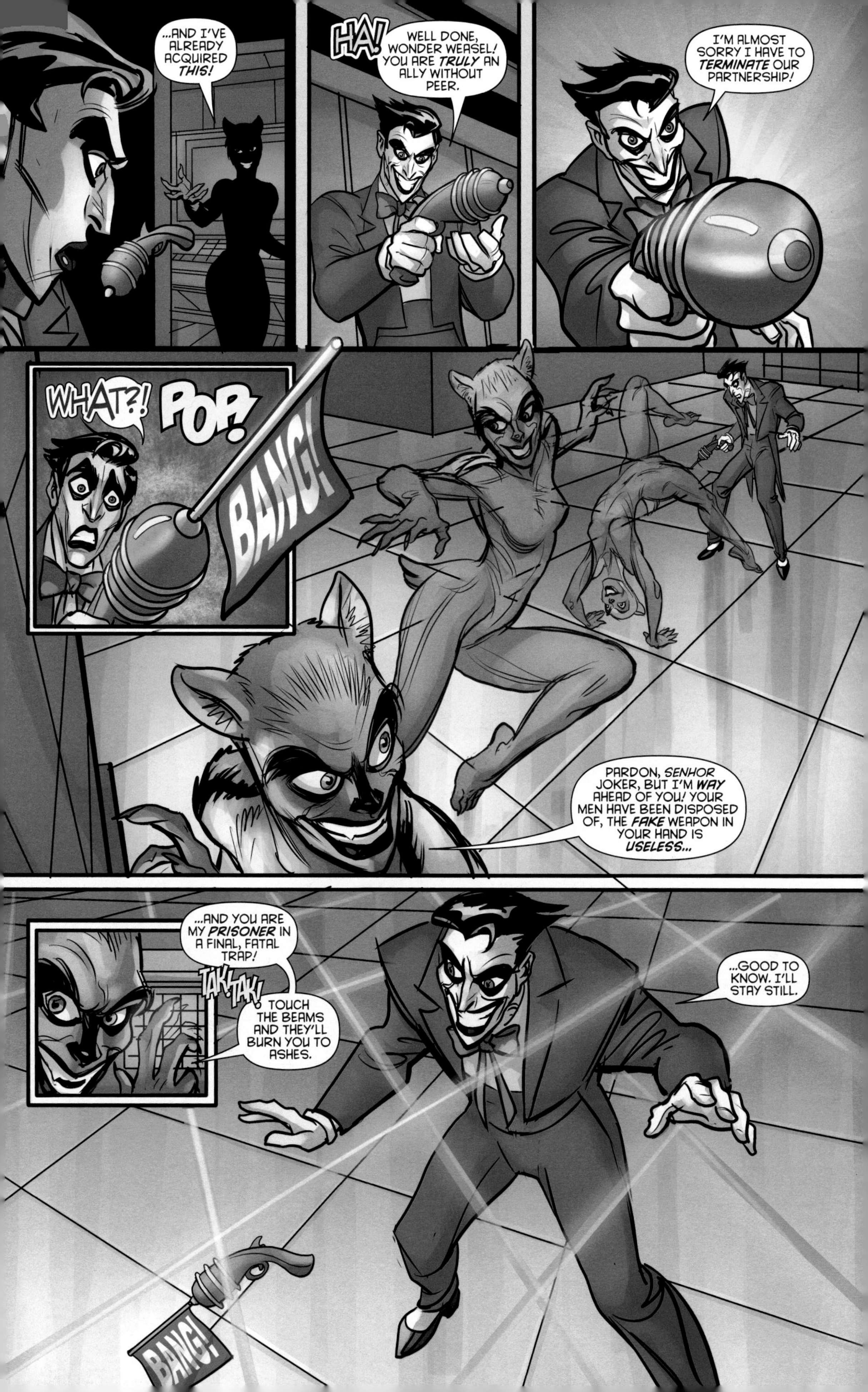
...AND I'VE ALREADY ACQUIRED THIS!
HA!
WELL DONE, WONDER WEASEL! YOU ARE TRULY AN ALLY WITHOUT PEER.
I'M ALMOST SORRY I HAVE TO TERMINATE OUR PARTNERSHIP!
WHAT?!
POP!
BANG!
PARDON, SENHOR JOKER, BUT I'M WAY AHEAD OF YOU! YOUR MEN HAVE BEEN DISPOSED OF, THE FAKE WEAPON IN YOUR HAND IS USELESS...
...AND YOU ARE MY PRISONER IN A FINAL, FATAL TRAP!
TAK! TAK!
TOUCH THE BEAMS AND THEY'LL BURN YOU TO ASHES.
...GOOD TO KNOW. I'LL STAY STILL.
BANG!

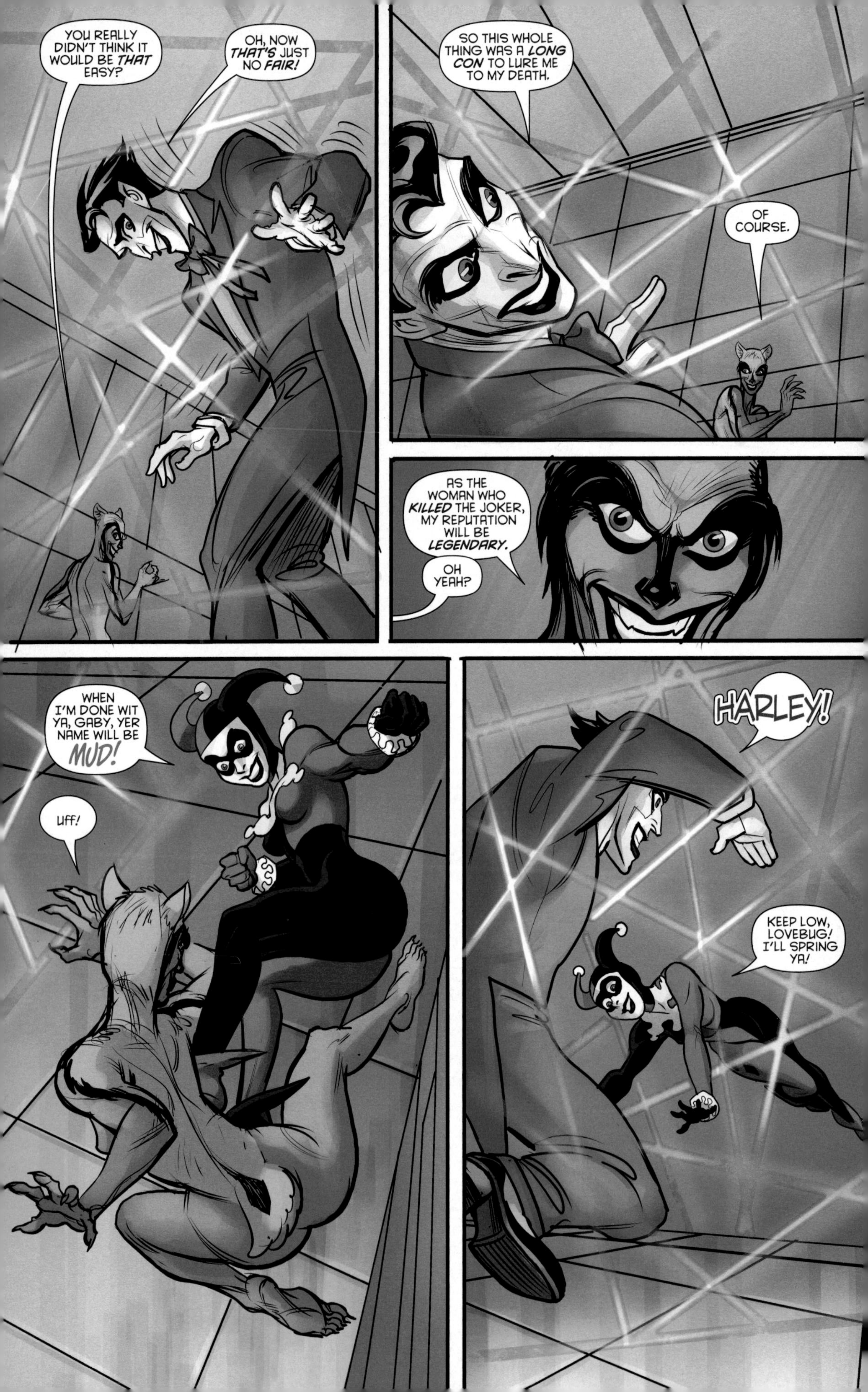
YOU REALLY DIDN'T THINK IT WOULD BE THAT EASY?
OH, NOW THAT'S JUST NO FAIR!
SO THIS WHOLE THING WAS A LONG CON TO LURE ME TO MY DEATH.
OF COURSE.
AS THE WOMAN WHO KILLED THE JOKER, MY REPUTATION WILL BE LEGENDARY.
OH YEAH?
WHEN I'M DONE WIT YA, GABY, YER NAME WILL BE MUD!
UFF!
HARLEY!
KEEP LOW, LOVEBUG! I'LL SPRING YA!

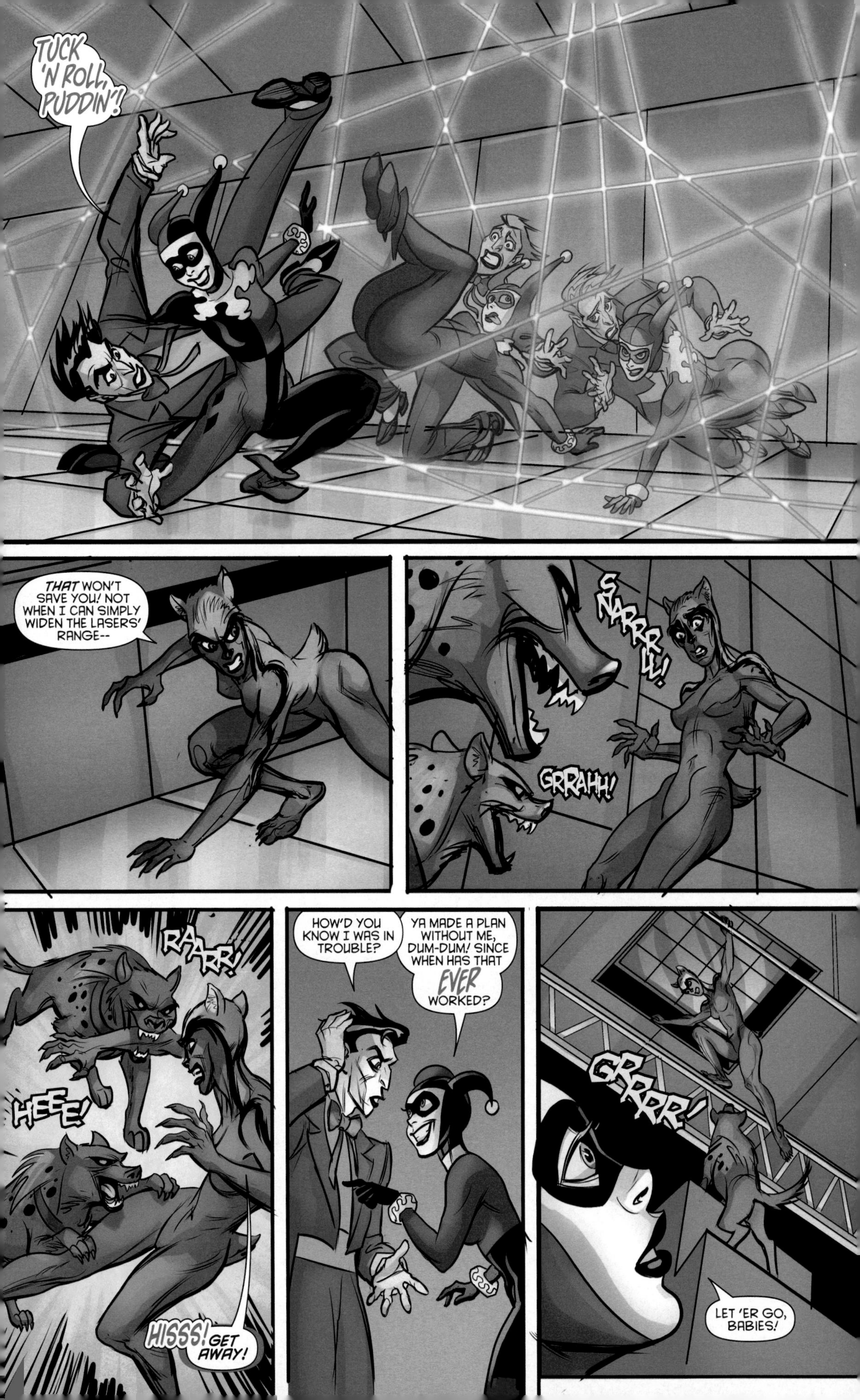
TUCK 'N ROLL, PUDDIN'!
THAT WON'T SAVE YOU! NOT WHEN I CAN SIMPLY WIDEN THE LASERS' RANGE--
SNARRRL!
GRRAHH!
RAARR!
HEEE!
HISSS! GET AWAY!
HOW'D YOU KNOW I WAS IN TROUBLE?
YA MADE A PLAN WITHOUT ME, DUM-DUM! SINCE WHEN HAS THAT EVER WORKED?
GRRRR!
LET 'ER GO, BABIES!

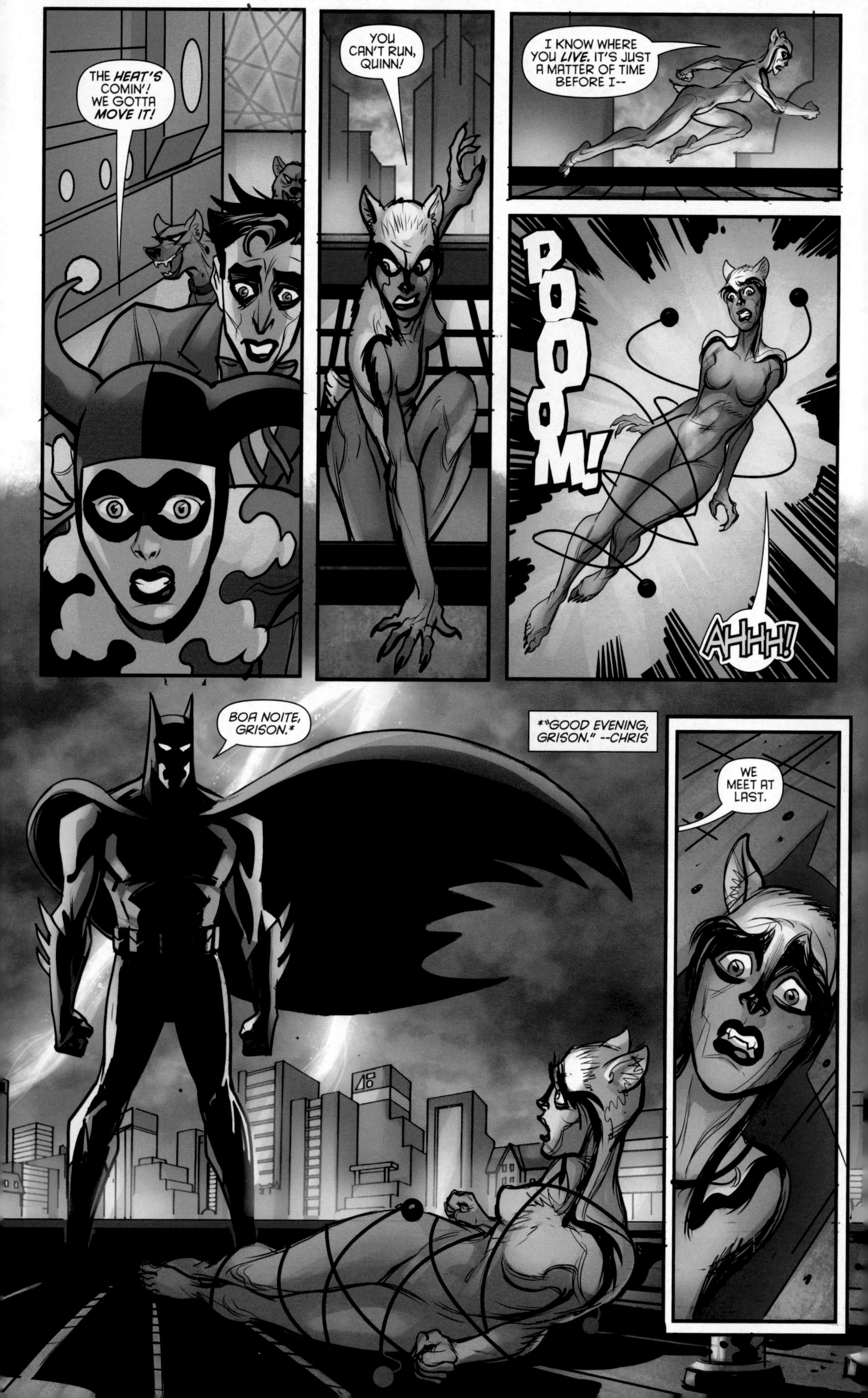

THE HEAT'S COMIN'! WE GOTTA MOVE IT!
YOU CAN'T RUN, QUINN!
I KNOW WHERE YOU LIVE. IT'S JUST A MATTER OF TIME BEFORE I--
POOOM!
AHHH!
BOA NOITE, GRISON.*
*"GOOD EVENING, GRISON." --CHRIS
WE MEET AT LAST.

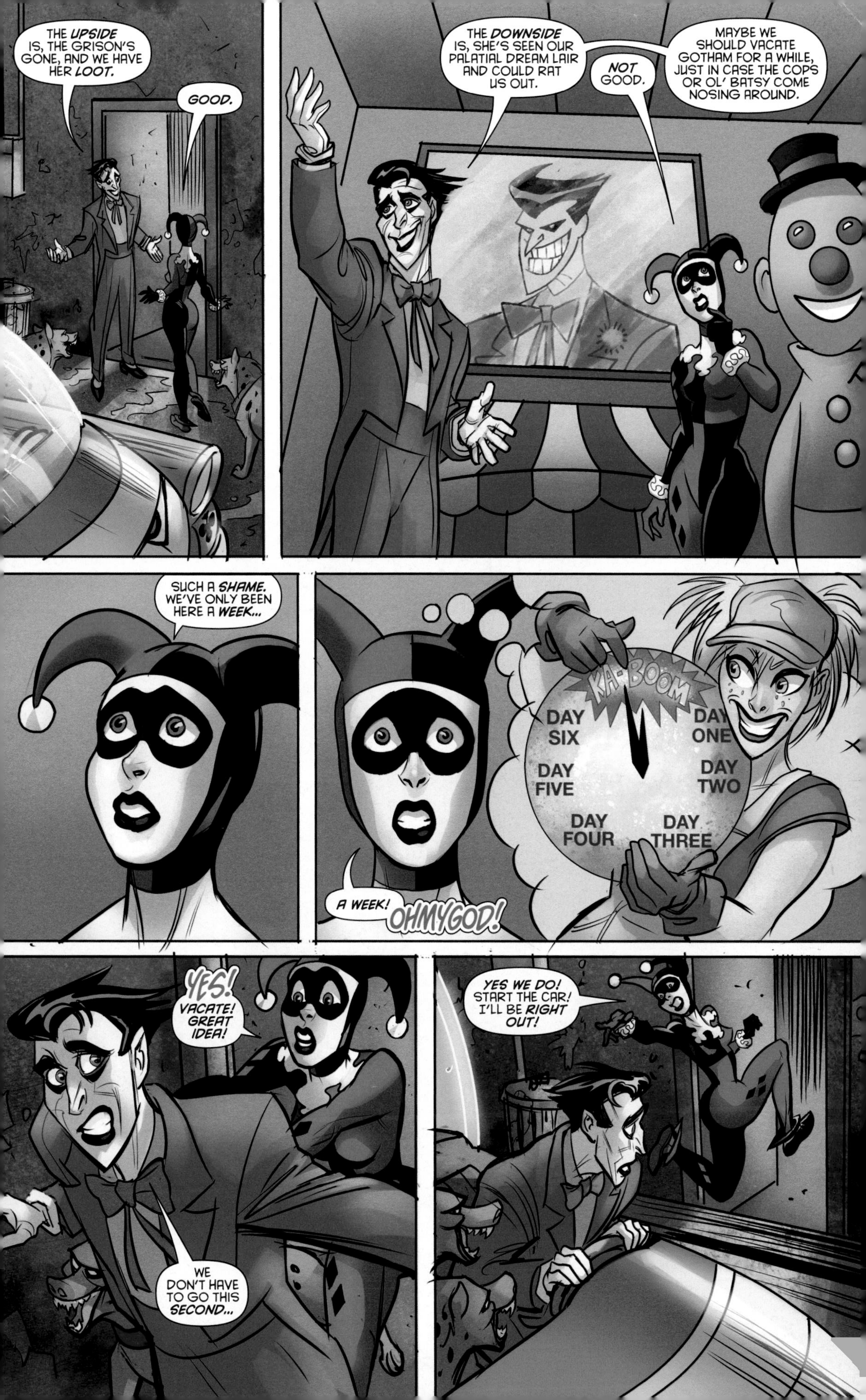

THE UPSIDE IS, THE GRISON'S GONE, AND WE HAVE HER LOOT.
GOOD.
THE DOWNSIDE IS, SHE'S SEEN OUR PALATIAL DREAM LAIR AND COULD RAT US OUT.
NOT GOOD.
MAYBE WE SHOULD VACATE GOTHAM FOR A WHILE, JUST IN CASE THE COPS OR OL' BATSY COME NOSING AROUND.
SUCH A SHAME. WE'VE ONLY BEEN HERE A WEEK...
KA-BOOM
DAY ONE
DAY TWO
DAY THREE
DAY FOUR
DAY FIVE
DAY SIX
A WEEK! OHMYGOD!
YES! VACATE! GREAT IDEA!
WE DON'T HAVE TO GO THIS SECOND...
YES WE DO! START THE CAR! I'LL BE RIGHT OUT!

AW, JEEZ!

TONIGHT'S TH' LAST NIGHT I HAD T' PAY OFF TH' *CARPENTER* BEFORE--

OY! *NOW* WHAT?!

BAM!

THERE SHE IS, DETECTIVE BULLOCK!

SHE'S THE ONE WHO ATTACKED US AND *STOLE OUR DEED!*

OF COURSE. WHY *WOULDN'T* THEY SHOW UP NOW?!

WELL, WELL! *HARLEY QUINN!* WE BEEN LOOKIN' FOR YOU AND YOUR PSYCHO PLAYMATE FOR A *LONG* TIME!

NICE DIGS.

THANKS, BULLSY. *DROP DEAD,* BULLSY.

SEEMS SOME LOWLIFE KNOCKED OUT THESE NICE FOLKS AND LOCKED 'EM IN A CARGO SHIP HEADED FOR NEW ZEALAND.

WHAT DO *YOU* KNOW ABOUT THAT?

I'LL TELL YA HARV, IT'S A *FUNNY* STORY...

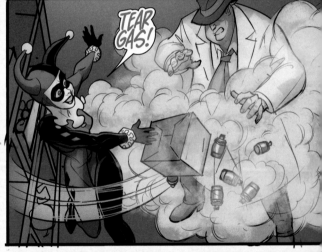

TEAR GAS!

DRIVE!

WHAT?

JUST DRIVE!

KRASSH!

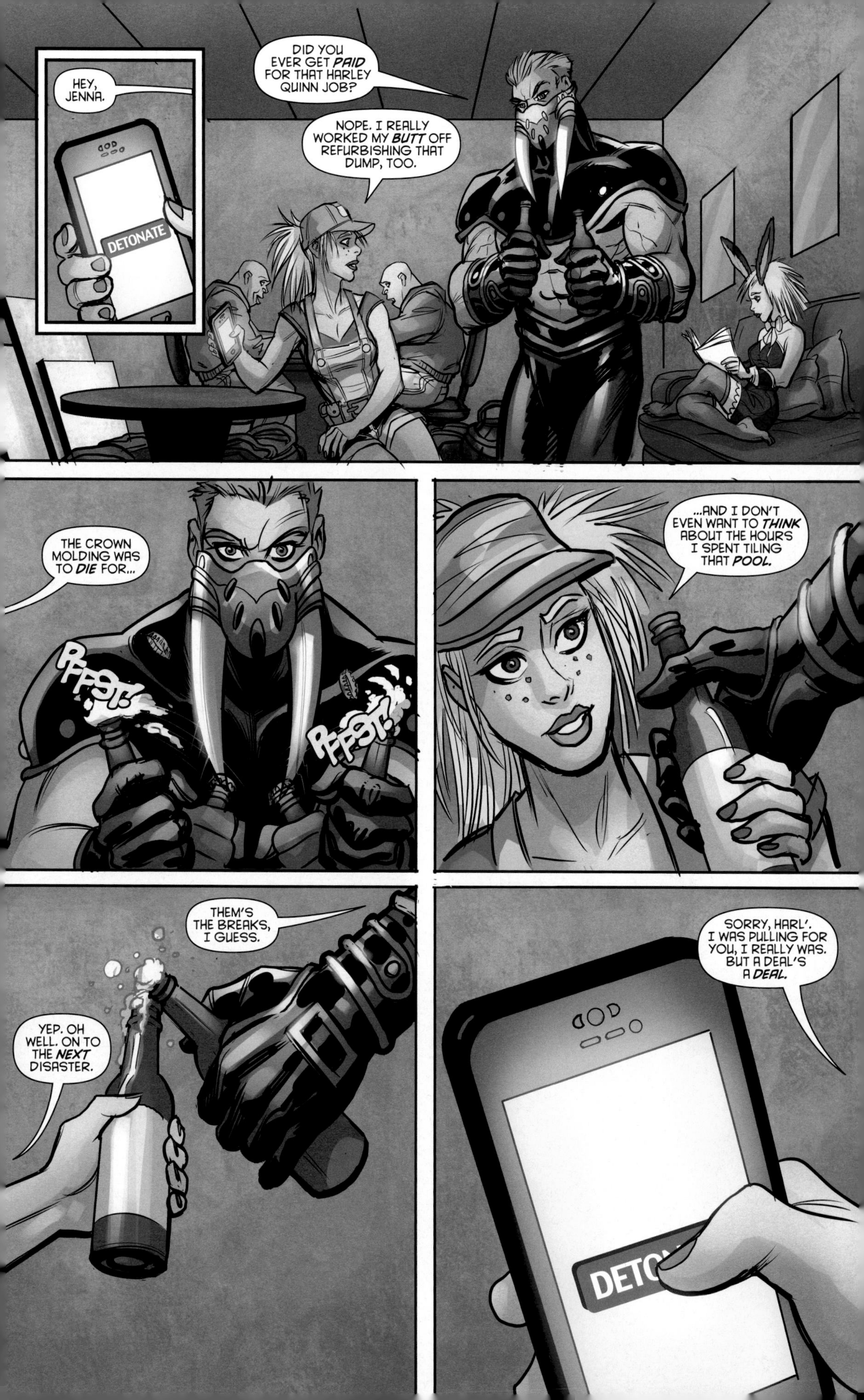
HEY, JENNA.
DETONATE
DID YOU EVER GET *PAID* FOR THAT HARLEY QUINN JOB?
NOPE. I REALLY WORKED MY *BUTT* OFF REFURBISHING THAT DUMP, TOO.
THE CROWN MOLDING WAS TO *DIE* FOR...
PFFST!
PFFST!
...AND I DON'T EVEN WANT TO *THINK* ABOUT THE HOURS I SPENT TILING THAT *POOL.*
THEM'S THE BREAKS, I GUESS.
YEP. OH WELL. ON TO THE *NEXT* DISASTER.
SORRY, HARL'. I WAS PULLING FOR YOU, I REALLY WAS. BUT A DEAL'S A *DEAL.*

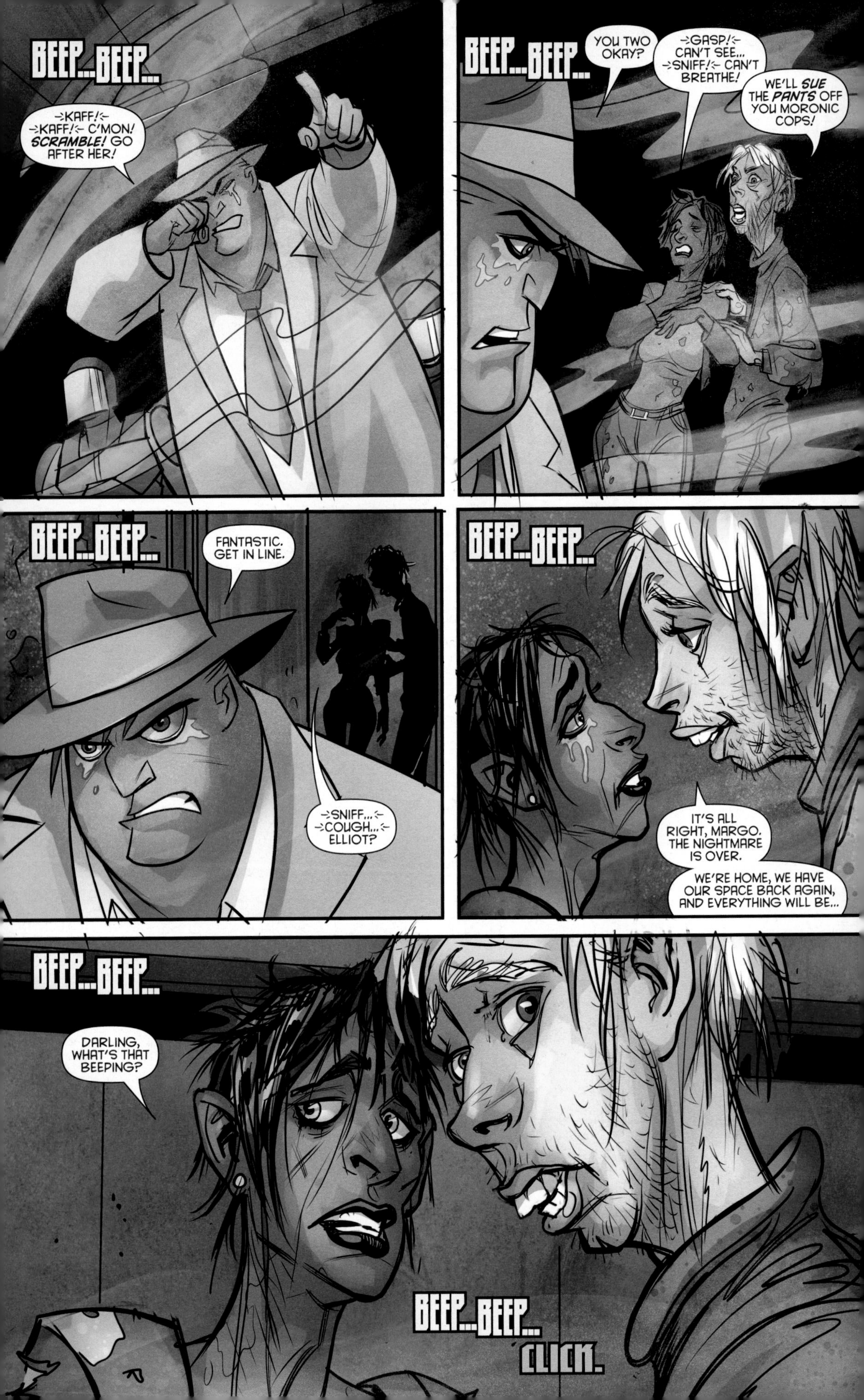
BEEP...BEEP...
-KAFF!- -KAFF!- C'MON! SCRAMBLE! GO AFTER HER!
BEEP...BEEP...
YOU TWO OKAY?
-GASP!- CAN'T SEE... -SNIFF!- CAN'T BREATHE!
WE'LL SUE THE PANTS OFF YOU MORONIC COPS!
BEEP...BEEP...
FANTASTIC. GET IN LINE.
-SNIFF...- -COUGH...- ELLIOT?
BEEP...BEEP...
IT'S ALL RIGHT, MARGO. THE NIGHTMARE IS OVER.
WE'RE HOME, WE HAVE OUR SPACE BACK AGAIN, AND EVERYTHING WILL BE...
BEEP...BEEP...
DARLING, WHAT'S THAT BEEPING?
BEEP...BEEP...
CLICK.

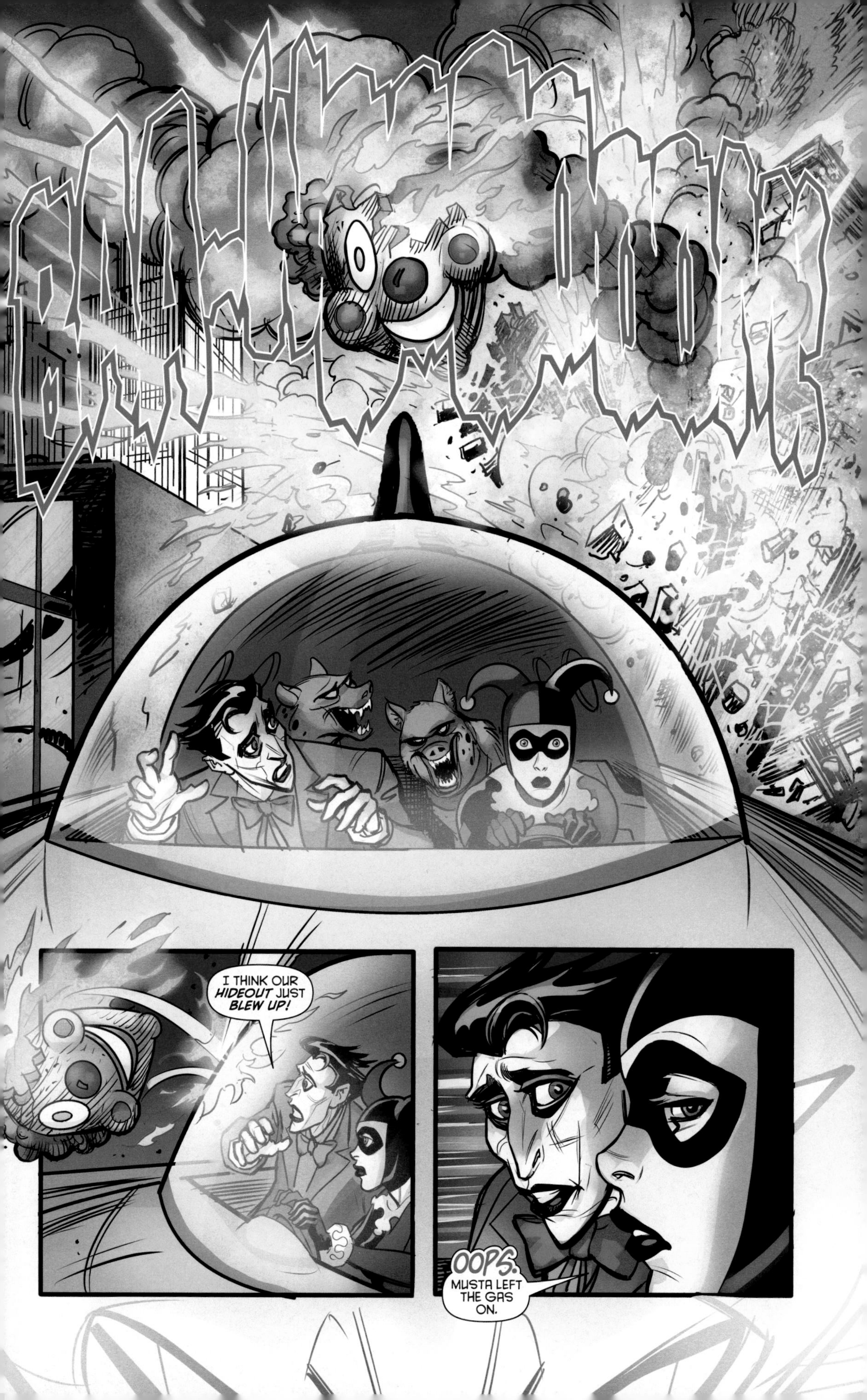
I THINK OUR *HIDEOUT* JUST *BLEW UP!*
OOPS. MUSTA LEFT THE GAS ON.

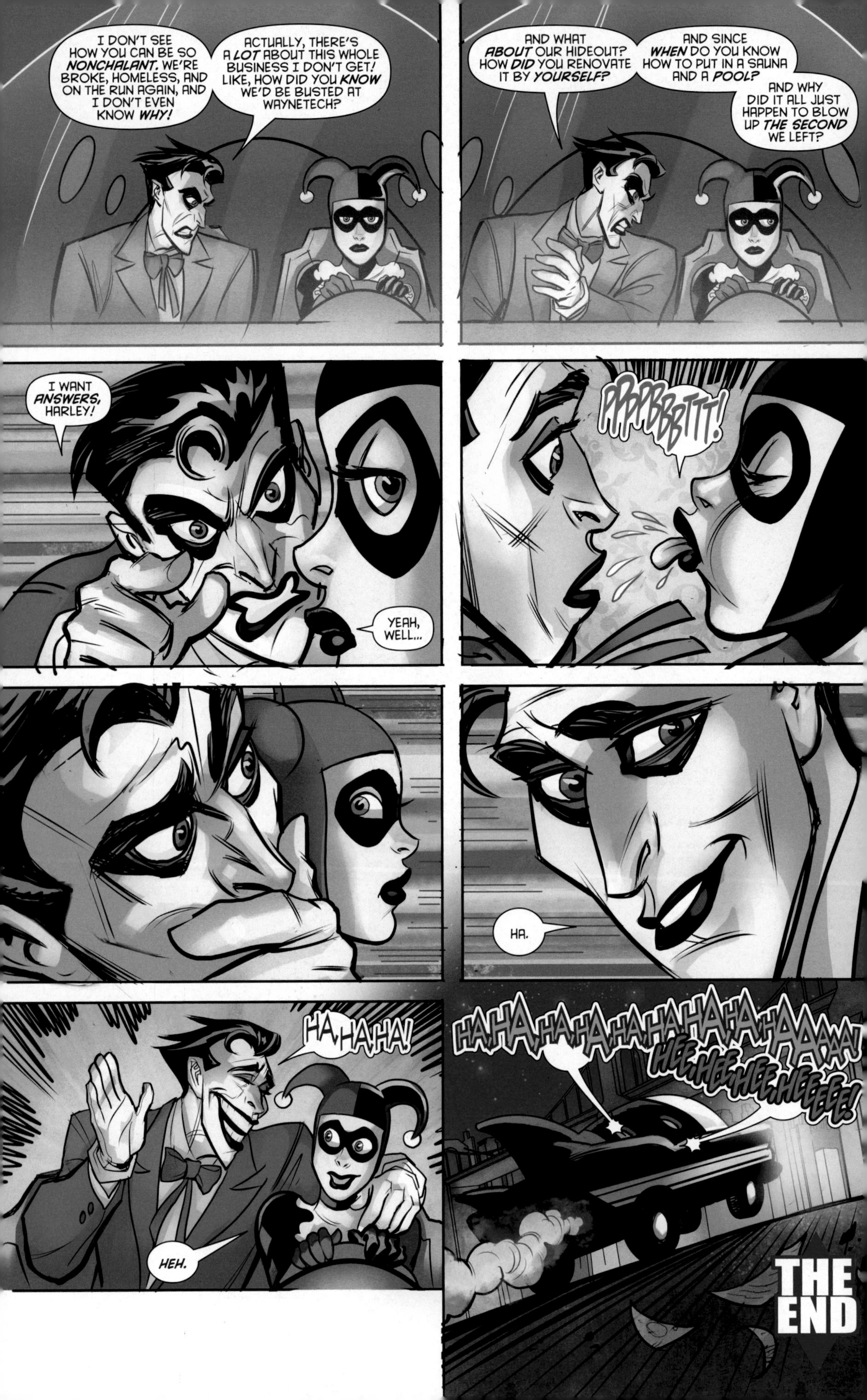
I DON'T SEE HOW YOU CAN BE SO *NONCHALANT.* WE'RE BROKE, HOMELESS, AND ON THE RUN AGAIN, AND I DON'T EVEN KNOW *WHY!*
ACTUALLY, THERE'S A *LOT* ABOUT THIS WHOLE BUSINESS I DON'T GET! LIKE, HOW DID YOU *KNOW* WE'D BE BUSTED AT WAYNETECH?
AND WHAT *ABOUT* OUR HIDEOUT? HOW *DID* YOU RENOVATE IT BY *YOURSELF?*
AND SINCE *WHEN* DO YOU KNOW HOW TO PUT IN A SAUNA AND A *POOL?*
AND WHY DID IT ALL JUST HAPPEN TO BLOW UP *THE SECOND* WE LEFT?
I WANT *ANSWERS,* HARLEY!
YEAH, WELL...
PPPPBBBTTT!
HA.
HA,HA,HA!
HEH.
HA,HA,HA,HA,HA,HA,HA,HA,HAAAAA!
HEE,HEE,HEE,HEEEEEE!
THE END

COVER GALLERY and SKETCHBOOK

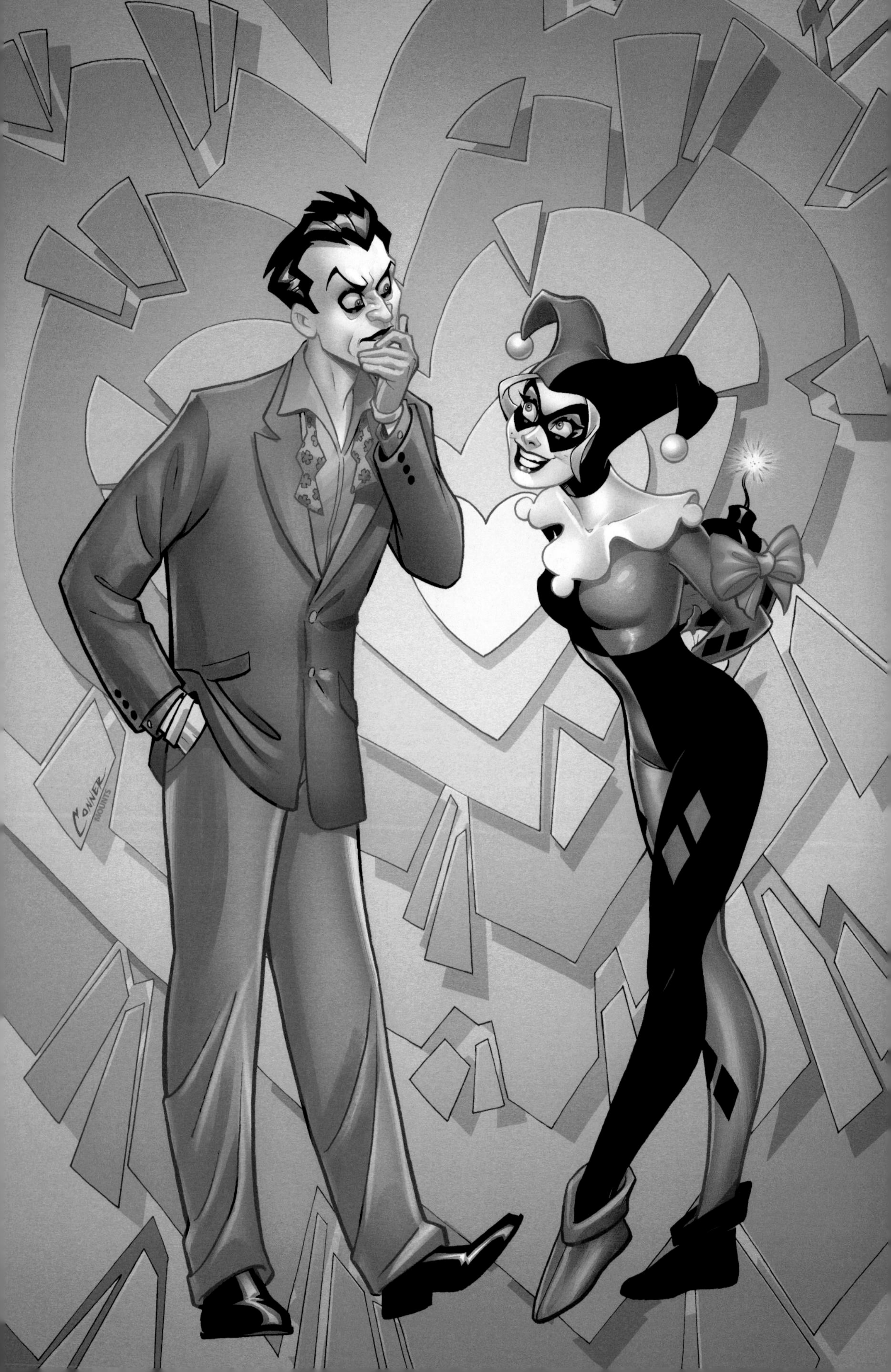
CONNER
MOUNTS
HARLEY QUINN: HARLEY LOVES JOKER #1 cover by Amanda Conner and Paul Mounts

HARLEY QUINN: HARLEY LOVES JOKER #2 cover by Amanda Conner and Paul Mounts

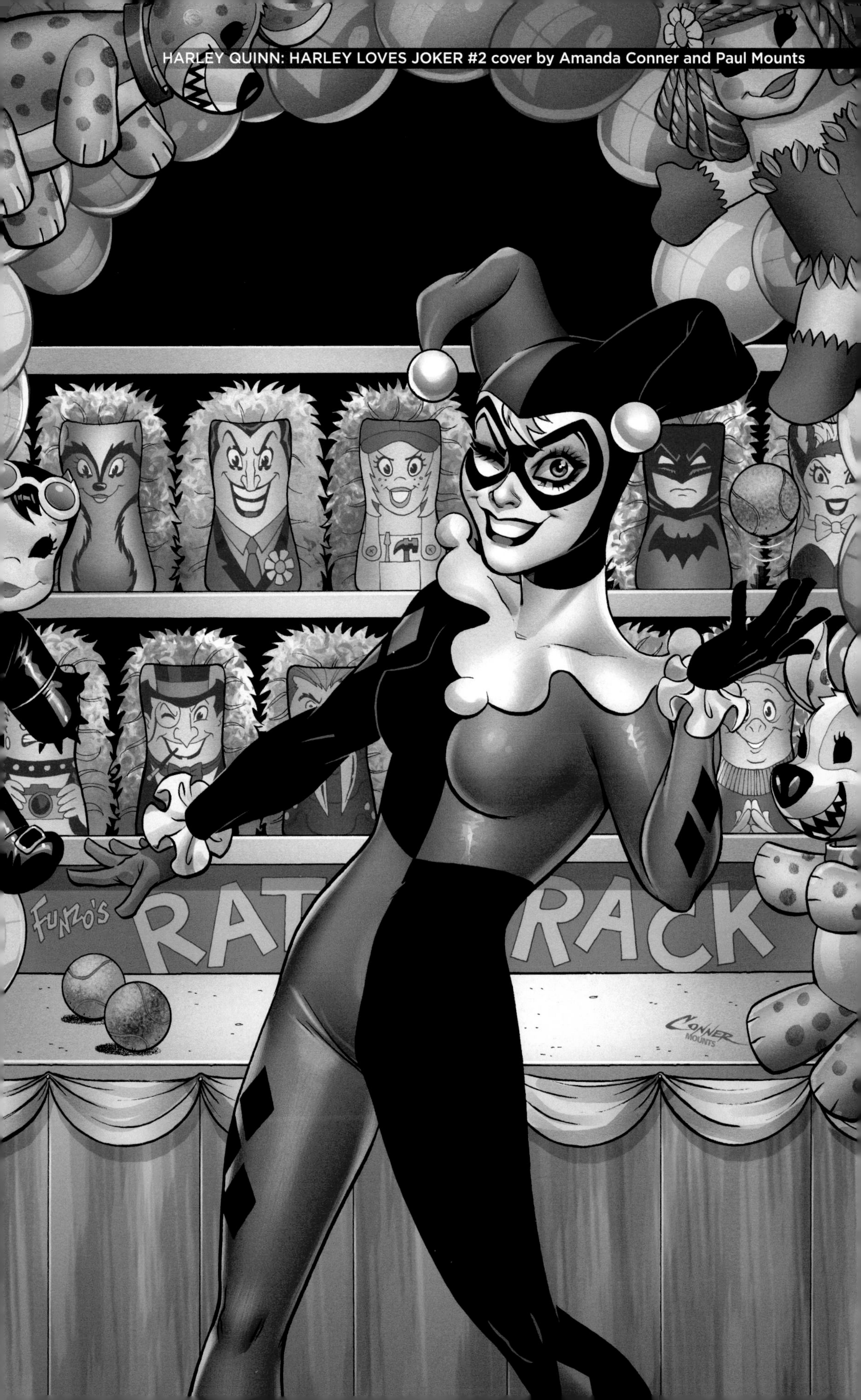

FUNZO'S
RAT RACK
CONNER
MOUNTS

HARLEY QUINN: HARLEY LOVES JOKER #1 variant cover by Frank Cho and Sabine Rich

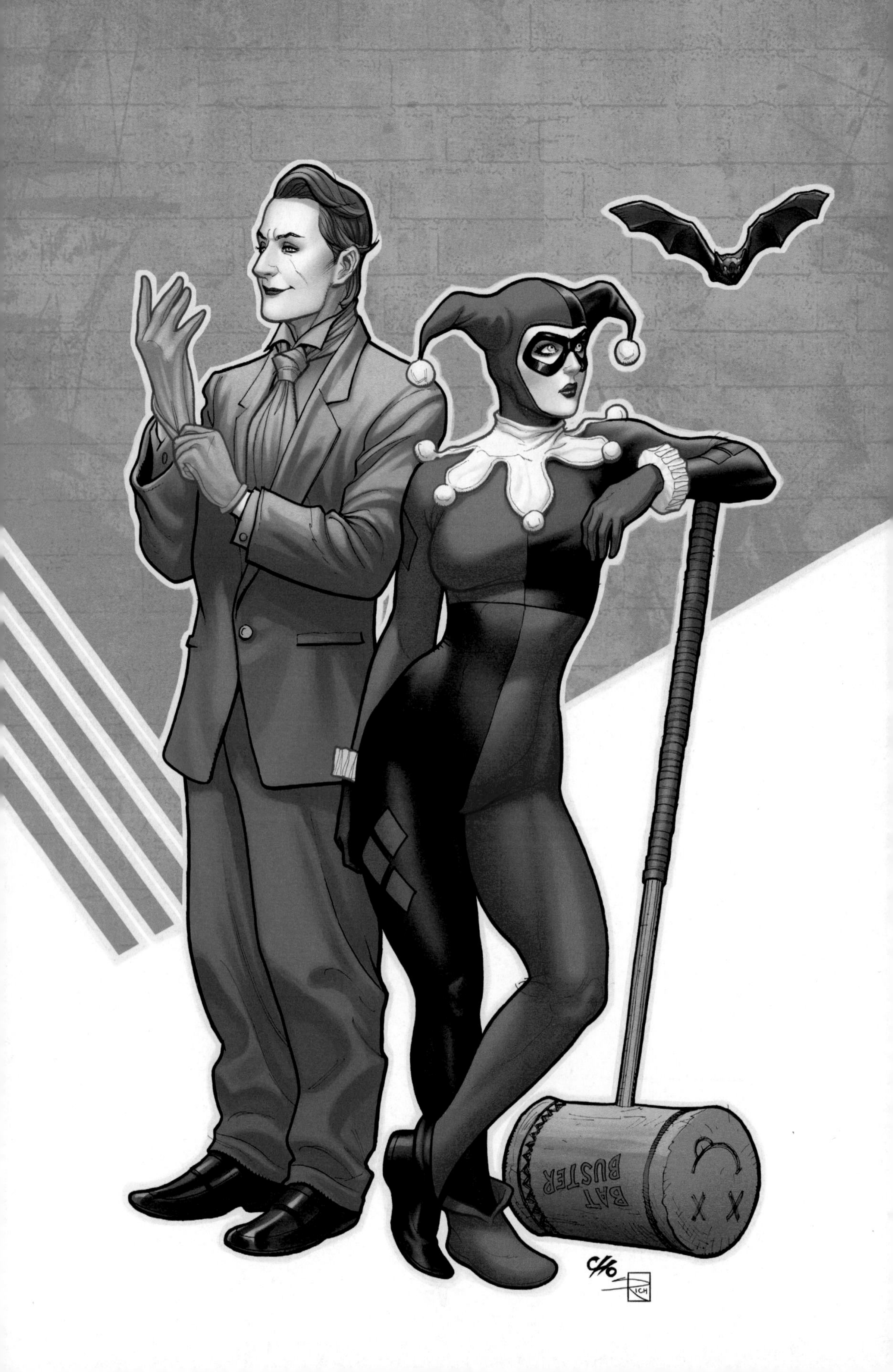
BAT BUSTER

HARLEY QUINN #17 cover by Amanda Conner and Alex Sinclair

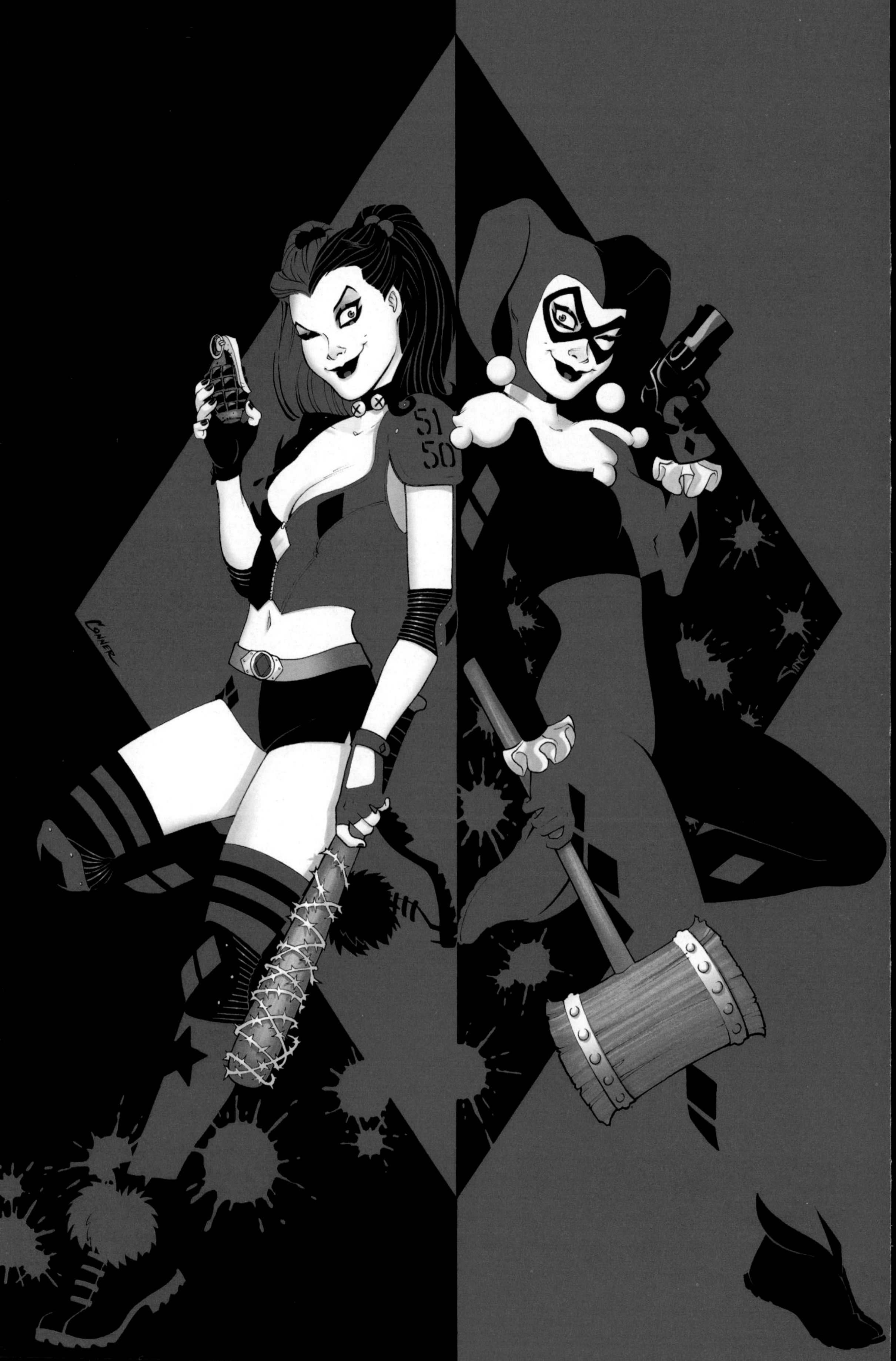

51
50
CONNER

HARLEY QUINN #19 cover by Amanda Conner and Alex Sinclair

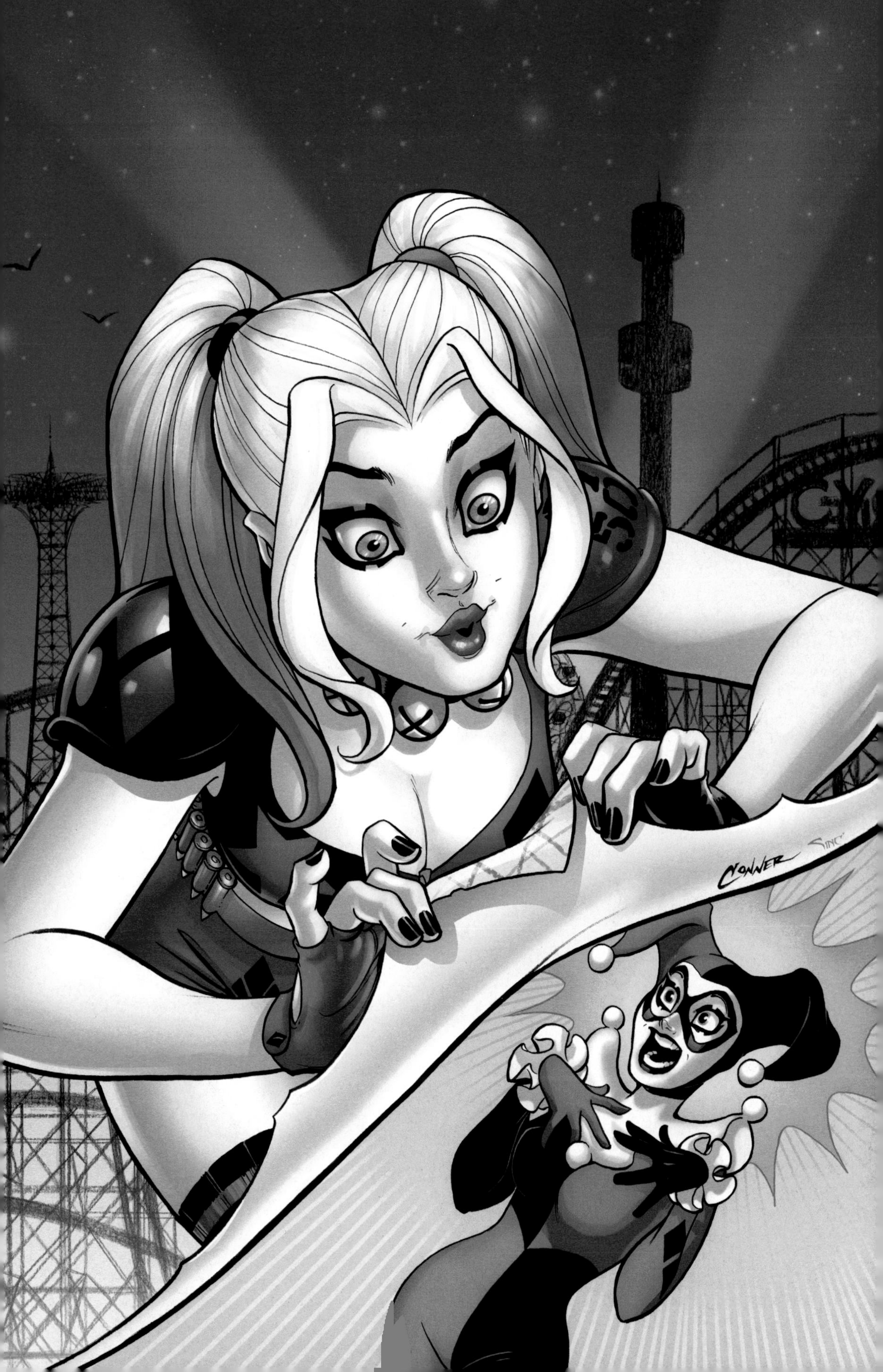

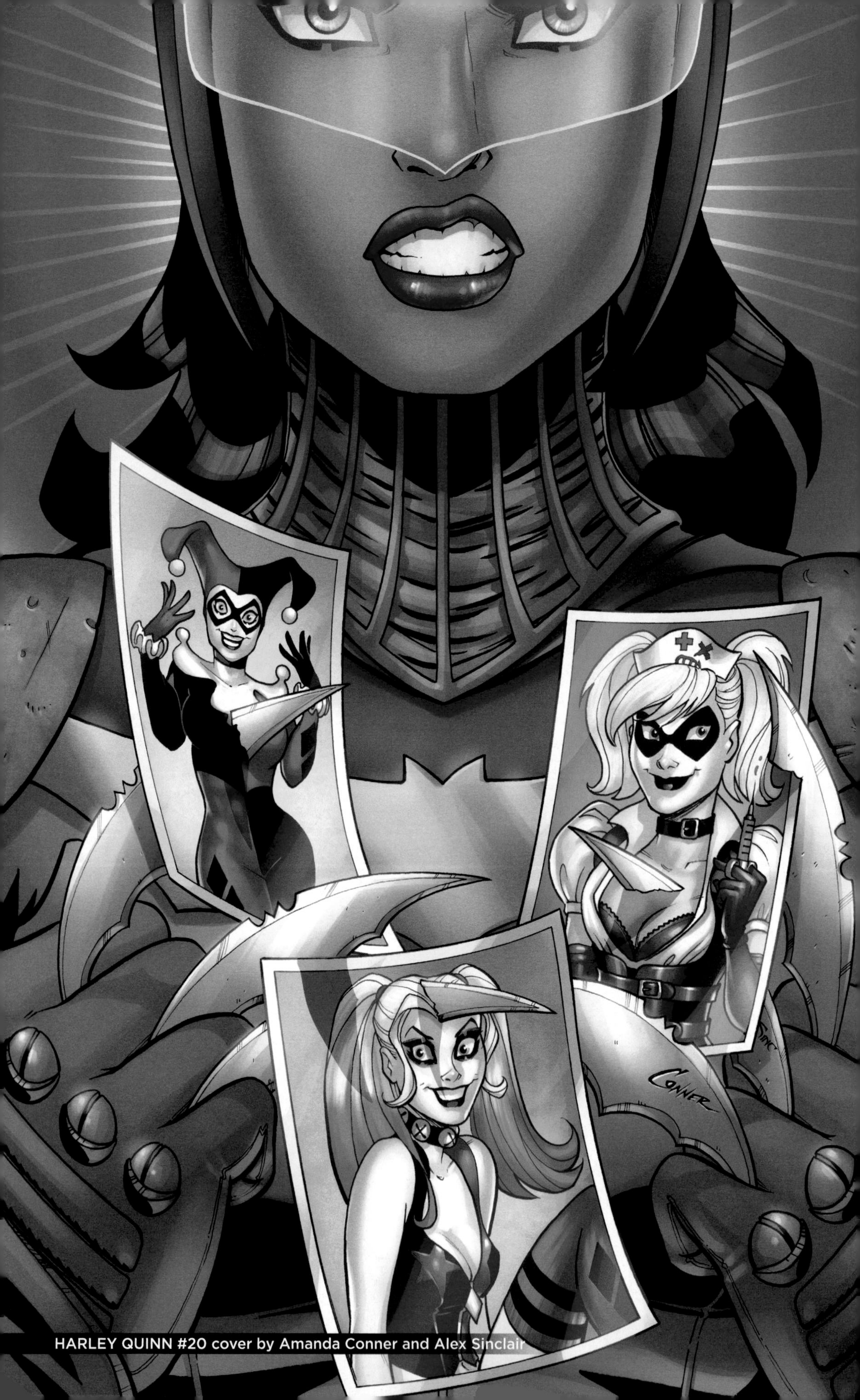
CONNER

HARLEY QUINN #20 cover by Amanda Conner and Alex Sinclair

HARLEY QUINN #21 cover by Amanda Conner and Alex Sinclair

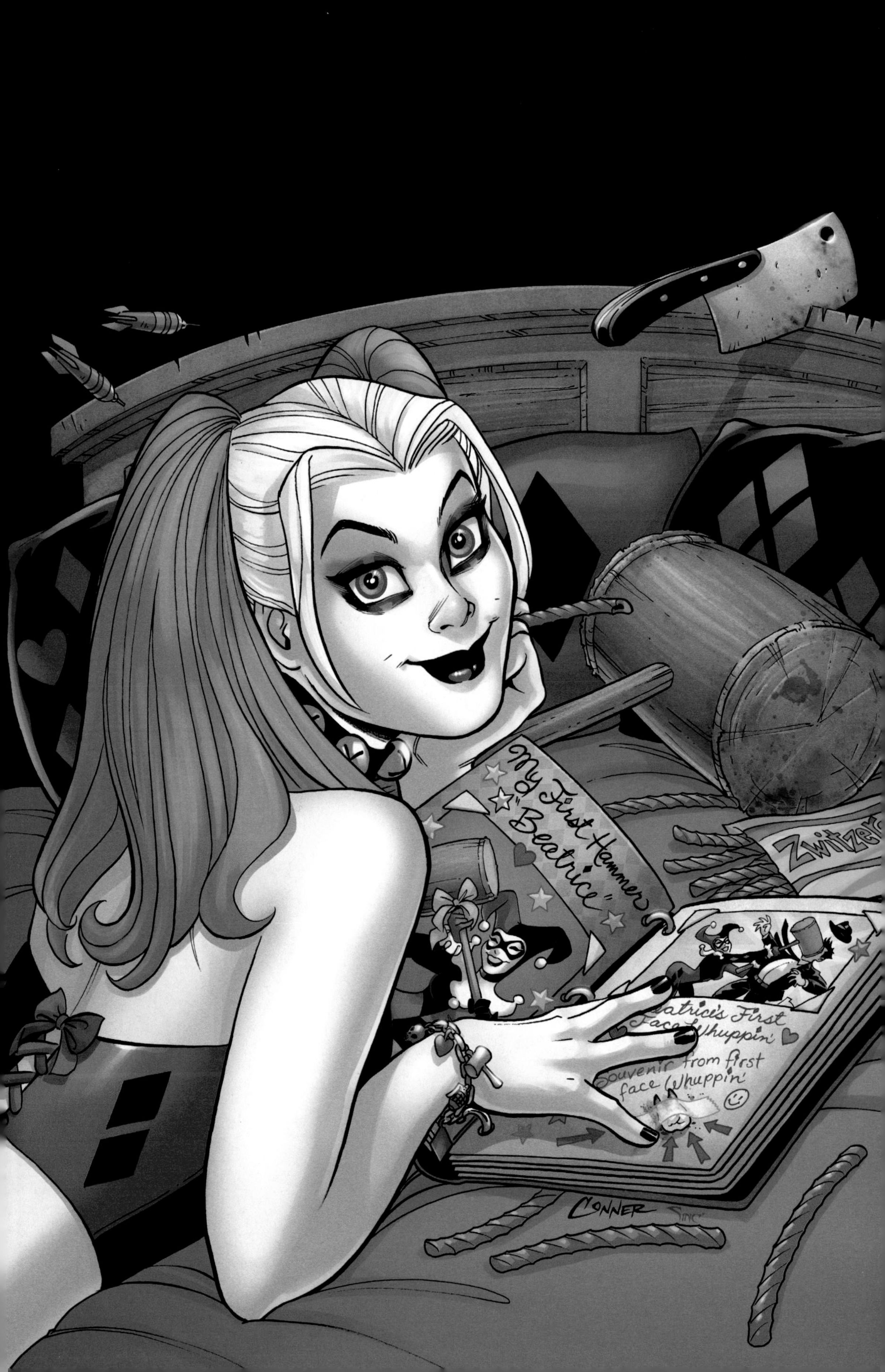

My First Hammer "Beatrice"
Souvenir from first face Whuppin'
CONNER

HARLEY QUINN #23 cover by Amanda Conner and Alex Sinclair

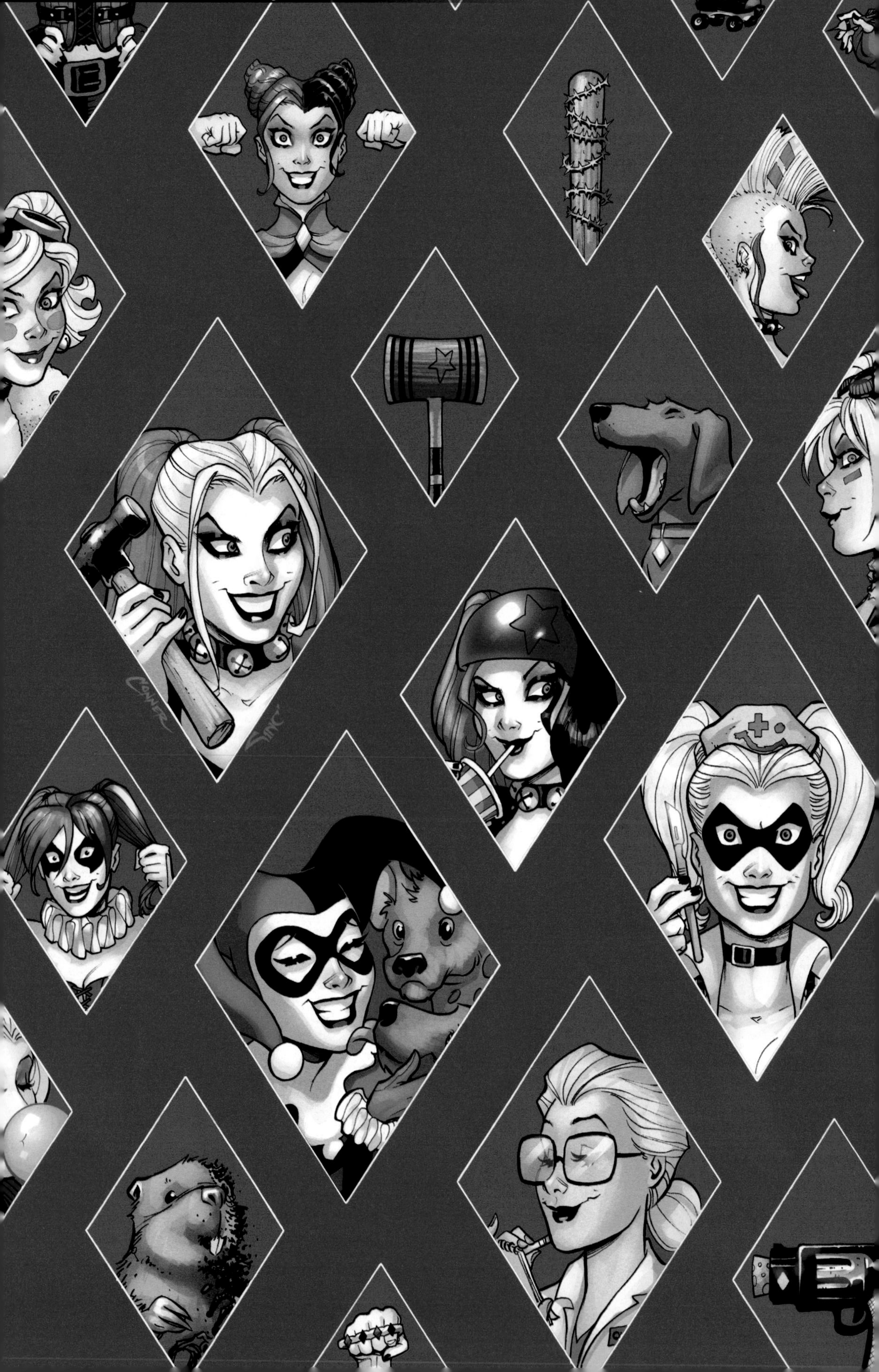
CONNER
SINC

HARLEY QUINN #17 variant cover by Frank Cho and Sabine Rich

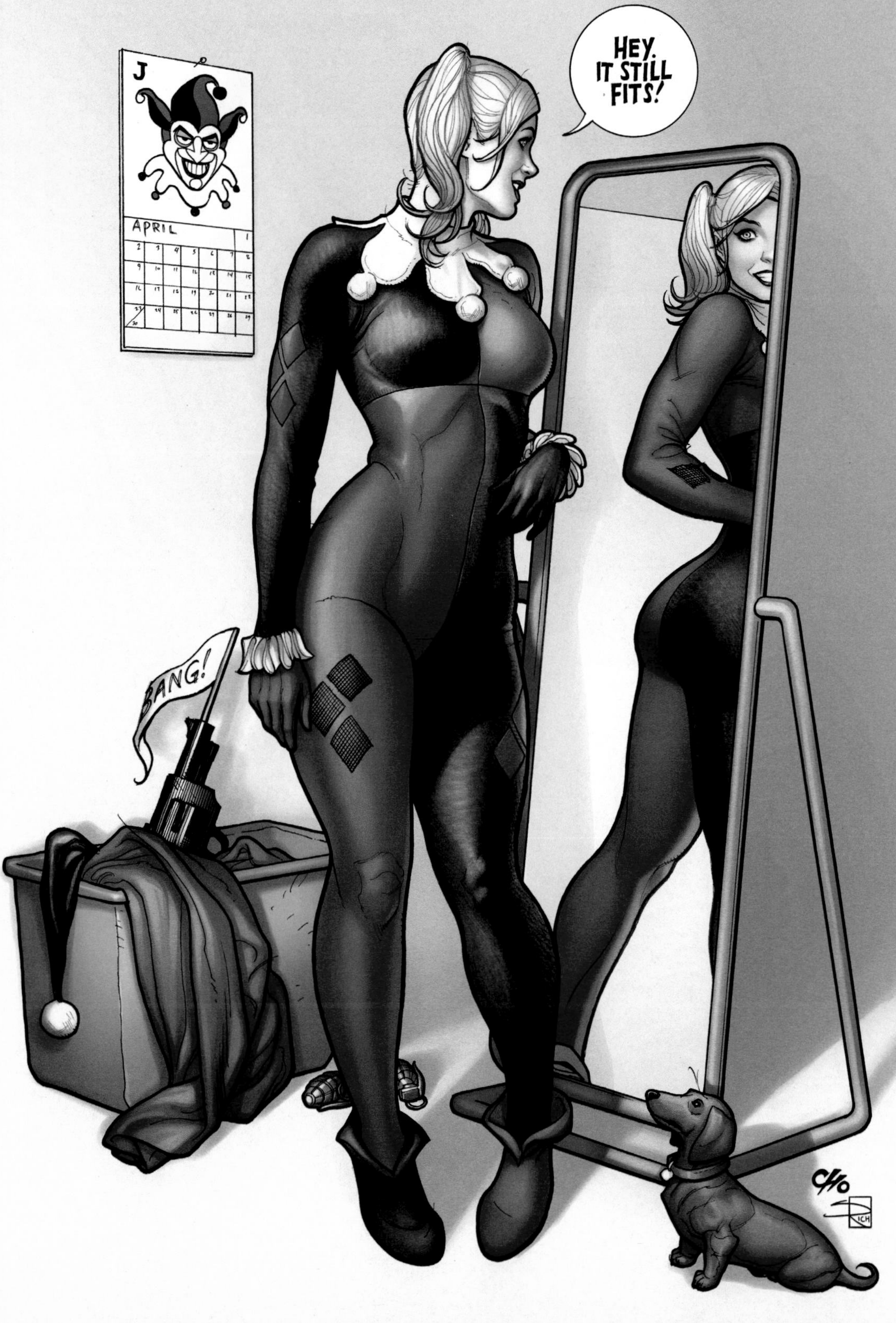
HEY. IT STILL FITS!
J
APRIL
BANG!

HARLEY QUINN #18 variant cover by Frank Cho and Sabine Rich

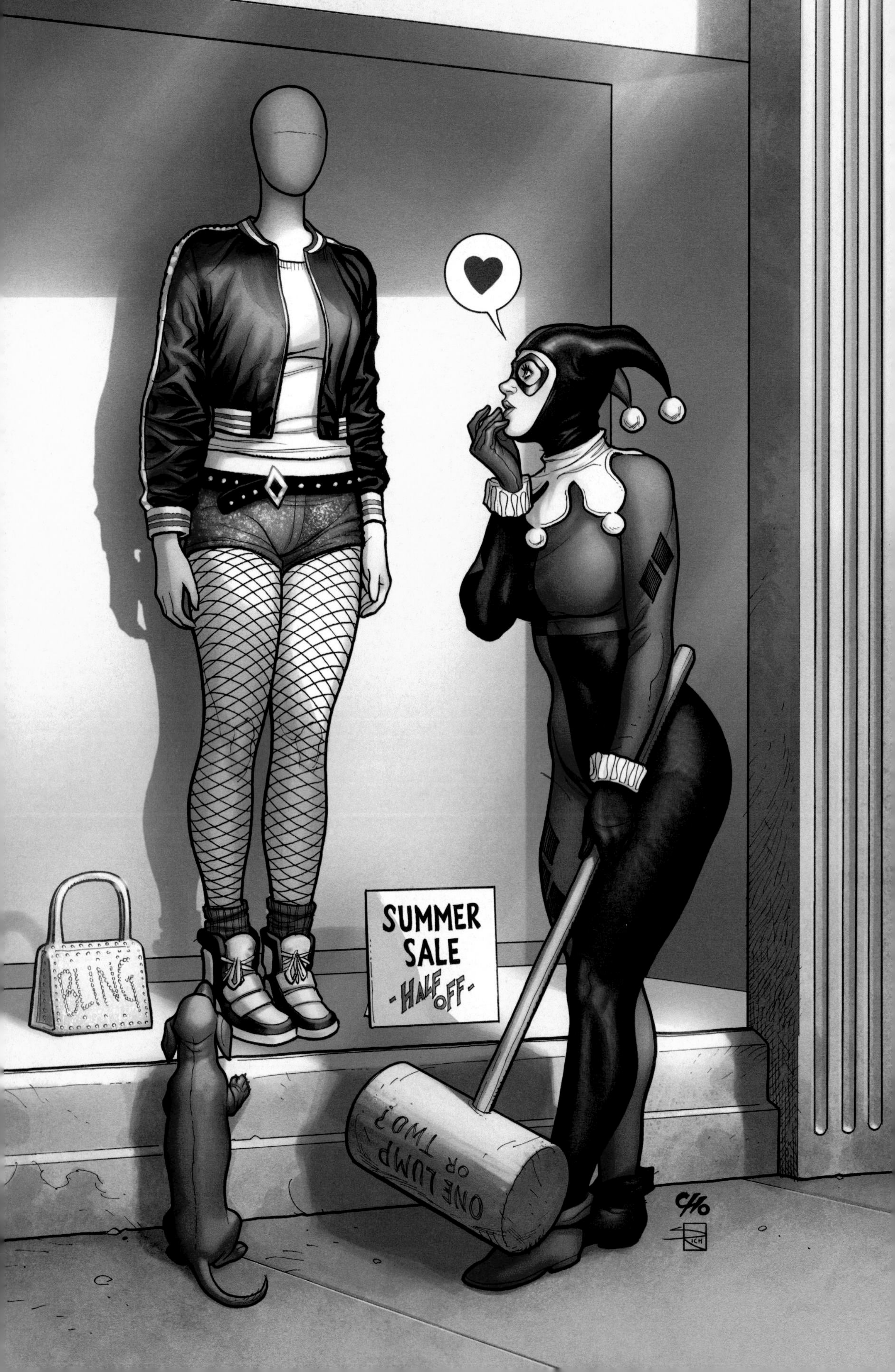

BLING
SUMMER SALE
-HALF OFF-
ONE LUMP OR TWO?

HARLEY QUINN #19 variant cover by Frank Cho and Sabine Rich

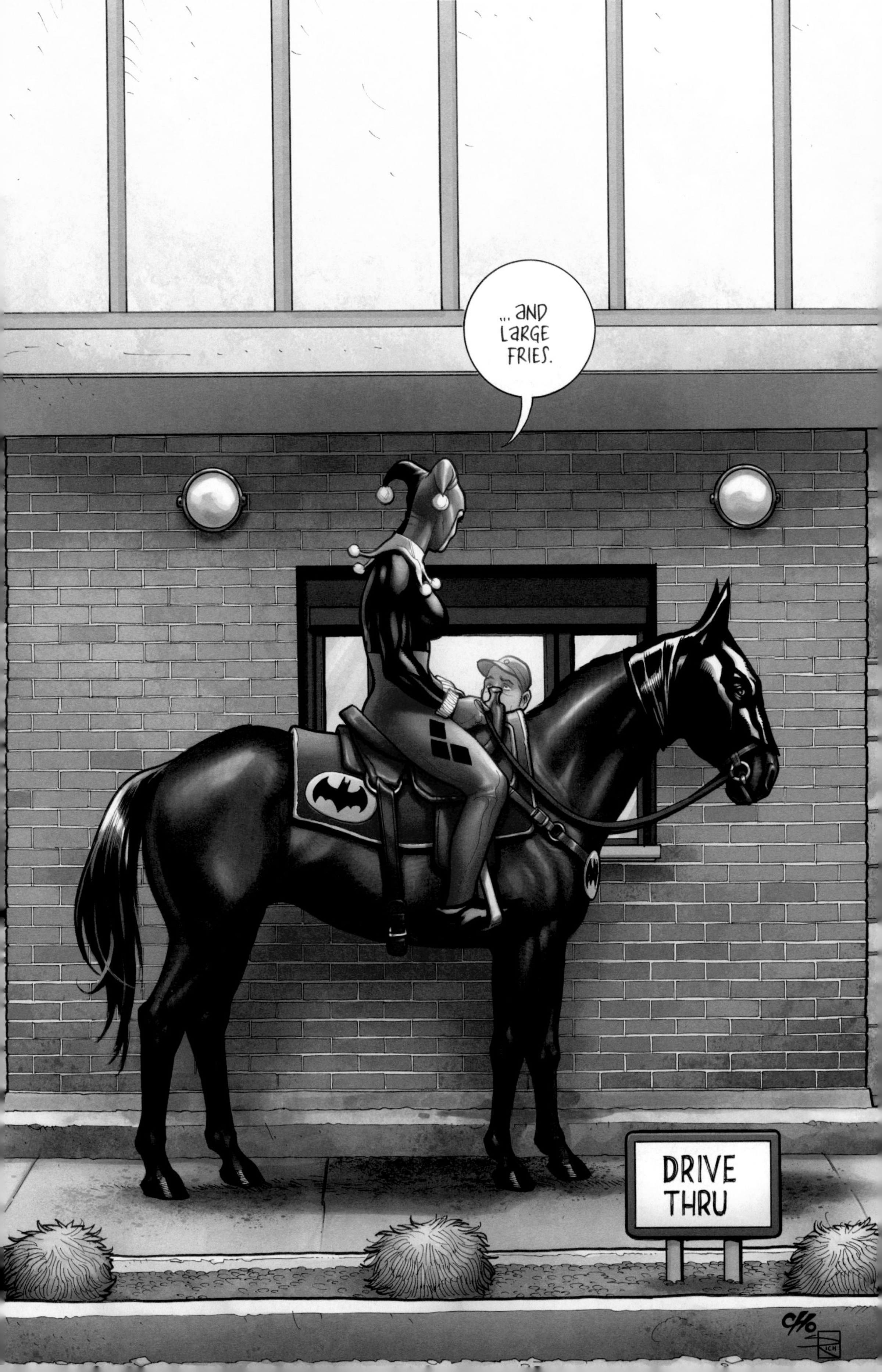
...AND LARGE FRIES.
DRIVE THRU
CHO
RICH

HARLEY QUINN #20 variant cover by Frank Cho and Sabine Rich

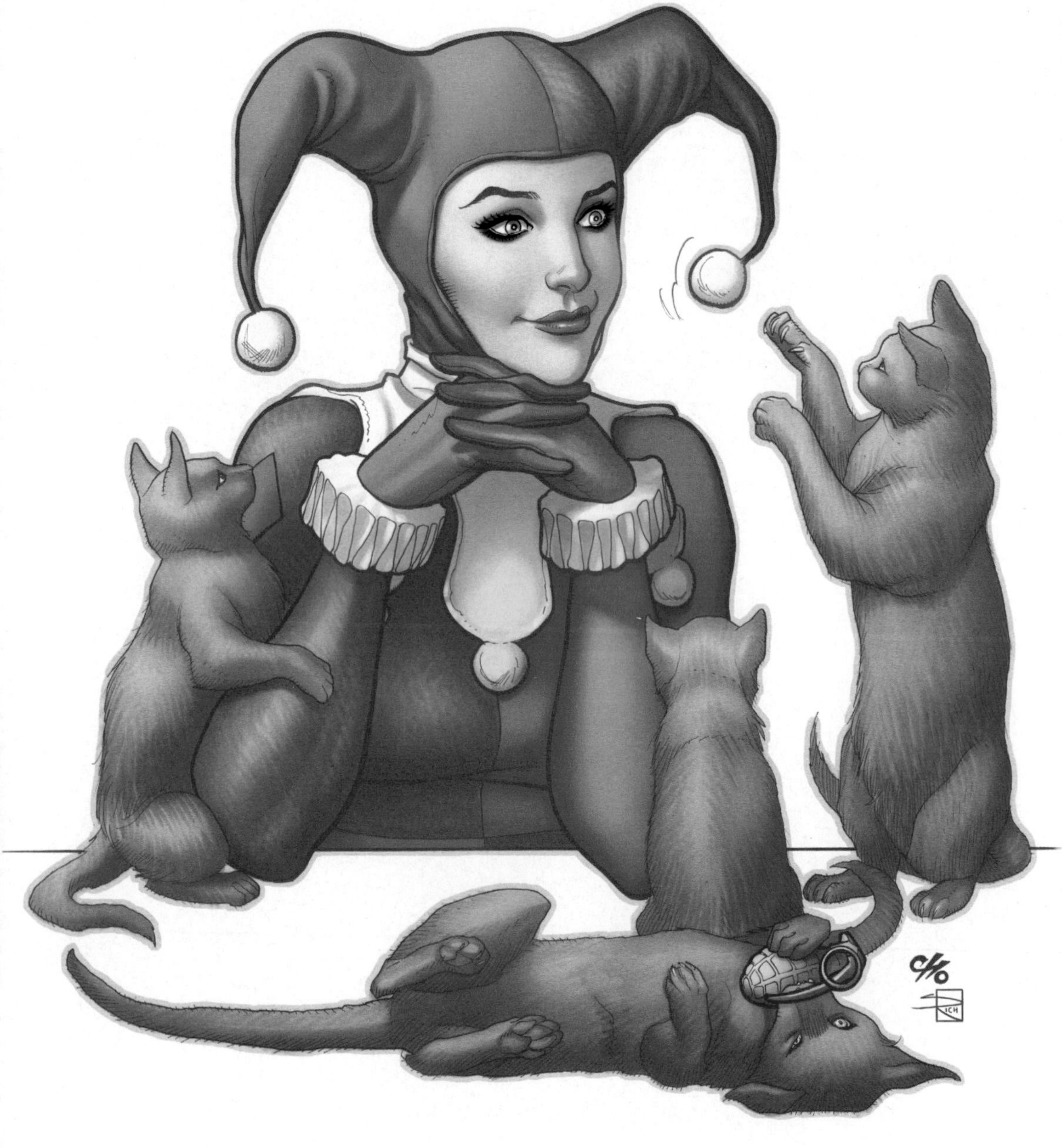

HARLEY QUINN #21 variant cover by Frank Cho and Sabine Rich

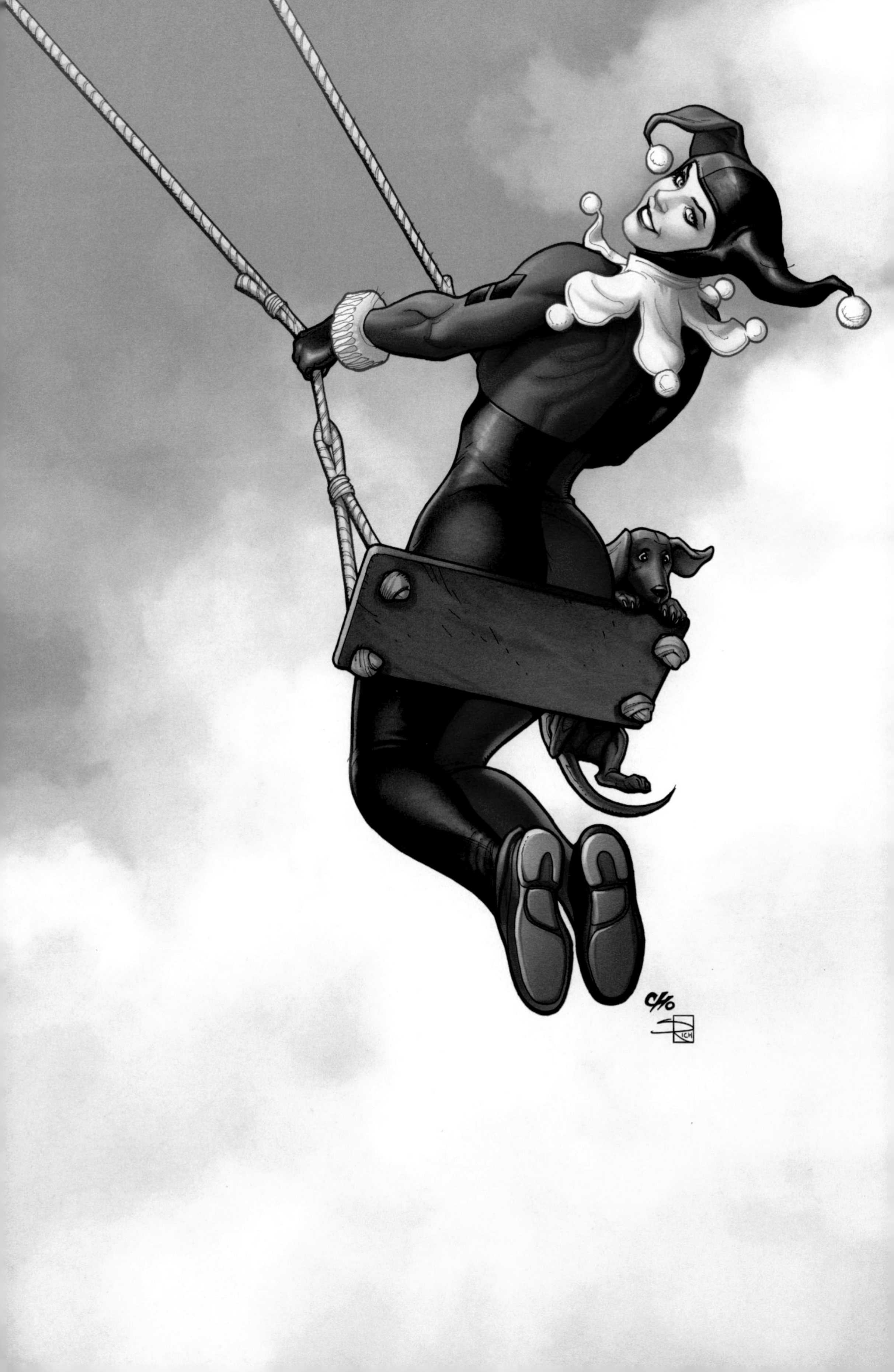

HARLEY QUINN #24 variant cover by Frank Cho and Sabine Rich

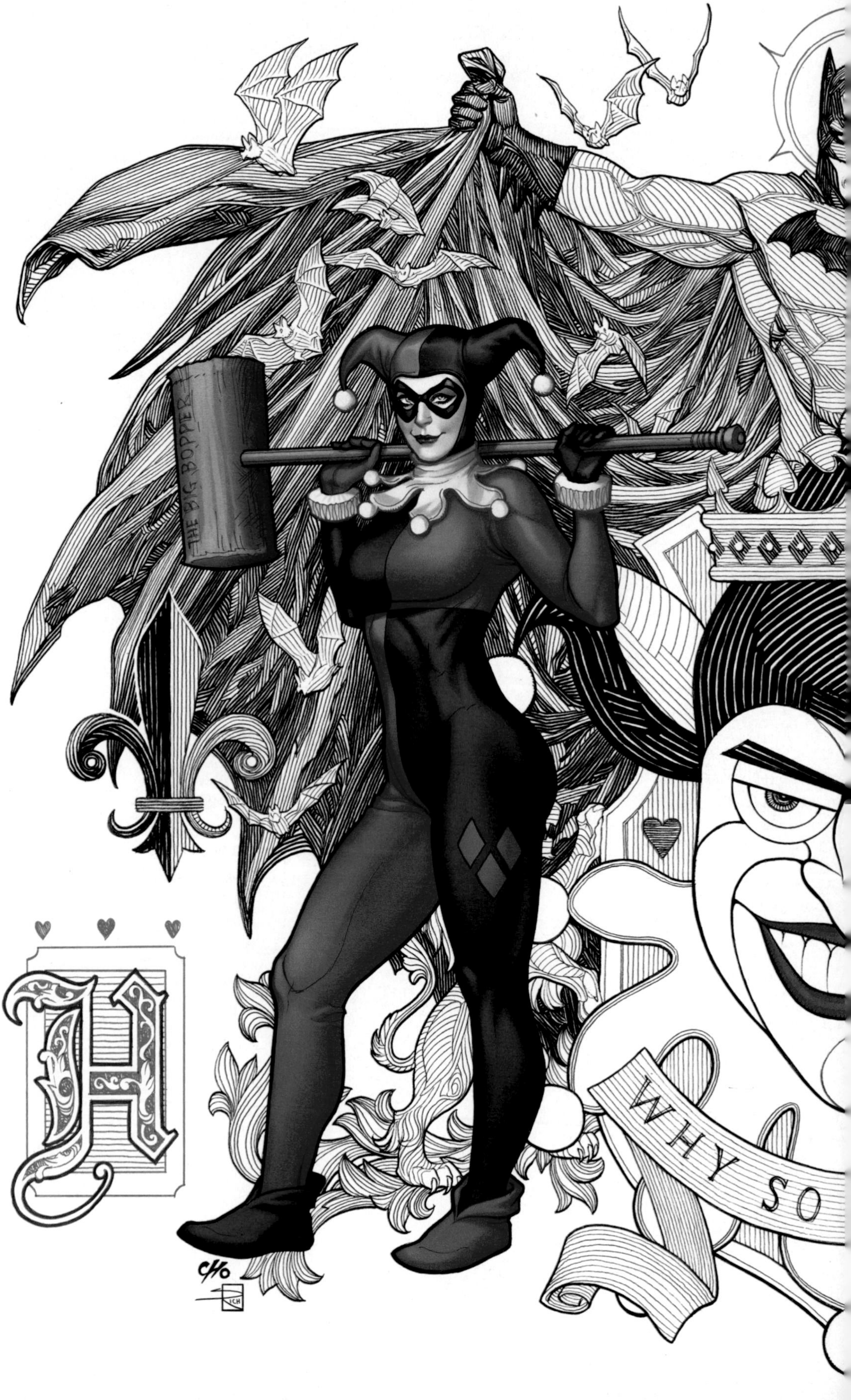
THE BIG BOPPER
H
WHY SO
CHO
RICH

HARLEY QUINN #25 variant cover by Frank Cho and Sabine Rich

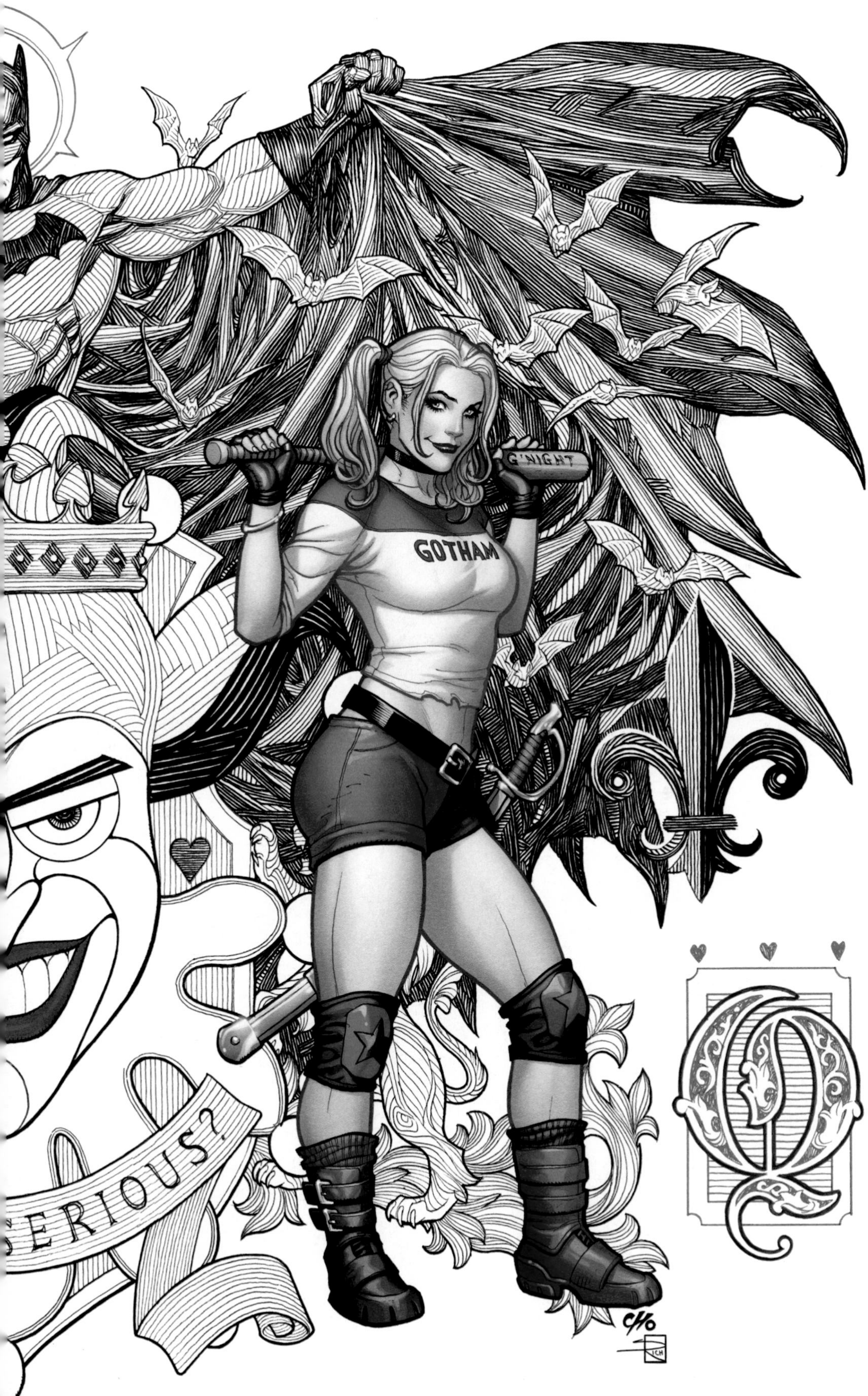
G'NIGHT
GOTHAM
SERIOUS?
CHO
RICH

HARLEY QUINN #22 variant cover by Frank Cho and Sabine Rich

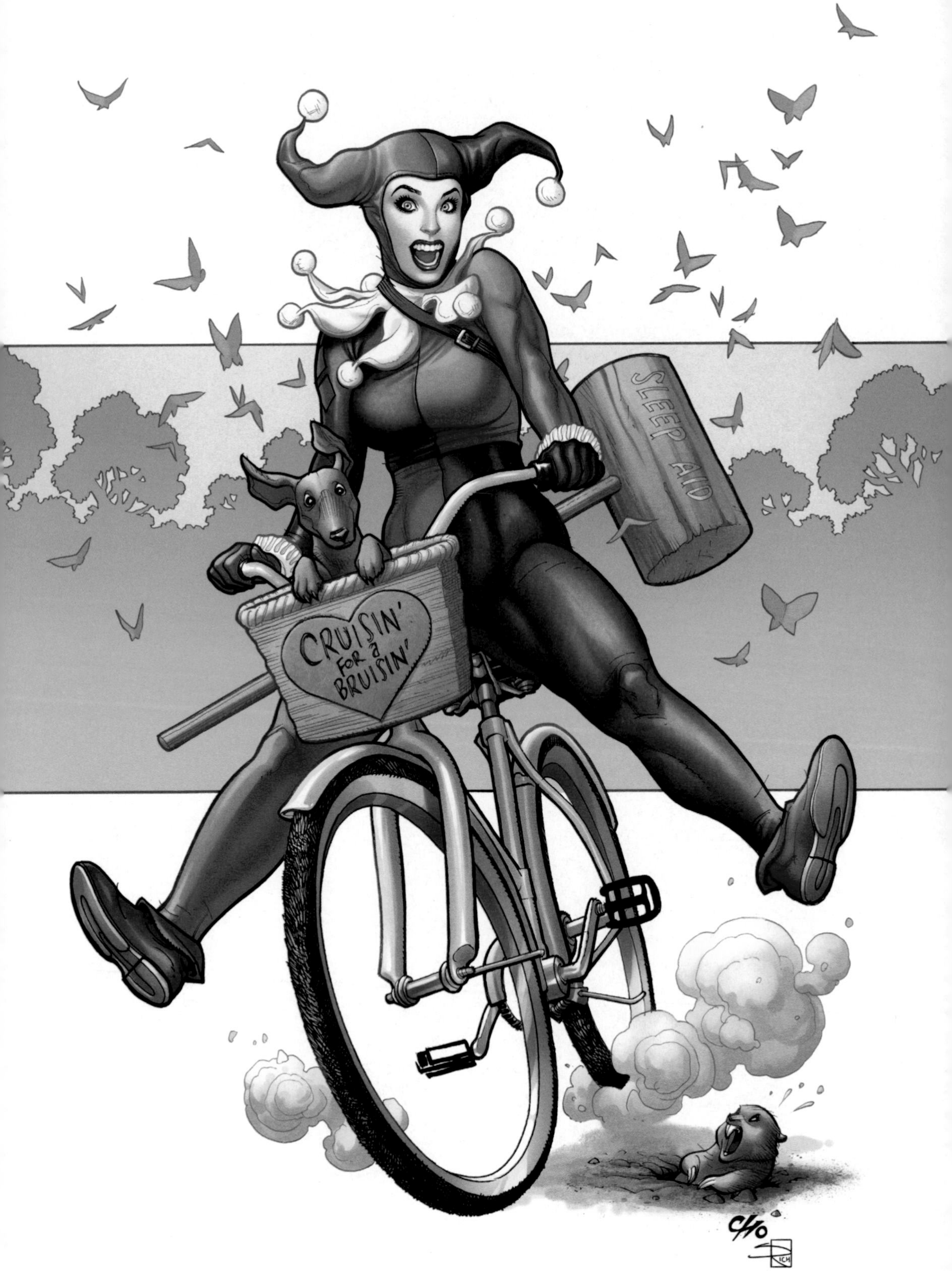
SLEEP AID
CRUISIN' FOR a BRUISIN'
CHO
RICH

I always work out all the storytelling, page layouts and compositions on small, rough "thumbnails" before drawing on the larger finished art boards. I don't like running into surprises on the final art when the deadline is bearing down! Here's a glimpse of the process—about 90 percent of the important decisions are made at this initial stage of intense thinking and doodling. —Bret Blevins

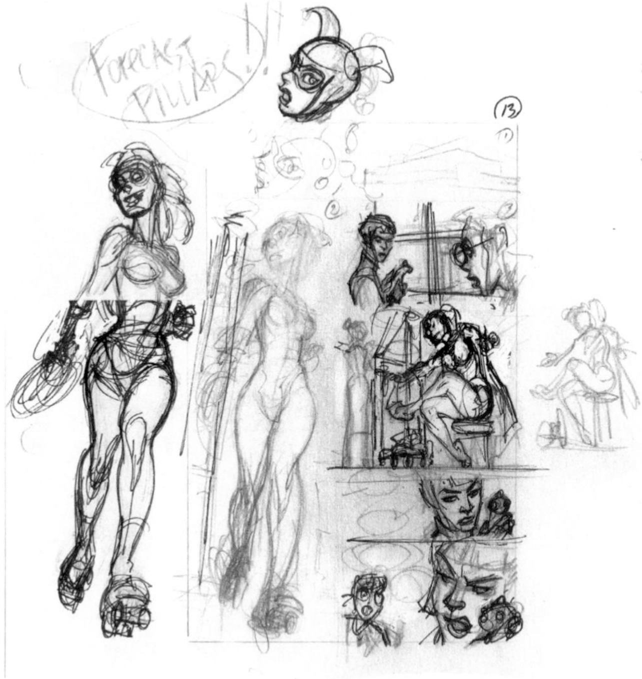
FORECAST PILLARS!
13

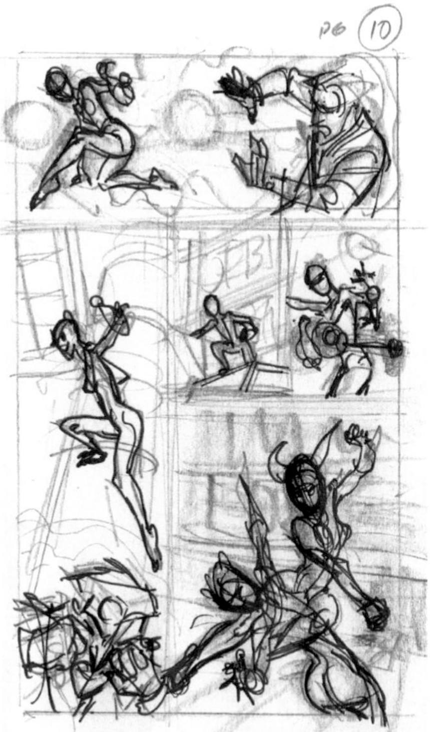
PG 10

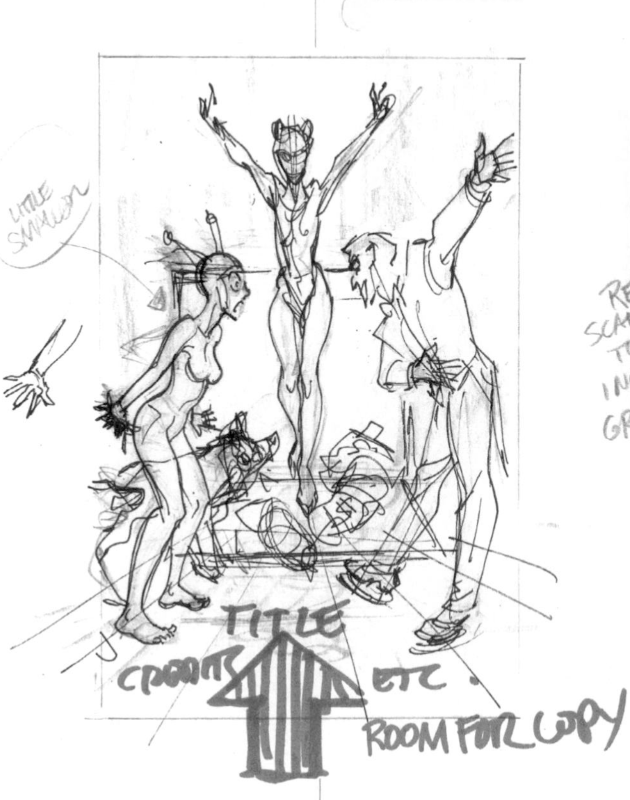
TITLE
CREDITS
ETC
ROOM FOR COPY

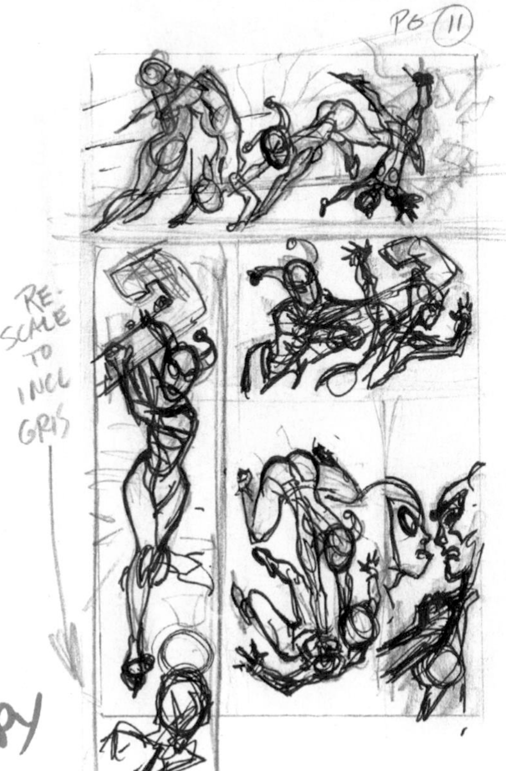
PG 11
RE-SCALE TO INCL

A rejected first attempt at the splash page—I like most of the changes I made for the final printed version, but I kind of like Harley dropping her gun in this one...not sure now why I took it out. I guess it made the lower corner too busy. —Bret Blevins

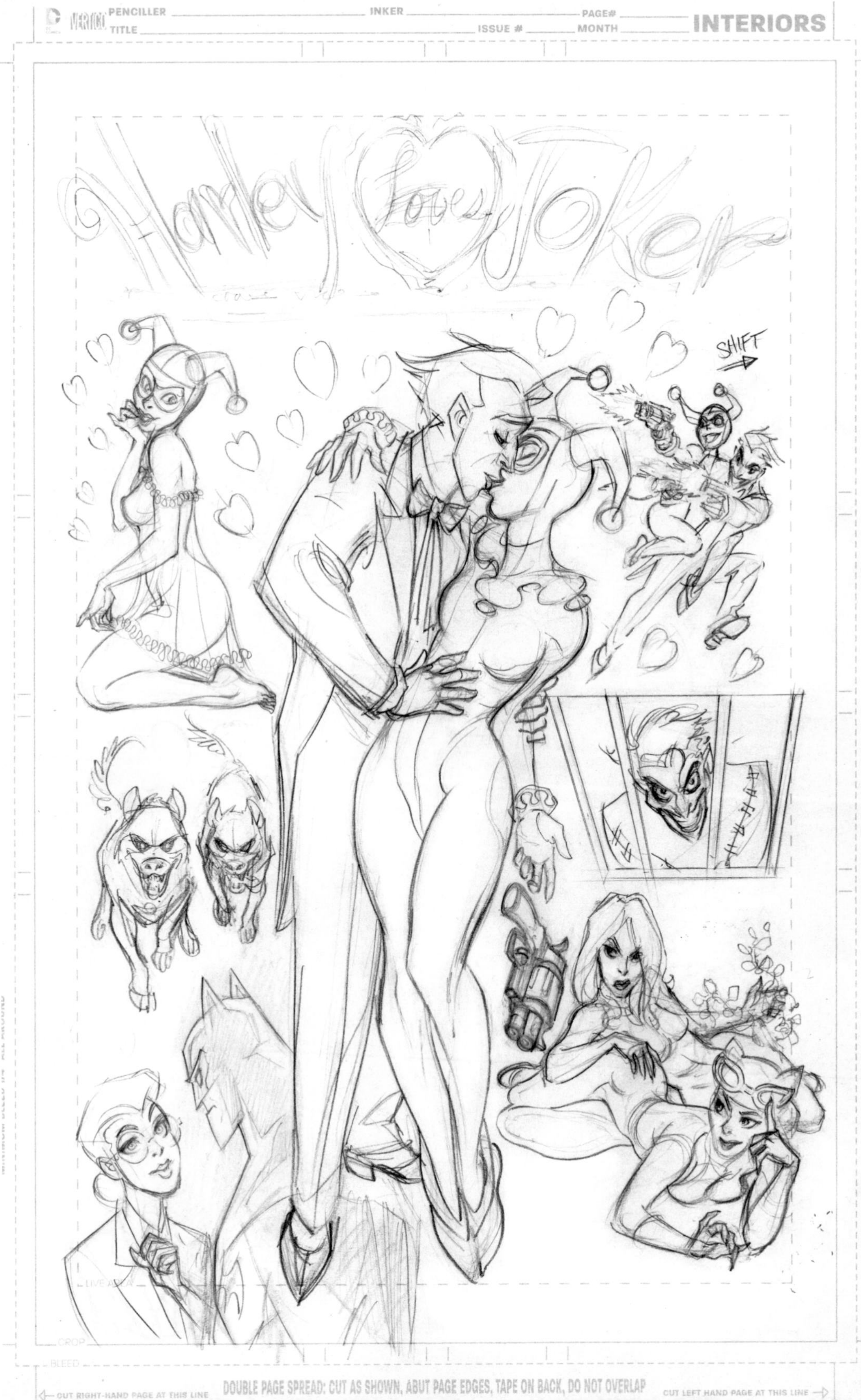
PENCILLER
INKER
PAGE#
TITLE
ISSUE #
MONTH
INTERIORS
Harley Loves Joker
SHIFT
DOUBLE PAGE SPREAD: CUT AS SHOWN, ABUT PAGE EDGES, TAPE ON BACK, DO NOT OVERLAP
CUT RIGHT-HAND PAGE AT THIS LINE
CUT LEFT HAND PAGE AT THIS LINE

There was a gap of several months between the first group of short stories and the final two 22-page chapters. When we picked up again I did this warm-up sketch to get back in the groove and made a few notes about reference I would need on the side. —Bret Blevins

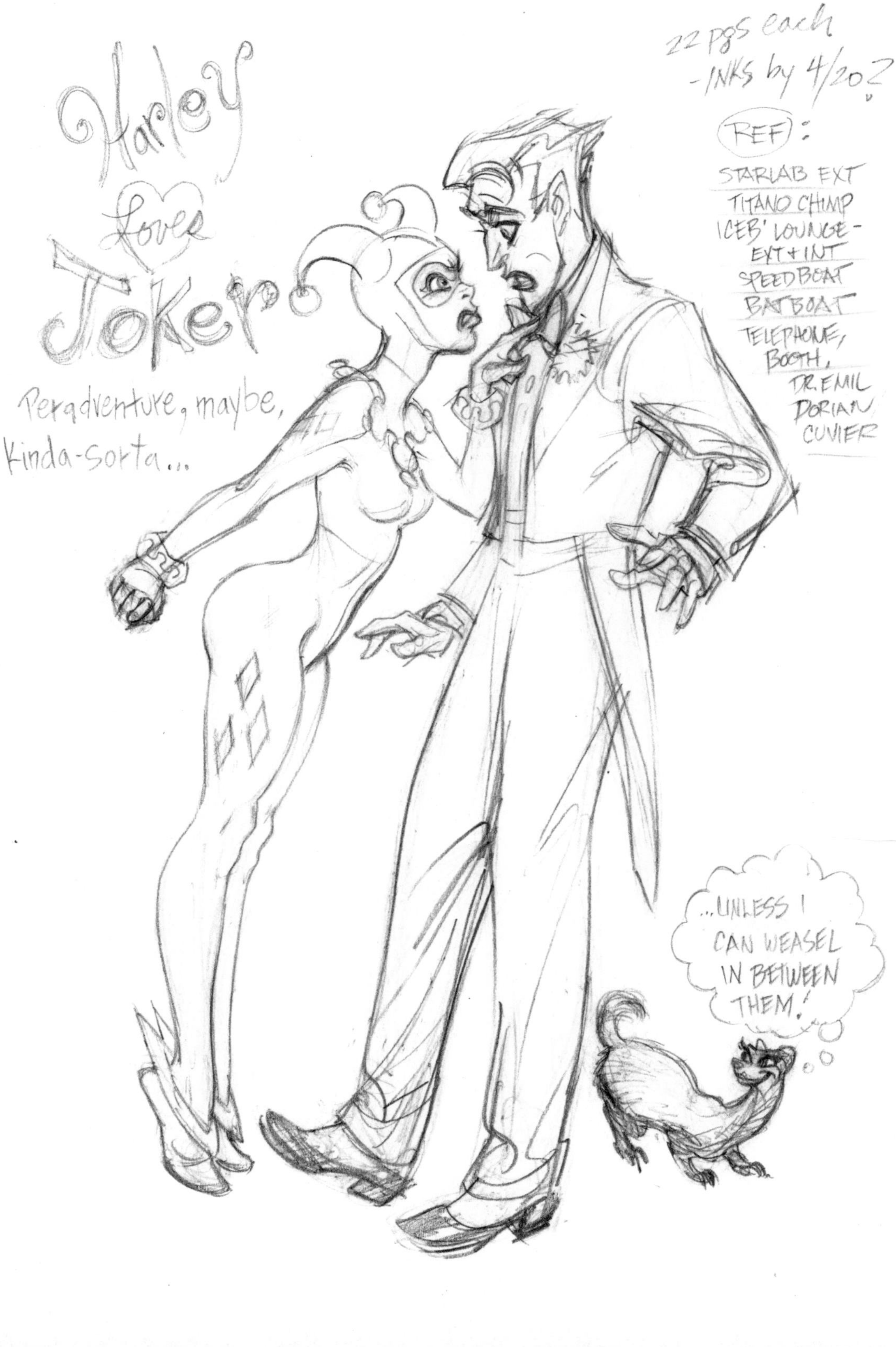
Harley Loves Joker
Peradventure, maybe, kinda-sorta...
22 pgs each
-INKS by 4/20?
REF:
STARLAB EXT
TITANO CHIMP
ICEB' LOUNGE - EXT + INT
SPEEDBOAT
BATBOAT
TELEPHONE, BOOTH,
DR. EMIL DORIAN CUVIER
...UNLESS I CAN WEASEL IN BETWEEN THEM!

Grison model sheet by Bret Blevins

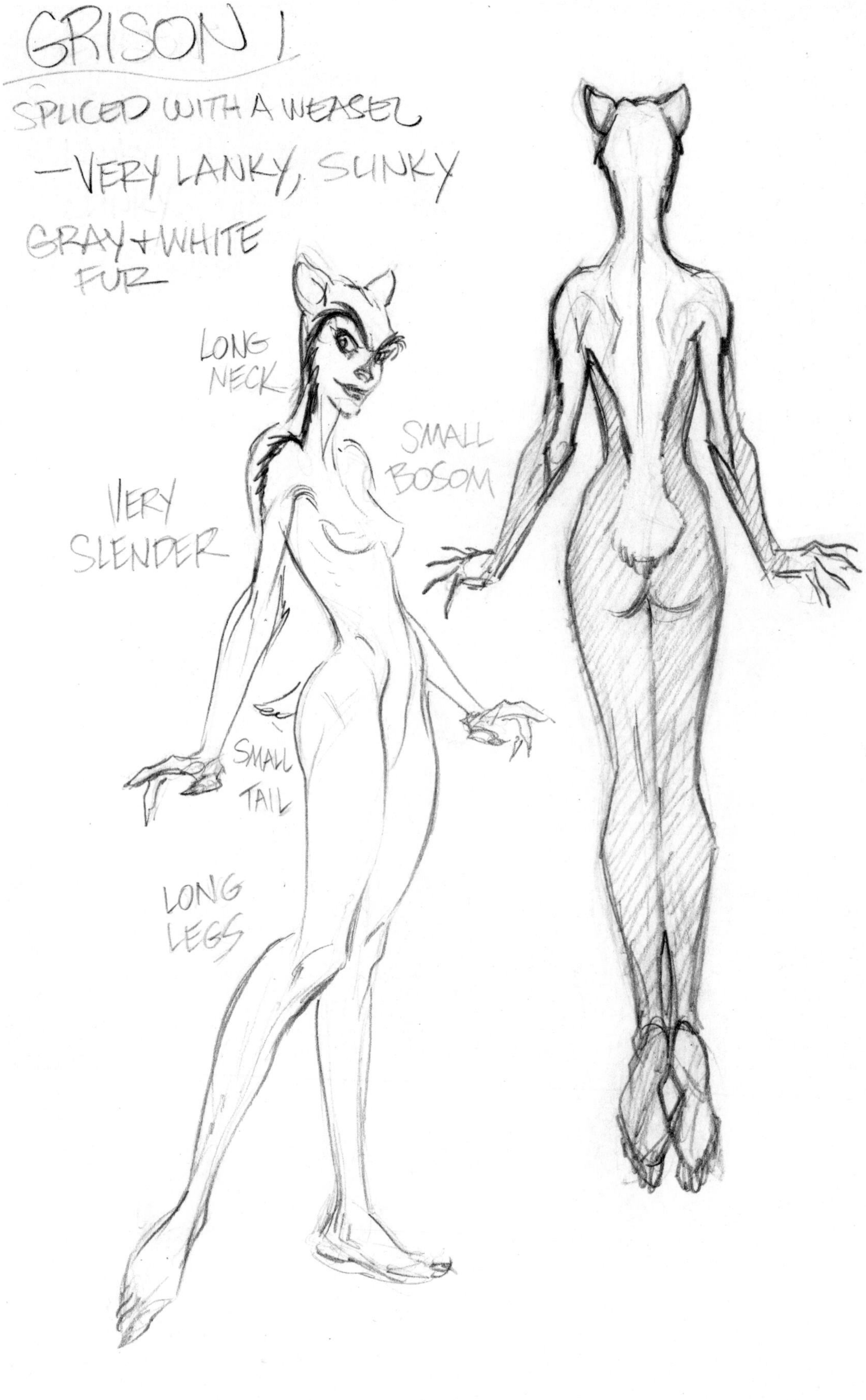

GRISON 1
SPLICED WITH A WEASEL
—VERY LANKY, SLINKY
GRAY + WHITE FUR
LONG NECK
SMALL BOSOM
VERY SLENDER
SMALL TAIL
LONG LEGS

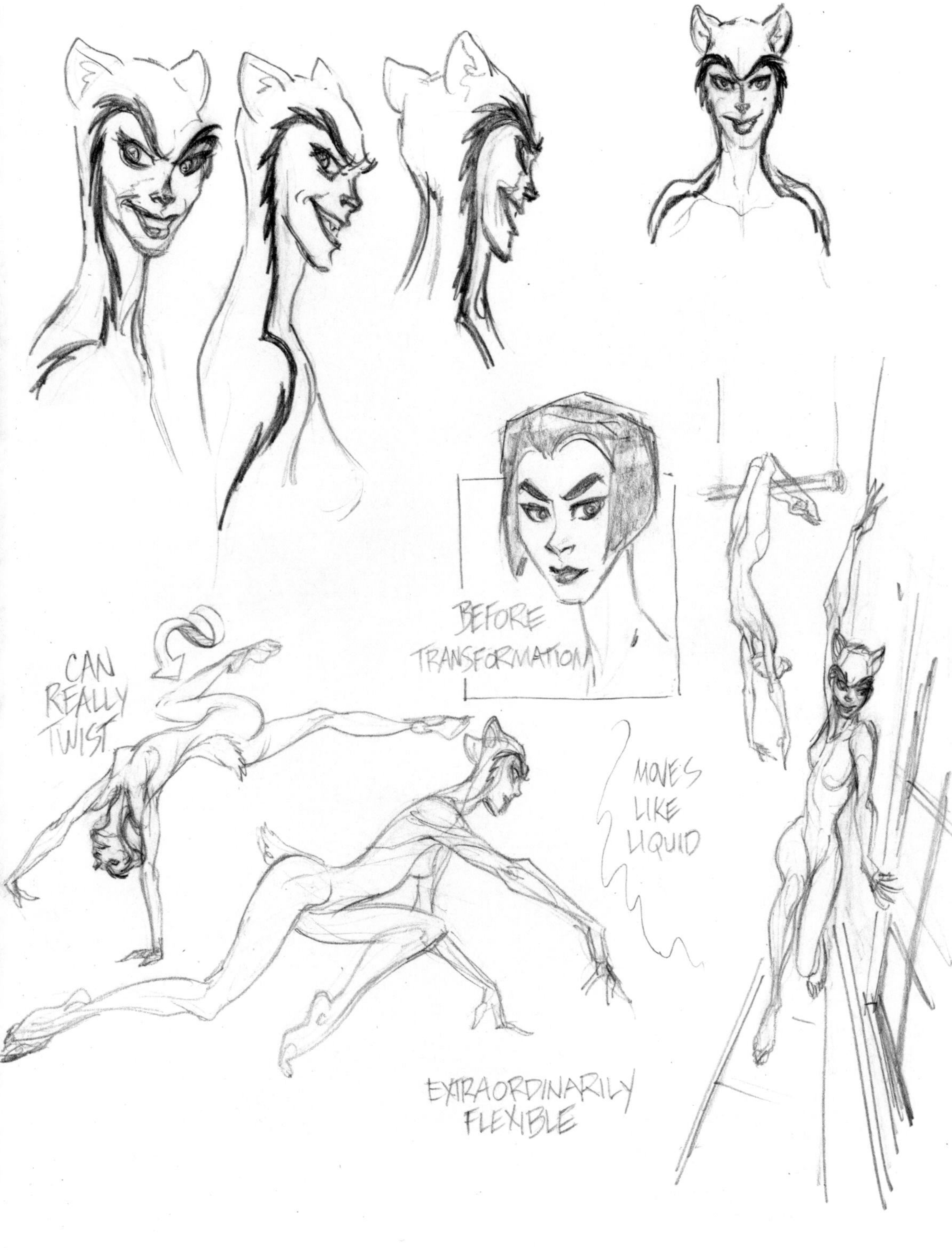
BEFORE TRANSFORMATION
CAN REALLY TWIST
MOVES LIKE LIQUID
EXTRAORDINARILY FLEXIBLE

Early Grison character sketch by Paul Dini

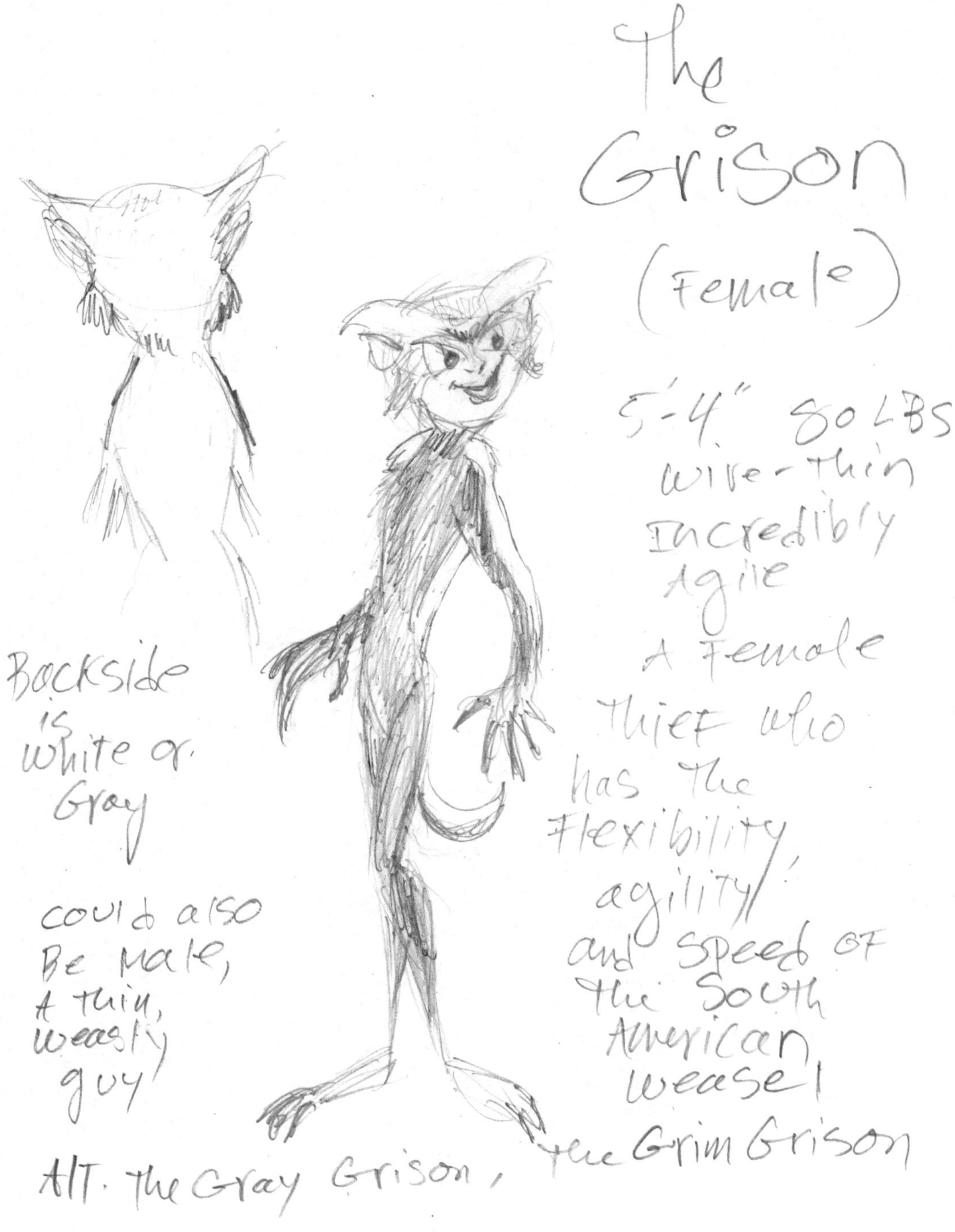
The Grison
(Female)
5'-4" 80 LBS
wire-thin
Incredibly
Agile
A Female
Thief who
has the
Flexibility,
agility
and speed of
the South
American
weasel
Backside
is
white or
Gray
could also
Be Male,
A thin,
weasly
guy
Alt. the Gray Grison, the Grim Grison